POPULAR POLITICS IN EARLY INDUSTRIAL BRITAIN:
BOLTON 1825–1850

Popular Politics in Early Industrial Britain: Bolton 1825–1850

PETER TAYLOR

RYBURN PUBLISHING
KEELE UNIVERSITY PRESS

First published in 1995
by Ryburn Publishing
an imprint of
Keele University Press
Keele University, Staffordshire

Composed by KUP Services
and printed by Hartnolls,
Bodmin, England

Popular Politics in Early Industrial Britain:
Bolton 1825–1850

ISBN 1 85331 059 X

Contents

List of Tables   6
Abbreviations   6

Introduction   7

1. The 'Cotton Districts' and the Origins of the   11
       Mid-Victorian 'Consensus': Issues and Debates

2. Local Politics 1827–1836: Petit-Bourgeois Radicals   25
       and Local Government
       Local government and politics before   29
       municipal incorporation
       The political outlook of the petite bourgeoisie   41
       in perspective: local campaigns and national politics

3. Local Politics 1837–1850: Middle-Class Social   57
       Formation and Municipal Reform
       The divided middle class: Bolton Liberals   60
       The divided middle class: Bolton Tories   65
       Municipal incorporation and the emergence of a   73
       middle-class consensus

4. Popular Politics 1837–1850: The Ideological Origins   105
       of the Mid-Victorian Consensus
       Middle-class Liberals and popular reform movements   107
       Toryism and the working class   120
       The ideological content of political protest movements   126

5. The Limits to Middle-Class Hegemony: 151
       Technological Change and Industrial Relations
       Workers and labour processes   154
       Economic conflict in perspective   170

6. Paternalism and Class Reconciliation   181
    Paternalism and authority   185
    Adult education   193
    Charity and philanthropy   197
    Temperance   200
    Factory reform   203

Conclusion   217
Bibliography   227
Index   245

List of Tables

3.1   Population Levels in the Townships Comprising   80
      the Bolton Poor Law Union, 1841
3.2   Population Levels in the Townships Comprising   81
      the Bolton Poor Law Union, 1851
5.1   Occupational Analysis of Selected South-East   154
      Lancashire Towns, 1841
5.2   Principal Occupations, Bolton Borough, 1851   155

Abbreviations

B.C.   *Bolton Chronicle*
B.F.P.   *Bolton Free Press*
B.A.   Bolton Archives section of the Bolton Reference Library
B.R.L.   Material located in the Local History section of the Bolton
         Reference Library
B.P.P.   British Parliamentary Papers
H.O.   Material from the Home Office files, located in the Public
         Record Office at Kew, London

Other references are given in full.

Introduction

This book is concerned with an area that has received much attention from historians. It is a study of popular politics and class relations in the 1830s and 1840s. Focusing on the experience of the community of Bolton, its aim is to outline and explain the developments leading to the marked transformation in social relations that took place in the years around 1850. The origins and nature of the mid-Victorian 'consensus' is a highly controversial subject, generally portrayed as a sudden and major shift in the years around 1850 and usually attributed to changes in the nature of work and British capitalism. This is held to be especially the case in the 'cotton district' of Lancashire and Cheshire, the region where industrial capitalism was most advanced and the area within which the findings of this work are primarily situated.[1]

The 'cotton towns' are considered to provide dramatic examples of discontinuities in working-class attitudes and behaviour at mid-century. An examination of events and developments in Bolton, however, shows that the transformation of class and political relations there was in fact a gradual process of social stabilisation. The second quarter of the nineteenth century did witness an intensification of economic struggle across a wide range of trades and, in common with other centres in the region, Bolton became a stronghold of militant Chartism. Yet local evidence suggests that the forces promoting conciliation between labour and capital and middle class and working class were never completely eroded by those promoting conflict. It was significant that workers primarily wished to restore threatened reciprocities with employers and not, as has been suggested, to create an alternative social and economic order.[2] Moreover, an examination of the ideological content, social composition and progress of reform movements in Bolton supports the view that radical and Liberal analyses of society were essentially inter-class in appeal[3] and further reveals that they promoted meaningful class cooperation before 1850, even during the particularly strife-torn years of 1838 to 1842. Of significance in this respect was the way in which those analyses attributed increasing exploitation primarily to political rather than economic causes. For this united middle-class and working-

class reformers in an assault upon aristocratic power at Westminster
which ensured that it was the national political framework, rather than
the local economic sphere, which acted as the major force shaping the
working-class response to industrial capitalism. The ability of middle-
class Liberals to attract a mass base of support before 1850 would appear
to have been unduly discounted by historians – historians who have
obscured their success through narrowly focusing on their relations
with a militant section of the Chartists. This section represented only a
minority of the working class, or indeed, the organised labour movement. Class-based tensions and contradictions often worked to divide
middle-class and working-class reformers, both before and after 1850.
Nevertheless, the widespread support of piecemeal Liberal 'reformism'
did not await the decline of militant Chartism or demands for major
changes in the political order. In the case of Bolton at least, the movement to social calm represented a gradual process, and not a climacteric
in the years around 1850, as many accounts of the regional experience
have portrayed.[4]

   In terms of approach, this book aims to further knowledge and
understanding of events and developments by placing at the centre of
the historical process the social formation of the middle class. The
owners of capital have only just begun to receive detailed examination
and much more needs to be done in this area.[5] This is in contrast to
the historical trajectory and experience of the working class, which has
received a far more comprehensive and satisfactory coverage. Yet an
examination of the local pattern of events suggests that a more coherent,
holistic and satisfactory historical synthesis can be gained through the
utilisation of an analytical framework incorporating the experience of
the middle class.

   The usefulness of such an approach is revealed in the fact that while
class relations were often bitter, it is significant that the predominant
endemic political rivalry in the town was one within an internally
divided middle class. This struggle for supremacy between rival middle-
class élites was at its most intense during the years 1838 to 1842, when
south-east Lancashire was perhaps the foremost centre of Chartism in
the country. But from the middle-class perspective, their own struggle
was more important than conflict between labour and capital and rich
and poor. By 1850, however, these internal divisions had been significantly alleviated and there was general agreement as to how the town
should be governed. This in itself served not only to confirm the consolidation of middle-class power, but also to complement the overall
improvements in class relations which were taking place.

   The foregoing perspective has been instrumental in shaping the organisation of the book. Chapter One elaborates upon some of the issues

raised above and attempts to set the general historiographical context. The leading explanations of change offered at the mainly regional level are outlined and set in national focus, as are the main arguments of the present work. Chapter Two examines the political activities of the town's middling groups, such as shopkeepers, small traders and small producers. The social strata between the extremes of working class and middle class played a greater role in Bolton's political life than this discussion has hitherto suggested, especially up to the mid-1830s. Although primarily motivated by a desire to bring greater accountability to local government, it is significant that the actions and political outlook of these strata played an important role in uniting reformers from all social classes in the national Reform Bill agitation against aristocratic power at the centre. Another theme of this chapter further helps to set the overall historiographical context. It contends that the connections between the spheres of local and national politics were more comprehensive in the minds of contemporaries than some historians of the regional experience have portrayed.[6] In Chapter Three attention turns to the social formation of the middle class and to further developments in aspects of local government and politics introduced in the previous chapter. By 1837 the Liberal section of the middle class had taken over the campaign for municipal reform from the petite bourgeoisie. It will be shown that although middle-class social formation was attended by a significant degree of fragmentation, by 1850 a meaningful degree of reconciliation had taken place against the background of municipal reform. In turn, this enabled the middle class more effectively to exercise their assumed social leadership over the whole community. Chapter Four focuses mainly on political relations between the middle class and working class throughout the Chartist period. By the mid-1830s middle-class activists dominated local politics and had further assumed the leadership in national political struggles. There were tensions with working-class radicals, but while it will be acknowledged that the relations between the major classes did deteriorate during these years, it will be argued that links between reformers were stronger than has sometimes been assumed and that Liberal analyses of social ills had a greater appeal than has usually been appreciated. Chapter Five concentrates on industrial relations. The argument that improvements in social relations owed much to changes in work organisation and practice is refuted and the case is made for the importance of the various continuities in this area between the second and third quarters of the nineteenth century. Finally, Chapter Six considers the contributions made to social stabilisation by the emergence of more mellow and socially-orientated middle-class practices and attitudes in the 1840s.

Notes

1. J. Foster, *Class Struggle and the Industrial Revolution: Early Industrial Capitalism in Three English Towns* (London, 1974); P. Joyce, *Work, Society and Politics: The Culture of the Factory in Later Victorian England* (London, 1980); N. Kirk, *The Growth of Working Class Reformism in Mid-Victorian England* (Beckenham, 1985).

2. Foster, *op. cit.*, pp. 74, 107, 148.

3. For examples of this view, presented from varying perspectives, see: E. F. Biagini and A. J. Reid, *Currents of Radicalism: Popular Radicalism, Organised Labour and Party Politics in Britain, 1850–1914* (Cambridge, 1991); B. Harrison and P. Hollis, 'Chartism, Liberalism and the life of Robert Lowery', *English Historical Review* LXXXII (1967); D. Nicholls, 'The English Middle Class and the Ideological Significance of Radicalism, 1760–1886', *Journal of British Studies* 24 (1985).

4. Foster, *op. cit.*; Joyce, *op. cit.*; Kirk, *op. cit.*

5. For the middle class, see, for instance: C. Barker and D. Nicholls, (eds), *The Development of British Capitalist Society: A Marxist Debate* (Manchester, 1988); Foster, *op. cit.*, ch. 6; D. Fraser, *Urban Politics in Victorian England: The Structure of Politics in Victorian Cities* (Leicester, 1976); J. Garrard, *Leadership and Power in Victorian Industrial Towns 1830–80* (Manchester, 1983); V. A. C. Gatrell, 'Incorporation and the Pursuit of Liberal Hegemony in Manchester 1790–1839', in D. Fraser (ed.), *Municipal Reform and the Industrial City* (Leicester, 1982); S. Gunn, 'The "Failure" of the Victorian Middle Class: A Critique', in J. Wolff and J. Seed (eds), *The Culture of Capital: Art, Power and the Nineteenth-Century Middle Class* (Manchester, 1988); Joyce, *op. cit.*; T. Koditschek, *Class Formation and Urban Industrial Society: Bradford, 1750–1850* (Cambridge, 1990); D. Nicholls, 'The English Middle Class and the Ideological Significance of Radicalism, 1760–1886', *Journal of British Studies* 24 (1985); Rubinstein, 'Wealth, Elites and the Class Structure of Modern Britain', *Past and Present* 76 (1977).

6. Foster, *op. cit.*; Gatrell, *op. cit.*

CHAPTER ONE

The 'Cotton Districts' and the Origins of the Mid-Victorian 'Consensus': Issues and Debates

This chapter attempts to set the general historiographical context. The leading explanations of change offered at the regional level are outlined and set in national focus, as are the main issues and debates, the arguments of the present work, and reasons for the choice of Bolton as a case study. Historians have spent much time exploring the nature and the processes leading to the social transformation that took place in the years around 1850, whereby the turbulent 1830s and 1840s gave way to the stability of the mid-Victorian period. The main forms which this mellowed state of social relations were seen to have taken were more cordial labour relations, the decline of militant 'independent' working-class political agitation, the firm assimilation of the working class into the two-party system, the passing of the phase of aristocratic govern-ment known as 'Old Corruption' and the ascendancy of middle-class values to a position of dominance in English society. Beyond the accepted view of the general contours of this social transformation, however, there has been much disagreement regarding the relative weight and priority of contributory factors and the extent and nature of the celebrated mid-Victorian 'consensus'.

The historical experience of the working class has received much attention from historians, but there have been conflicting interpre-tations as to the extent to which the years around 1850 constituted a 'watershed' in the history of labour. This question was first posed by the Webbs, who proposed a complete break in the structure and ideology of the labour movement.[1] Similarly, Briggs described the co-operative movement as passing from community-building to shopkeeping and trade unions, as becoming less like 'schools of war' and more like the workman's equivalent of the public school.[2] Royden Harrison assumed a 'massive transformation' of the labour movement, unequalled before or since.[3] Conversely, however, there is a view which suggests that notions of 'discontinuity' in working-class consciousness and behaviour have little general application. The general line of argument proposed here suggests that because some historians have exaggerated the extent of working-class consciousness in the Chartist period, this, in turn, has led them to overstate the degree to which the working class became quiescent in the years after 1850. Malcolm Thomis, for instance, in support of his argument that a highly fragmented labour movement betrayed the low degree of class consciousness among nineteenth-century English workers, has emphasised the extent of sectionalism in working-class activity and organisation. According to his portrayal, the high-water marks of the Chartist agitation indicate only the potential, and not the actuality, of the situation. Only a minority of workers became Chartists and enthusiasm was generally short-lived, the reality of labour politics for the most part being massive working-class apathy to the endeavours of their would-be political leaders.[4] Another leading advocate of this general line of argument is A. E. Musson, who has also highlighted the separateness of working-class economic and political activity and the various continuities evident in the structure and policies of the labour movement (especially its trade union aspect) before and after 1850.[5]

It is not necessary to rehearse the finer points of detail of these disagreements.[6] For the purposes of this study, it is sufficient to take account of a regional pattern of developments which has already been placed into a national context by other historians. As suggested by Kirk, the cotton towns of Lancashire and Cheshire – within which this study of Bolton is situated – constitute a useful testing ground of the case for discontinuities or 'breaks' in working-class experience. Thus he argues that the transition to social calm was particularly well marked in his test cases of Ashton, Stalybridge and Stockport, which had seen intense industrial conflict and militant independent working-class political agitation before 1850.[7] This position is supported by evidence from two other well-known studies of the region. John Foster's study of Oldham sought to explain what the author saw as a major shift in the class consciousness of that town's workers from about the mid-1840s, when some supposedly early variant of a 'revolutionary class consciousness' suddenly gave way to 'class collaboration and a "labour aristocracy" type of social structure'.[8] Patrick Joyce looked most closely at Blackburn, a town situated in north Lancashire, but he drew evidence from other factory towns in the county. In his account the onset of social stability was closely linked with technological changes that brought about a transfer of control of the productive process from labour to capital. Nowhere was this situation more advanced than in the cotton districts of Lancashire, the two decades after 1830 witnessing the thorough consolidation of mechanised production in the most advanced parts of the county. This ushered in a situation where a complex system of employer paternalism and worker deference replaced the open class hostility of the Chartist era. By way of contrast, in those areas where handworking traditions survived longer and male labour was mechanised later –

especially in the West Riding, but also in late-mechanising north-east Lancashire towns like Burnley – radical traditions continued to make an impact and the transition to social harmony was correspondingly delayed.[9] Places like Robert Gray's Edinburgh and Geoffrey Crossick's Kentish London can also be mentioned in this context, for they lend further support to the received picture of the Lancashire experience. These towns never had any strong tradition of militant working-class action or acute class conflict and while they did experience improvements in class relations from the later 1840s, it is questionable as to whether they experienced any sharp break in class relations in the years around 1850.[10]

Within this field of debate on the regional experience, there are different interpretations of the extent to which class relations mellowed after 1850. Controversy still surrounds interpretation of the complex interrelations between conflict and reconciliation and of the significance of evidence for continuing class tensions against the background of increasing social tolerance. Regarding industrial relations, Joyce has argued that although conflict continued after 1850 and trade unions remained as potential and actual organs of class struggle, there was a significant reduction in the frequency and intensity of industrial conflict. Trade unions actually served to complement deference by removing conflict from the point of production – post-Chartist Lancashire being notable for its advanced system of institutionalised industrial relations and distinguished by its general class harmony.[11] But most of his evidence on this clearly relates to the fourth quarter of the century. While conflict did decline in frequency and intensity in the mid-Victorian years, Kirk is correct to suggest that the centralisation and bureaucratisation of trade union affairs were insufficiently advanced to contain industrial conflict until beyond the 1870s. Until then at least, such conflict continued at a level sufficient to dispel Joyce's portrayal of widespread class harmony and internalised worker-deference.[12] Turning to political developments, Kirk again takes issue with Joyce's 'deferential proletariat' explanation. He plausibly attributes the unprecedented Conservative gains in Lancashire in the 1868 general election to the exploitation of ethnic and religious tensions, rather than to the political influence exercised by paternalistic employers over their allegedly deferential operatives. And as regards popular Liberalism, Kirk rightly warns against accepting a picture of an untroubled movement of Chartists into Liberalism when Chartism lost its capacity for mass mobilisation after 1848. Kirk is therefore justified in his insistence that the mid-Victorian period represented a process of social stabilisation rather than class harmonisation.[13]

Despite these disagreements, it is generally accepted that, in much of the cotton districts of Lancashire and Cheshire at least, the mid-nineteenth century saw a marked transformation in social and political relations from the disturbed 1830s and 1840s. The literature on the region has provided varying explanations of the change and historians have placed differing degrees of emphasis on a number of factors. Although echoes remain of the traditional viewpoint that the onset of social stability can be primarily attributed to straightforward economic improvement, this is now widely considered to be theoretically simplistic and empirically unsound. More recent accounts, while not totally discarding the overall role that economic improvement played in the growth of social stability, have generally employed the notion within more sophisticated frameworks of analysis. These emphasise the material advances and class concessions and compromises permitted by the stabilisation and expansion of capitalist market relations. Some historians, highlighting important structural changes, have pointed to the demise of certain occupational groups such as the hand-loom weavers and block calico-printers, whose attempts to halt their decline had supposedly provided Chartism with much of its strength. Similarly, others have described the rise to dominance within the labour movement of a relatively privileged 'labour aristocracy' able to impose its moderate views on the rest of the workforce. One account which dismissed this notion has nevertheless pointed to the very real gains made by sections of the labour movement (especially its trade union, Friendly Society and co-op movement elements) which promoted a greater acceptance of, and integration within, capitalist society.[14] Another critic of the labour aristocracy thesis emphasised the long-term effects of technological change. This was first seen as promoting a precarious unity between those whose status, skill and security it threatened, but having been carried through to its logical conclusion, via the passing of the control of the labour process from worker to employer, it produced a workforce firmly subjected to the authority structures of industrial capital.[15] Another factor recognised by historians as playing a role in easing class tensions was the mellowing of middle-class attitudes and behaviour, manifest in the spread and consolidation of employer paternalism and more benign social policies.[16] Also important is the rise of ethnic tensions between sections of the host and immigrant communities in the wake of the massive Irish Roman Catholic immigration into the region during the post-famine years, which is seen as reducing the potential for class solidarity and as promoting a greater working-class attachment to the framework of middle-class politics.[17] All of these factors are seen as contributing in some way to the improvements in class relations that occurred.[18] As previously mentioned, however, disagreements abound over the relative weight and priority that historians have attached to them.

As suggested above, in the more recent accounts little credence is attached to the view that Chartism was the creed of hard times, with political radicalism inevitably giving way to social moderation with the onset of mid-Victorian prosperity. Foster argues that while 'economic recovery', consequent upon changes in the town's economic base, undoubtedly did lead to a lessening of unemployment and distress in mid-nineteenth-century Oldham, it is questionable that such changes could have acted quickly enough to produce the shifts in working-class attitudes and behaviour evident by 1850.[19] Therefore, it can only serve as a 'very partial explanation'. Wages remained low throughout the 1840s and the capital-cheapening effects of new technology, the price-inflating effects of cheap gold, and the boons of cheaper food and increasing foreign profits all came later. Moreover, the circumstances that led to the loss of the 'mass influence of the working-class vanguard' were produced in the years 1846 and 1847, during a depression which Foster ranks as perhaps the worst of the second quarter of the century, a period marked by the frequency and acuteness of its commercial depressions.[20] Further comments on the limited overall explanatory power of the improvement thesis have been made by David Gadian, who suggests that although Chartism in north-west England probably was fuelled by economic distress, there was no simple correlation between deprivation and reform movements. He further argues that while prosperity was certainly conducive to the maintenance of social stability, the decline of Chartism is equally attributable to such factors as the demoralisation, tactical confusion, government repression and internal policy divisions among the movement's leaders following the failure of petitioning movements.[21] Joyce also suggests that prosperity served to enhance rather than to create social stability. According to his account, the passing of the control of the productive process from man to master heightened the dependence of the worker upon the employer as a supplier of work. This, together with the presence of reservoirs of trained workers and pools of unskilled and often cheaper Irish labour, left the factory worker vulnerable in the labour market. Prosperity did not, therefore, necessarily increase labour's bargaining power. But it did promote social peace by playing a role in healing the wounds of increasing dependency.[22] All this suggests that the demise of popular protest cannot simply be attributed to the direct stimulus of economic improvement, a point comprehensively demonstrated by Kirk's survey of wage trends and living conditions, which shows that the decline of Chartism preceded discernible widespread economic improvement.[23]

A consensus that economic improvement served to enhance rather than to create social stability has not prevented disagreement in other areas of debate. In terms of the national picture, from Hobsbawm's classic essay on the subject in 1954, dissatisfaction with the overall explanatory value of the improvement theory led to increasing interest in the labour aristocracy thesis. This suggested that although it was true that the benefits of economic prosperity were not universally felt, their distribution among an identifiable and privileged 'aristocracy of labour' – distinguished by its higher wages and by the moderate political viewpoint it was able to impose upon the mass of workers – was instrumental in blunting the revolutionary potential of the working class.[24] In attempting to explain the rupture in Oldham's working-class politics in the mid-1840s, Foster utilised his own particular definition of this concept when he pointed to what he saw as 'a deliberate bourgeois attempt at restabilization', the key component of which lay in the creation of new systems of labour control at the workplace.[25] These emerged after technological advancement in the key cotton and engineering industries facilitated the breakdown of traditional craft controls in the 1830s and 1840s – a breakdown which paved the way for the creation of a 'labour aristocracy'. Foster emphasises that this stratum is not to be confused with the traditional 'artisan élite', distinguishable by its on-the-job autonomy, security, status, high wages and opposition to employers. Rather, it comprised a segment of workers stripped of craft control, exercising discipline over the mass of the semi- and unskilled workforce on behalf of capital, and altogether firmly identified with the culture and interests of the employers. This new class-collaborationist stratum thus buttressed the authority of the employers by acting as pace-makers and supervisors over the rest of the workforce in the production process and by assimilating their values in the outside community. According to Foster, the co-ops, temperance societies and adult education institutes were the preserve of the labour aristocracy and constituted an institutional network that came within the cultural orbit of the bourgeoisie.

Patrick Joyce has provided some telling criticisms of Foster's views and further suggests that the labour aristocracy thesis is irrelevant in the context of the cotton districts of Lancashire. Thus he contends that Foster's claims rest on insubstantial empirical foundations, and that Gray and Crossick's sophisticated application of the thesis to areas dominated by workshop production does not take us very far in understanding the experience of workers in areas of advanced factory production. When the empirical evidence is considered, he maintains, 'there are no grounds for imagining that the revolutionary, class-conscious potential of the majority was choked back by a reformist labour aristocracy.' On the contrary, far from being the 'moderates', the labour aristocrats were always at the forefront of radical politics.[21] Kirk has provided further theoretical and empirical weight to the case against Foster and the labour aristocracy thesis in general. Thus neither Edinburgh nor Kentish London experienced major changes in class relations or working-class attitudes at mid-century and, as such, it is difficult to see just what, in Gray and Crossick's application of the thesis, is revealed about the broader patterns of social relations in those places. It is in the cotton districts that the thesis stands or fails and Kirk has deployed sufficient evidence to show the empirical weaknesses in Foster's use of his particular variant of the thesis. Perhaps the most damaging of these is the fact that the introduction of the self-acting mule in cotton did not involve the creation of a new pace-making grade, the supervisory role of the cotton-mule spinner being a feature before, during and after the period of Oldham's 'heroic' class struggle. Moreover, Kirk's discussion of respectability shows that occupational divisions were not faithfully reproduced in cultural ones; the various co-ops, temperance societies and adult educational institutions were not the labour aristocratic preserves that Foster claimed them to be.[27] In general, the fact that the labour aristocracy has been variously defined and characterised by historians (whether in terms of wages and status or Foster's authority-wielders) only underlines the general imprecision and unconvincing nature of the concept in terms of those overall changes it seeks to explain.

Dissatisfaction with the labour aristocracy thesis provoked studies which utilised wider frameworks of explanation and, given the various weaknesses of the improvement and labour aristocracy theories, it is with these that this examination of the Bolton evidence is primarily concerned. It should be noted that, in describing the development of a labour aristocracy in Oldham, Foster was aiming to further understanding of the nature of changes which English capitalism under-went in the middle years of the nineteenth century.[28] And in his (1975) review of Foster's book, Gareth Stedman Jones also developed a framework of analysis that similarly associated the mellowing of class relations with changes in British capitalism. However, Stedman Jones was more concerned with the *overall* nature of change and, in seeking to explain the altered behaviour of the working class as a whole, he eschewed the notion that social calm was somehow linked to the supposed moderation of a particular stratum within the working class.[29] He attached special importance to two developments. Firstly, a 'new stage of industrialisation' brought about the stabilisation of capitalist market relations. The crisis in profitability in the cotton industry, which had so adversely affected social relations in Lancashire in the second quarter of the century, was the result of an extreme imbalance between the industrialised sector and the rest of the economy. The result of the new phase of capitalist development was the removal of this imbalance.

The 'most obvious feature of this new stage of industrial capitalism' was railway building, which although not a primary industry in Oldham, was nevertheless of great effect in that it 'lessened the impact of cyclical crisis, stimulated coal, iron, steel and machine production, and resolved the crisis of profitability. More than any other single factor, it assured the successful transition to a modern industrial economy.' This gave a renewed stability to the cotton and engineering industries which – against the background of Britain's confirmed position as the workshop of the world – experienced a slackening of the pace of technological change which had proved so disruptive to industrial relations. Secondly, Stedman Jones followed Foster to some extent in locating the onset of moderate 'reformism' with changes in the organisation and execution of work. Focusing upon the distinction made by Marx between the 'formal' and 'real' subordination of labour to capital – involving the replacement of a division of labour based upon handicrafts by a division of labour based upon machines – he notes that Chartism had been underpinned by struggles for the control rather than the ownership of production. With the resolving of these in favour of Oldham's capitalists, 'the vision of a different society and economy' lost its relevance and disappeared in the face of what now seemed to be the permanency of industrial capitalism. Economic struggles continued, but they no longer possessed a political dimension. New conditions and structures led to the adoption of new tactics and narrowed perspectives on the part of the labour movement, characterised by a piecemeal, gradual and moderate reformism.[30]

These avowedly tentative conclusions were largely theoretically rather than empirically based. Nevertheless, they provided a framework of analysis which proved to be subsequently influential and the important studies of Joyce and Kirk both took their cue from Stedman Jones.[31] Joyce's theoretical debt to Stedman Jones will become apparent by referring back to his views on the nature of the transition to social calm outlined above. To reiterate, he utilised a wide conceptual framework which located the key to changes in working-class attitudes and behaviour in technological advances which brought about a transference of the control of the labour process from labour to capital, and which in turn increased the level of working-class dependency, the seedbed of deference.[32] Kirk's 'materialist explanation of the onset of mid-Victorian stability' similarly made use of a wide framework of explanation, though less emphasis was placed on changes in the labour process. Taking issue with 'labour aristocratic' and 'deferential proletariat' explanations, central importance was attributed to the emergence of a restabilised and dynamic capitalism. This provided the economic background to class manoeuvre and compromise which saw concessions from above and the advancement of sections of the working class within the system. It was also responsible for a many-sided process of working-class fragmentation along occupational, cultural and ethnic lines.[33]

As the above discussion indicates, studies of the relationship between changing structures (especially economic, manifest in changes in work practice and the stabilisation of industrial capitalism) and consciousness have been central in the employment of wider explanatory frameworks which have embraced discussions on the role of factors such as economic improvement, increased working-class dependency, employer paternalism, worker deference, ethnicity, cultural convergence, and the new-found moderation of labour leaders and their institutions. While these explanatory frameworks have accorded primacy to economic conditions and relations, however, the precise nature and role of ideology has been unduly neglected. The ideological content of the political critiques of the 1830s and early 1840s has generally been assumed to be reflective of social bases. Since his review of Foster's book, Stedman Jones has persuasively argued for a more political interpretation of Chartism, in which the roots of exploitation and oppression are attributed to political and not economic causes and in which the decline of radicalism is accorded to changes in the character of the state.[34] He now insists that ideology was prefigurative and not merely reflective of social bases, and claims that neither trade unionism, Owenism nor Ricardian Socialism produced a breakthrough to a more proletarian ideology. This represents a change of intellectual direction from his earlier insistence that changes in working-class ideological, political and cultural formations could be understood in terms of their interrelations with changing economic structures. Kirk has berated as unconvincing and idealistic Stedman Jones' reversal of the explanatory priorities of labour history, contending that the class-based nature of Chartism has been falsely denied through an improper detachment of the material determinations of Chartist ideology and practice.[35]

Stedman Jones' study was nationally based, while Kirk's argument that economic and social structures exerted considerable influence within Chartism was primarily based on an examination of selected material from the area where industrial capitalism was most advanced, the cotton districts of Lancashire and Cheshire constituting the severest testing ground of Stedman Jones' formulation of Chartism. Stedman Jones has certainly understated the force of class tensions and contradictions which did exert some influence within Bolton's reform movements. It seems to me, however, that the '"other" language of Chartism' which Kirk has identified did not displace the emphasis on Old Corruption as the central radical image. What he has termed '*de-facto* anti-capitalist' perspectives were really a set of themes within Chartism which should properly be located as having their greatest influence in the years between 1840 to 1842, when Chartists such as McDouall and Leach showed greater tactical awareness of the possibilities of a trade union base of support. Greater efforts were thus made at persuading trade unionists that there could only be a political solution to their problems and during this phase of the movement themes from the trade union and factory movements were pushed to the fore in Chartist arguments. But these and other economic themes nevertheless continued to be referred back to the political system. Within radicalism, political and not economic roles and relations were seen as primary.

Based on the assumption that developments in the labour process were central to changes in working-class political consciousness and behaviour, all the explanations of change in the cotton districts offered so far still accept broad chronological parameters of change, maintaining that the centrally important contributory factors produced their effects in the late 1840s and early 1850s. This book differs from existing lines of interpretation on the south-east Lancashire experience by suggesting that the origins of middle-class hegemony can be found earlier, in the apparently strife-torn 1830s and early 1840s, and that the restructuring of economic relations, while important, was not necessarily of crucial significance in the overall process of change. Rather, it is suggested that a significant degree of class cooperation in reform movements took place in the 1830s, drawing its strength from a shared political critique and political traditions that operated with a significant degree of autonomy and which were only partly consistent with shifts in economic developments. It was significant, for instance, that both middle-class and working-class reformers defined liberty as against the state and that the campaign against the New Poor Law took on a popular rather than a class-based form. Working-class protest on this issue was further muted by the refusal of Liberal guardians to implement the worst rigours of the new regime and by the fact that changes in administrative forms were not matched by corresponding changes in the treatment of the poor. In the Reform Bill agitation of the late 1820s and early 1830s, the focus on political and not economic roles and relations within the radical analysis of society facilitated cooperation between working-class and petit-bourgeois radicals, who joined forces under a single organisation, the Bolton Political Union. Organisational unity between reformers was not achieved to the same degree in the Chartist period, but Bolton Chartism nevertheless grew out of the revival of both middle-class and working-class radicalism and alliances were formed which again drew their strength from the essentially inter-class appeal of the radical analysis of society. These alliances were subject to periodic bouts of tension and disunity – indeed, class divisions and considerations did not altogether disappear from the field of popular

Liberalism after 1850 – but economic conflict was not necessarily the primary influence in this. Workers' economic aspirations amounted to the restoration of threatened reciprocities with employers and for a more regulated system of market relations, but they did not amount to plans for an 'alternative social system', a 'non-capitalist society', a 'vision of an alternative social order',[36] or the overthrow of capitalist relations of production as such. Moreover, it is suggested that attention to the often strained relations between militant Chartists and Liberals should not be allowed to obscure the fact that, at least in Bolton, Chartism never completely subsumed movements aiming for more gradual change and that there always was a significant number of non-Chartist and moderate working-class reformers from which Liberalism drew considerable support. The movement of labour leaders into the Liberal camp was not as sharp as Kirk has portrayed in his particular test cases,[37] and did not wait for either Foster's 'liberalization' process or Joyce's consolidation of mechanised production. The emphasis, therefore, is on a slow convergence, not a climacteric in the mid-century years. While accepting the views of other historians that the process was far from complete by the 1850s, an attempt will be made to show that it had progressed far more than is often recognised even before the major Chartist uprisings.

Something has to be said about the organisation and presentation of evidence and the choice of Bolton as a case study. The cotton districts of Lancashire and Cheshire are usually held to constitute major examples of breaks or shifts in working-class attitudes and behaviour at mid-century. However, in this book most attention is focused on the broad historical experience of the middle class, developments being considered against the background of the remodelling of the town's local governing institutional network and the alleviation of a number of other problems that confronted the consolidation of a satisfactorily smooth middle-class rule. These included intense industrial conflict across a wide range of trades and 'independent' working-class political insurgency. But internal conflict was also important and it was significant that intra-class relations were usually more important in defining the parameters of middle-class action than relations with either central government or the working class. The latter made only brief and limited forays into local politics on their own behalf and the predominant endemic political rivalry in the town was one within a middle class divided internally along political, denominational, cultural and kinship lines. Conflict was particularly bitter during the struggle for incorporation over the years 1838 to 1842, a period which saw south-east Lancashire gain national significance as a hotbed of Chartism. From the middle-class perspective, however, their struggle was always more important than the parallel Chartist agitation and conflict between labour and capital.[38]

The propriety of presenting developments from this angle is further suggested by considering that, despite the qualifications that the findings of this study may offer to the received historical picture, and notwithstanding the persistence of disagreements, labour historians have in general satisfactorily reconstructed the overall trajectory and historical experience of the working class. As Simon Gunn has recently remarked, however, there is an absence of a similar coherent history of the middle class, which hinders development towards a more scrupulous and perhaps more useful historical synthesis.[39] This is not to deny the importance of those works in this area which have gone some way to incorporating the role of the middle class in power relations within Victorian society, especially those of Foster, Howe and Joyce,[40] which have heightened our understanding of the pattern of nineteenth-century social development. Nevertheless, the role of the middle class in social and political relations within Victorian society has rarely been incorporated into a suitable holistic analytical framework. In this respect, historians still lack a sufficient geographical range of case studies on its culture, institutions, social formation, perceptions and experiences of the elementary constituents of social relations to enable the formulation of firm conclusions. Thus, while John Garrard has already – to some extent – covered themes relating to the municipal history of Bolton in the period under consideration here,[41] for the sake of completeness I thought it necessary to go over some of the main ground in order to explore areas unexplored or inadequately treated in his study. In so doing, it was further necessary to incorporate local politics into a framework of analysis which pays particular attention to the overall nature of the local political system and the interrelations between local and national political developments and movements. Social relations with the working class are considered within this framework as further areas within which the middle class exercised its leadership and power in the local community.

Finally, a study situated in the region where the factory system and the capitalist mode of production were most advanced is favourably placed to examine questions relating to the wider social importance of developments in the labour process, changes in the policies and social practices of employers, the progress and social composition of reform movements, the role of ideology, and the ideological content and social forms taken by mass discontent. Bolton's greater and growing share of medium-fine spinning firms and engineering enterprises helped to differentiate its experience, to some extent, from the other large towns in a region where coarse spinning predominated. Nevertheless, Gadian's examination of the 1841 Occupational Abstract reveals that it had a similar socio-economic profile to most of the other major south-east

Lancashire towns.[42] Textiles accounted for some 43 per cent of the occupied population. A further 29 per cent were to be found in the building industry, metal trades and 'general workshop' category. Mining, labouring and miscellaneous accounted for a further 13.5 per cent, trade and retail another 10 per cent, and the professional and white-collar sector 4.5 per cent.

Notes

1. S. and B. Webb, *The History of Trade Unionism* (New York, 1920), chs. 3–4.
2. A. Briggs (1954) is cited in R. Harrison, *Before the Socialists: Studies in Labour and Politics 1861–1881* (London, 1965), p. 6.
3. *Ibid.*, p. 4.
4. M. I. Thomis, *The Town Labourer and the Industrial Revolution* (London, 1974), ch. 10.
5. A. E. Musson, *British Trade Unions 1800–1875* (London, 1972).
6. They have received attention in H. F. Moorhouse, 'The Marxist Theory of the Labour Aristocracy', *Social History* 3, no. 1 (1978).
7. N. Kirk, *The Growth of Working Class Reformism in Mid-Victorian England* (Beckenham, 1985), p. 7.
8. J. Foster, *Class Struggle and the Industrial Revolution: Early Industrial Capitalism in Three English Towns* (London, 1974), intro.
9. P. Joyce, *Work, Society and Politics: The Culture of the Factory in Later Victorian England* (London, 1980), ch. 2.
10. G. Crossick, *An Artisan Elite in Victorian Society: Kentish London 1840–1880* (London, 1978); R. Q. Gray, *The Labour Aristocracy in Victorian Edinburgh* (Oxford, 1976).
11. Joyce, *op. cit.*, pp. 64–82.
12. Kirk, *op. cit.*, ch. 6.
13. Joyce, *op. cit.*, ch. 6; Kirk, *op. cit.*, pp. 161–166, chs. 6–7.
14. Kirk, *op. cit.*
15. Joyce, *op. cit.*, ch. 2.
16. *Ibid.*, ch. 4; Kirk, *op. cit.*, pp. 291–300.
17. Foster, *op. cit.*, pp. 243–6; Kirk, *op. cit.*, ch. 7.
18. Foster, *op. cit.*; Joyce, *op. cit.*; Kirk, *op. cit.*
19. Foster, *op. cit.*, p. 205.
20. *Ibid.*, pp. 205–6.
21. D. S. Gadian, 'A Comparative Study of Popular Movements in North-West Industrial Towns 1830–1850', Lancaster University Ph.D thesis (1976), pp. 167–9.
22. Joyce, *op. cit.*, p. 96.
23. Kirk, *op. cit.*, ch. 3.
24. For a useful summary of the debate of the labour aristocracy thesis, see D. G. Wright, *Popular Radicalism: The Working-Class Experience 1780–1880* (Harlow, 1988), pp. 162–9.

25.   Foster, *op. cit.*, pp. 206–38.
26.   Joyce, *op. cit.*, pp. xiv–xv, 51–2.
27.   Kirk, *op. cit.*, pp. 6–11, ch. 5.
28.   Foster, *op. cit.*, p. 1.
29.   G. S. Jones, 'Class Struggle and the Industrial Revolution', *New Left Review* 90 (1975), especially pp. 66–7.
30.   *Ibid.*, especially pp. 65–9.
31.   Joyce, *op. cit.*, p. xix; Kirk, *op. cit.*, p. 24.
32.   Joyce, *op. cit.*, chs. 2–3.
33.   Kirk, *op. cit.*, preface.
34.   G. S. Jones, 'The Language of Chartism', in J. Epstein and D. Thompson (eds), *The Chartist Experience: Studies in Working-Class Radicalism and Culture, 1830–60* (London, 1982); G. S. Jones, 'Rethinking Chartism', in his *Languages of Class: Studies in English Working Class History 1832–1982* (Cambridge, 1983).
35.   N. Kirk, 'In Defence of Class: A Critique of Recent Revisionist Writing Upon the Nineteenth-Century English Working Class', *International Review of Social History* XXXII (1987).
36.   Foster, *op. cit.*, pp. 107, 148; Kirk, *op. cit.*, p. 66.
37.   Kirk, *op. cit.*, p. 162.
38.   A similar pattern of events occurred in Manchester, which also experienced a struggle for municipal incorporation. See V. A. C. Gatrell, 'Incorporation and the Pursuit of Liberal Hegemony in Manchester 1790–1839', in D. Fraser (ed.), *Municipal Reform and the Industrial City* (Leicester, 1982).
39.   Simon Gunn, The "Failure" of the Victorian Middle Class: A Critique', in J. Wolff and J. Seed (eds), *The Culture of Capital: Art, Power and the Nineteenth-Century Middle Class* (Manchester, 1983), pp. 17–18.
40.   Foster, *op. cit.*; A. Howe, *The Cotton Masters 1830–1860* (Oxford, 1984); Joyce, *op. cit.*
41.   J. Garrard, *Leadership and Power in Victorian Industrial Towns 1830–80* (Manchester, 1983), chs. 9–10.
42.   Gadian, *op. cit.*, Appendix One.

CHAPTER TWO

Local Politics 1827–1836:
Petit-Bourgeois Radicals and
Local Government

Chapters Two and Three are in a sense complementary. They aim to show the nature of the conflicts that dominated local politics in the second quarter of the nineteenth century, to locate their significance in both the local political arena and national campaigns, and to put municipal reform into historical perspective. The local political system described in these chapters was inhabited almost exclusively by middle-class and petit-bourgeois activists. From the late-1820s to the mid-1830s, the period surveyed in this chapter, a radical petite bourgeoisie – mainly composed of a mixture of shopkeepers, traders and small producers – maintained a vigorous challenge to the rule of the Tory-Anglican oligarchy. In the years from 1837 to 1850, which come under focus in the next chapter, the initiative passed to the Liberal section of the 'big' bourgeoisie, as the endemic political rivalry in local politics became one between a middle class divided internally along political, kinship and denominational lines.

This periodisation will help to locate and put into perspective the significance of the historical role of the petite bourgeoisie. Many historians who have reconstructed the experiences of English industrial communities in the early nineteenth century have adopted a two-class model of society, in which economic and political power is concentrated in few hands and in which the social structure is polarised into antagonistic classes of rich and poor.[1] From this, the politics, values and attitudes of the petite bourgeoisie are usually portrayed, implicitly or explicitly, as fundamentally culturally and ideologically derivative of the big bourgeoisie. For although the concentration on political and not economic roles and relations in the radical analysis of society allowed cooperation between all classes of reformers, the more moderate bases of support were the first to be detached whenever working-class militancy threatened the sanctity of property relations. This was usually sufficient to impel the radical section of the petite bourgeoisie towards a more moderate Liberalism – sharing many affiliations with radicalism and the stratum as a whole towards social conservatism.[2]

While local events tend to support this general view, however, a chronological approach to social developments highlights the early importance of a vigorous petit-bourgeois radicalism in the town. This not only enables a more accurate description of long-term social developments, but also allows the portrayal of a more militant, independent and dynamic strand of radicalism than a concentration on the politics of the two major classes would allow. For with the Liberal élite maintaining a low profile in both national and local politics until 1837, and with the working-class political challenge confined to demands for parliamentary reform, the major radical voice in the local political arena in the period was actually that of the radical section of the petite bourgeoisie. However, to argue for the existence of an independent petit-bourgeois strand of radicalism in this fashion is to encounter the arguments of one historian who has accounted for the political motivation of the petite bourgeoisie in quite a different manner. As John Foster's account of Oldham[3] was based on another town – like Bolton, closely associated with the development of the cotton industry – it will be useful to consider it briefly before going on to the main body of this chapter.

In his portrayal of the south-east Lancashire town, Foster employed a two-class model of society in which capitalists and wage labourers were identified as the major conflict groups, with the relations between the two being seen as primary in shaping the nature of popular politics in the town. Tradesmen, shopkeepers, and small masters were placed into their own sub-groups, and accorded only a subordinate role. The working class based its strategy on control of the local political system and were able to do this because of the vulnerability of shopkeepers and tradesmen to 'exclusive dealing' and other forms of organised working-class pressure. Foster's arguments have received some sceptical reactions from other historians and one of his critics, D. S. Gadian, accorded the town's petite bourgeoisie a more independent role and argued that 'class collaboration rather than class war' was the key to radical success. Gadian saw Oldham's pattern of social relations as more harmonious than towns like Manchester and Bolton, and attributed this to a social and economic structure which he viewed as more closely resembling Birmingham than the other major cotton towns in the region. Accordingly, greater cooperation between social groups resulted primarily from the smaller concentration of ownership in Oldham's cotton industry and the employment of most adult male labour outside that industry in small-scale workshop production, permitting a degree of closeness between masters and men not to be found in most of the neighbouring towns.[4] However, Gadian has been shown to be statistically naive by Sykes, who shows that Oldham's mainstream cotton industry was not significantly smaller than in other towns in the region and indeed, that the town's industry in general was not particularly small-scale by early Victorian standards. Moreover, it is doubtful that

Oldham's pattern of social relations was particularly harmonious and, as Sykes further argues, there would appear to be no simple correspondence between class relations, political radicalism and size of industrial enterprise.[5] This would appear to be the case even in Birmingham. Here historians have usually portrayed the existence of exceptional class harmony and attributed it to an economic structure dominated by small-scale workshop production. Behagg, however, has shown that this picture has little to recommend it, as conflict was endemic and relations between reformers far from amicable.[6]

Despite the shortcomings in Gadian's critique, however, Foster's arguments are nonetheless unconvincing. His claims regarding exclusive dealing – designed with the town-centre shopkeepers in mind – are a case in point, but it is far from clear that the shopkeepers were heavily dependent on direct working-class custom. There is some evidence that shopkeepers were subject to political pressures, both from above and below, but this is inconclusive and more plausible factors exist to explain their political motivation and activities.[7]

Typically, the larger retailer and trader can be identified as active in Bolton politics. Along with small masters, they were strategically important in their own right. Their numerical strength in municipal and parliamentary electorates was greater than that of the middle class 'proper' and it was clearly important for the fortunes of the major parties that they recruited a significant level of support among this stratum. In the first parliamentary election of 1832, for instance, shopkeepers were by far the largest occupational group among the electorate, comprising 212 voters out of an overall total of 935.[8] Relations with working-class radicals were dictated less by coercion than by the primacy of political critiques of oppression over economic explanations of exploitation within radical ideology. As such, the radicalism described in this chapter differed in important respects from the kind described by Foster.

To put it in a wider context, it also differed in significant respects from that described by Behagg for Birmingham. There, widespread industrial conflict, based on a struggle for control in the workplace between labour and capital, is said to have produced two forms of opposing radicalism in which the issue of universal suffrage was central.[9] In Bolton at least, however, it will become clear that it is difficult to establish the existence of a distinctly working-class variant of radicalism, grounded in workers' struggles to maintain control of the 'labour process' in the face of capitalist encroachments. This is not to overlook the fact that divisions did periodically surface between groups of what may be loosely termed middle-class and working-class reformers. In the agitation for the parliamentary reform in the early 1830s, for instance, the rejection of the second Reform Bill in October 1831 served temporarily to disrupt the alliance between the predominantly petit-bourgeois opponents of the Tory-Anglican oligarchy in local government and the mainly working-class supporters of the more radical 'Huntite' programme. However, it is difficult to link this split directly to conflicts at the workplace. Such economic themes did not feature prominently in radical arguments until the early 1840s, and even then, as will be seen later, this can be attributed primarily to tactical political considerations – which, in any case, were always ultimately referred back to the political system.

The radicalism of the petite bourgeoisie initially turned on nothing more than their hostility to an unequal local property assessment – proportionately greater for the middling rather than the larger property owners – imposed by the self-appointed local authorities. However, this situation accorded well with a radical analysis which attributed society's ills to a political source – an unrepresentative and corrupt Parliament which taxed the people not for the general good, but to maintain a spendthrift aristocracy and its parasitic allies. During the parliamentary reform agitation of the early 1830s, a political alliance with the working class was facilitated by a degree of convergence on ideological and economic grounds. Although the alliance was subject to class tensions, this does not mean that it was historically insignificant in the long term; for the petit-bourgeois radicals were able to maintain this tradition of class collaboration into the Chartist period, when they were to play an important role in helping to maintain links between middle-class and working-class reformers at a time when society experienced an increasing degree of social polarisation. This helped to ensure that reformers from all social strata were united in the belief that a more democratic constitution would be the best protection against oppression and, beyond Chartism, it bestowed on 'advanced' Liberalism the aim of a more just society through the opening up of a state machine firmly in the grasp of property-owning élites.

The purpose of this chapter is thus to show how a radical petite bourgeoisie used minor political institutions from which to challenge the authority of the Tory-Anglican oligarchy from the late 1820s. This will involve an outline of the structure of the local governmental system before the introduction of the New Poor Law in 1837 and municipal incorporation in 1838, including consideration of the functions played by the following parochial and township institutions: vestries, churchwardens, overseers, highway surveyors, county magistrates, court leets and improvement trusts. The independent viability of the various institutions will receive some attention, but the emphasis will be on their relationship to the operation of local politics as a whole. Moreover, it will be shown that contemporaries were aware that they were operating in a comprehensive political system whose ramifications engrossed the whole urban experience and extended beyond the local level and into national politics. Thus, whilst we can agree to an extent with Gatrell's verdict that local politics in the nineteenth century operated at a considerable level of autonomy from the Westminster scene and that for most of provincial England, 'they were what politics was "about"',[10] it is important to consider that the radical analysis of society linked instances of local abuse and tyranny with the rule of Old Corruption centred on Westminster, which meant that radicals did not base their strategy solely on control of the local political system. This chapter is thus not exclusively concerned with local politics. It will show how the campaign for changes in local government was the foundation of the leading role played by petit-bourgeois radicals in the agitation for parliamentary reform in the early 1830s.

Local government and politics before municipal incorporation

By the 1820s power in Bolton was exercised through a range of parochial and memorial institutions. As far as any popular participation in the local political system was concerned, the most important points of access were the township vestry meetings of Great Bolton and Little Bolton and the parish meetings of Bolton-le-Moors. The importance of the vestry as a political institution has been highlighted by Fraser, who shows how it related to the politicising of all the minor institutions of local government in Victorian towns. In the context of Oldham, Foster has argued that radicals based their strategy on the control of the local political system and that this was achieved through their control of vestry institutions.[11] Doubts concerning Foster's arguments have already been raised, but the importance of the vestry did not escape Oldham radicals. Bolton radicals also considered vestry institutions to be important and were usually able to gain the upper hand at township and parish meetings. However, they were unable to shake the stranglehold exercised over local affairs by the Tory-Anglican oligarchy.

The importance of the vestry came from its role in matters of finance and taxation. The court leets of Great Bolton and Little Bolton had the sole right to appoint the boroughreeves and constables who, along with various lesser officials, were responsible for maintaining law and order. However, the rates levied to pay these officers' salaries had to be nominally approved by the ratepayers in vestry, who had the right to refuse to sanction the constables' accounts, presented every quarter. As voting at vestry meetings was open to all who paid rates, they could thus become the forum for the expression of ratepayers' grievances about public expenditure and the operation of the police. Moreover, authority to appoint many parochial and local administrative offices resided in the vestry. Ultimately, however, decisions made at this level could be – and were, when it mattered – overridden by the Tory-dominated county magistrates, who had the authority to reinstate rejected accounts and to discard township nominees for the offices of overseer and highway surveyor.

The movement for the reform of local government began in the late 1820s. Most radical energy was concentrated in Great Bolton, the larger and more southerly of the two townships that constituted the town and the place where Tory domination was more strongly entrenched. Depression in 1826 brought distress, most conspicuously to the town's large numbers of hand-loom weavers, but it was the consequent increases in the poor rate that provided the conditions for the emergence of the radical challenge. An unequal assessment of property rates placed most of the burden on the middling ranks of the ratepayers, such as shopkeepers, owners of cottage property and other small property owners. In February 1827 a Leypayers' Committee was formed at a meeting of ratepayers, with the intention of correcting this situation and of bringing 'existing abuses before the public'.[12] The depression also affected poor ratepayers and it was claimed by the radical draper William Naisby – a regular spokesman for the radicals – that in 1828 alone the bench had issued over 1,000 summonses against poor people who had failed to pay their rates.[13] However, throughout the whole of the period under consideration the working class was to make only brief and limited forays into the local political system on its own behalf. Moreover, the committee was largely composed of the likes of shopkeepers and small masters, acting independently and not manipulated into supporting the labour community. Their demands were typical of much of mainstream radicalism, but we need not follow Foster in struggling to identify as exclusively working class the causes they promoted.[14]

A general meeting of ratepayers, convened by the Leypayers' Committee early in March 1827, declared its lack of confidence in the activities of the 'Junta' or 'self-elected body' of assessors and overseers of Great Bolton (it was the custom for retiring overseers to nominate their own successors) and further stated the committee's determination not to recognise any future measures that they might adopt. The intention to serve legal notice to the churchwardens to call a general vestry meeting for the purpose of electing a 'select vestry' was also revealed.[15] The main appeal of this to the radicals lay in the prospect of exerting a greater control over finance. The Select Vestries Act of 1819 gave vestries the choice of surrendering complete responsibility for poor relief to the magistrates or of annually electing a select vestry –

in effect, a parish committee with a maximum membership of 24 – composed of 20 elected ratepayers together with overseers and church-wardens. Along with the Parish Vestries Act of 1818, which provided for the principle of cumulative voting at vestries, whereby a ratepayer would be entitled to between one and six votes depending on the size of his property (this was known as a 'Sturges Bourne poll'), it was originally designed to reduce popular access to the political system.[16] But, although the 1818 Act was occasionally used to restore the balance in favour of wealth at Bolton vestry meetings, the terms of the 1819 Act conveyed slightly different connotations in the context of local politics; for Naisby and the radicals, it was a measure that was eminently suitable for the purposes of transferring the control of local taxation and public expenditure away from the very wealthy and into the hands of the middling ranks of the ratepayers.[17] As police and church rates were traditionally levied as an integral part of the general poor rate, a select vestry would carry the potential of a real political counterweight to the rule of the Tory-Anglican oligarchy. Comparison with Foster's account of Oldham will illustrate this point more fully. There the ratepayers appear to have opted for the select vestry by 1820. Certainly, by the 1830s petit-bourgeois radicals were able to manage elections to ensure that they carried a permanent majority of radicals and, invariably, a radical chairmanship. This enabled them to retain control of poor relief in the town until the delayed takeover of the New Poor Law in 1847.[18]

In Bolton, however, the overseers and churchwardens refused to comply with the committee's demands for a general vestry meeting, and in fact a select vestry was never established. A general meeting of the ratepayers of Great Bolton then followed early in April, which resolved not only to appeal to the Quarter Sessions to secure a more equitable assessment of property, but also, as 'several Hundreds of Pounds per Annum, might be saved in the salaries of the different public officers in this town ... to allow no salaries whatever to be taken out of the Poor Leys, unless they have a voice in electing such officers and fixing their salaries according to law'. To further these aims, the radicals, in declaring themselves to be dissatisfied with the recently appointed overseers, further resolved 'to appeal, or take other measures as the law authorizes, for the purpose of superseding their re-appointment'.[19] This had the desired effect and the overseers now agreed to an immediate revision of the assessments, to be supervised by a committee composed of members of both sides.[20] But this was hardly sufficient to appease the increasing aspirations of the radicals, now flushed with success and assured of continuing ratepayer support as poor rates continued to rise, reaching fifteen shillings in the pound by December 1828.[21] The radicals did not immediately resort to the tactic of refusing to sanction the constables' accounts, however, but first adopted a strategy suggested by Naisby at a meeting held shortly before the one in April, whereby the scale of the salaries allowed to the various officials of the town was to be challenged in vestry.[22] The radicals were to attempt to raise the political conscious-ness of ratepaying groups by raising issues concerned with the alleged inefficiency and extravagance of the present administration, popular with vestry audiences, and linking them to wider questions concerning power and authority in local affairs.[23]

At the August 1827 township meeting the Leypayers' Committee revealed plans to reduce the salaries paid to the various officials of Great Bolton from over £1,000 to £380. The governor of the workhouse, who allegedly enjoyed 'more feasting at that house, than in any gentleman's house in Bolton', whilst providing food barely fit for human consump-tion for the inmates, was accused of sheer extravagance and was to have his salary and board reduced from £250 to £100. Other proposed cuts, which included the abolition of the charge for the salary of the deputy constable's assistant ('That officer ought to pay it out of his own salary') and for the services of the market regulator (his duties were to be per-formed by the bellman), brought into question the efficiency of the present administration. The question of the liability of the ratepayers for some of the charges imposed was also raised (Naisby contended that it was illegal to pay salaries out of the poor rate). Underlying these accusations of extravagance and inefficiency, however, was the real issue of the control of taxation. After the boroughreeve, James Scowcroft, remarked that 'the observations respecting the deputy constables were foreign to the meeting. The lord of the manor would have his consta-bles, and whatever the committee might do at a town's meeting, would be of no avail,' Mr Morley (a hatter) replied that he 'cared not who appointed the town's officers, if the ley payers had not to pay them', to which Naisby added the demand that 'a general vestry ought to be called, to regulate these salaries'. In short, even if the court leets retained the right to select the town's officers, an increase in the authority of the vestry to regulate their salaries promised to make many of their powers ineffectual. This meeting ended in confusion when the unceremonious departure of the town's officers brought it to a premature halt.[24]

The radicals had gained little ground and now took to persuading the ratepayers to disqualify the constable's accounts outright, on the grounds that the town's officers ought to be more accountable to those that subsidised them. The demands remained basically the same: the court leets were to continue to have the right to select the town's officers, but the ratepayers ought to have the power to fix their salaries. When the radicals were successful in the first vestry meeting of the following year, the boroughreeve and constable 'appeared panic struck at the result of the decision of the meeting, and were incapable for some time of replying'.[25] The authorities did not attempt to circumvent this decision by a Sturges Bourne poll and all subsequent Great Bolton township vestry meetings throughout 1828 achieved the same result. For reasons that are not clear, the radicals then apparently abandoned the tactic in 1829 and all the accounts for that year were passed without opposition.[26] It seems likely, however, that their problem was the readiness of the Tory-controlled Bolton division of the county magistrates to use its formal power to reinstate rejected accounts upon their presentation to the bench by the constables. At least, this is what happened in 1831 – and also in 1832 when, in the context of the parliamentary reform agitation of that year, the radicals extended their demands and called for the parish constables to be not only subsidised but also elected by the rate-payers.[27] Thus the first vestry meeting of 1832 refused to sanction the constables' accounts and carried Naisby's amendment that 'no salaries be paid out of the poor rates, unless the persons by whom such salaries are received, be elected by the leypayers once a year'. The magis-trates subsequently reinstated the accounts, but had been divided on the issue and one of the five then present indicated that in future they would reinstate no more accounts unless the ratepayers had the 'privilege' of fixing their salaries.[28] The prospect of a ratepayer-elected police may have caused the magistrates to suffer a temporary loss of nerve and their actions certainly made the radicals feel that many of them were ready to make concessions. But any hopes of concrete gains were dashed as disqualified accounts continued to receive magisterial sanction.[29] The year 1832 was the last in which the radicals maintained any sustained challenge in vestry to the prerogatives of the court leets (and indirectly to the magistrates who vetted the accounts). But radical agitation continued nonetheless at other points in the institutional system outside the immediate jurisdiction of the court leets.

We have already seen how the radicals questioned the propriety of paying the salaries of unelected officials out of the poor rates and objected to the mode of appointing overseers. The overseers' role in collecting poor rates had always made them important, and from 1832 their function in compiling the electoral register made them even more so. In 1833 the radicals made their first real attempts to secure the appointment of their own nominees. In March a requisition signed by 165 of the ratepayers of Great Bolton was presented to the overseers and churchwardens of that township, calling upon them to convene a vestry meeting for the purpose of adopting a list of names to be considered eligible for the position of overseer in the forthcoming year. The same list was then to be presented before the magistrates – who again constituted the formal authority in such matters – from which they were expected to make their appointments. The overseers declined to call the meeting, 'because the custom from time immemorial was for the retiring overseers to appoint their successors'. But as this system *was* merely founded on custom, the Liberal lawyer Winder felt that the magistrates might consider the wishes of the ratepayers on the subject, and the radicals therefore convened their own public meeting at which they adopted a list of ten names. The magistrates concurred with the ratepayers on this issue and appointed the three overseers for the township from their list, in opposition to one presented by the overseers and churchwardens.[30]

After 1833 the magistrates usually chose overseers from lists adopted at township meetings dominated by reformers, but when occasion suited them, they could still intervene to restore the balance in favour of the Tories. In March 1836 the constables wished to augment the police force and, in preparation for this, some Tory employers marched their spinners to the vestry in an attempt to carry the Conservative list. Many of the workers subsequently refused to bow to their employers' wishes and the reformers' list was adopted. However, although it had become 'customary' for the magistrates to appoint the first three names on the adopted list, they now 'broke with custom' and struck off the name of Naisby, appointing Richard Daly, from the defeated Tory list, in his place, a Great Bolton trustee and former constable and boroughreeve.[31] Because at this particular time the Tories controlled the two churchwardens of the parish of Bolton-le-Moors, who also functioned as overseers, they had now effectively regained control. The significance of this move proved to be the overseers' role in collecting rates. The authorities pressed ahead with their plans to increase the police force, and although a Great Bolton township meeting refused to sanction the appointment of an extra six police officers, these were appointed regardless and paid for out of the poor rates collected by the overseers. The radicals challenged the legality of this move at the subsequent vestry meeting and, accusing the overseers of 'robbery', tried to get the accounts disqualified. But many shopkeepers and small traders had since become convinced of the need for extra police protection and, after a Sturges Bourne poll, the accounts for the quarter were passed by 291 votes to 185.[32] In April 1837 the reformers were again successful at a Great Bolton township meeting, but controversy over the impending introduction of the New Poor Law had raised the stakes and this time the magistrates rejected the adopted list in its entirety.[33] As shall be seen in the next chapter, the magistrates also intervened in 1838, when the overseers were drawn into the struggle for municipal incorporation.

If, because of its function in collecting rates, the office of overseer was important to all parties, then so too, in similar respects, was that of churchwarden. As we have seen, even when the magistrates appointed reformers as overseers, the Tories were still often able to exercise an overall control through the churchwardens. For this and other reasons, the office was politically contested from 1831. The churchwardens derived much of their authority and status from their power to levy a church rate to maintain the fabric of the church. This meant that the intrinsic status of the office was worthy of consideration. But as the legitimacy of church rates was being challenged by Dissenters in Bolton and elsewhere in the 1830s, it was drawn into the conflict between the established Church and nonconformity which underlay much of the political life of nineteenth-century England.[34] Churchwardens were also important because of their power to convene vestry meetings for the regulation of township or parish affairs.

Churchwardens in Bolton were formally appointed at a parish vestry meeting convened for that purpose. By 1830 this appears to have become a matter of mere convention, for the Anglican vicar was clearly taken by surprise when, in April 1831, his right to appoint both the churchwarden and sidesman was challenged by a number of leading radicals who had attended in order to contest the election. They contended that, while the vicar had a perfect legal right to appoint one churchwarden, he had no right to appoint more than one, and therefore the election of the sidesman (i.e. the churchwarden's assistant) was a matter for the parishioners. For the radicals, 'the question was of importance to the inhabitants, because the churchwardens for the time being were overseers of the poor.'[35] Thus attempts by the radicals to gain access to the rate-collecting points in the institutional system began at the office of churchwarden. As in the case of the overseers, the Reverend Slade contended that his right to appoint both officers was based on customary practice, on 'the immemorial custom for the Vicar of Bolton to chuse these officers'. The radicals followed up the vestry meeting by sending a deputation to remonstrate with Slade, who, after thus becoming acquainted with the legal position, subsequently conceded, though insisting that those appointed for the ensuing year remain in place and that his right to elect the senior officer remain intact.[36]

It does not appear to have mattered too much to the radicals at this stage whether their nominee served as churchwarden or sidesman. However, they eventually won the right for the ratepayers to elect their own full churchwarden to serve alongside the vicar's nominees (a churchwarden and a sidesman). For Naisby, although the Tories retained overall control of the office, this success was nevertheless of importance because the additional churchwarden was also to function as an overseer and 'because the people never had any voice in the appointment of the overseers, and the last appointment was not approved of by any of them'.[37] The radical pawnbroker Charles Nuttall was duly elected churchwarden in 1832 and 1833.[38] Yet the radicals failed to contest the elections of 1834 and 1835. This would appear to be because the magistrates were by then appointing overseers from lists of names adopted at township meetings. For when, in 1836, the magistrates began to reassert their authority and reject township nominees for overseer, the radicals moved to ensure that they were not excluded from this office by successfully contesting the election for churchwarden, with Naisby being returned.[39]

Although the main interest that the office of churchwarden had held for the radicals was in its role as overseer, religious tensions nonetheless provided an important motivation for political action against the established Church. Locally, the attack on church rates was focused on the vestry and was directed by the same radical leaders who were assailing the Tory–Anglican oligarchy in all the minor institutions of local government. These do not appear to have been particularly imbued with any religious fervour and economic and political motives were primary. Nevertheless, during the period of this vigorous petit-bourgeois challenge, from the late 1820s to the mid-1830s, it was in this particular form of attack on privilege and monopoly that religious differences most strongly infused political ones. Naisby, for instance, was 'a Quaker in principle' for whom 'there was nothing just in one congregation paying the expenses of another'.[40]

Church rates were supposed to be levied for the forthcoming twelve months at a rate set at a parish vestry meeting, but as they were usually collected along with the poor rates, the customary practice was for the past year's accounts to be presented for the approval of the ratepayers of the parish in vestry, similar to the way in which the constables' accounts were presented quarterly. The campaign against church rates began in July 1832, shortly after the radicals had first got their own nominee appointed as churchwarden. Some of those opposed to church rates, led by the radicals Naisby and Joseph Skelton (linen draper), gathered at the parish vestry meeting in July, where they expressed their disapproval of the accounts in a show of hands, with 75 votes in favour of church rates and 65 against at a Sturges Bourne poll.[41] However, the radicals also took other steps by putting pressure on the overseers and, in the case of the unequal assessments episode, this brought another notable success. They now served the churchwardens notice that no more church rates should be collected along with the poor rate as it was illegal to do so, arguing that some ratepayers would object to their own accounts unless the practice was ceased forthwith. The object of this strategy was to raise the awareness of a public that was apparently apathetic to the issue of church rates. The only publicity that parish vestry meetings usually received was the posting of a notice on the door of the parish church. The meeting to appoint churchwardens in 1832 was 'numerously and respectably attended', but had received no greater announcement than the reading out of a notice in the parish church on the Sunday beforehand. And while the collecting of church rates along with the poor rates saved the ratepayers the expense of a separate survey and collection (estimated at over £180), it was believed that the present method did not alert the ratepayers to their true interests; Naisby claimed that 'People now did not know that they paid any church rate, but by dividing it from the poors' rate, they would know it, and ... He did not think that the rate would be able to be collected legally.' However, the radicals recorded an even more immediate success. The refusal of the overseers to collect any more church rates along with the poor rates meant that a rate for the ensuing twelve months now had to be levied, and the boroughreeve, the wealthy cotton-spinner Peter Ormrod, moved that a rate of a halfpenny in the pound be laid on the parish of Bolton-le-Moors. However, the prospect of having to collect the rates via the churchwarden was enough to change the minds of many. Even Anglicans like the Reverend Thistlewaite, incumbent of St George's, considered that a separate collection was extravagant and that, in these circumstances, church expenses were better defrayed by their own congregations. Naisby was able to pass an amendment, to the effect that no rate at all be levied, by 'a very large majority', with only five persons supporting the original motion.[42]

The church postponed the next meeting from July until December, so that the costs of completing the building of the walls around Trinity Church could be accommodated in the rate to be set. However, Naisby was of the opinion that Parliament was about to change the law relating to church rates and, by a large majority, the meeting carried his amendment to the effect that the meeting be adjourned for twelve months to see if Parliament would take any action.[43] The church could have taken a strictly legal line and insisted on levying a rate, but it did not do so. This effectively marked the end of church rates in Bolton. The building of Emmanuel Church (completed 1839) foreshadowed an expansion of Anglican church building in the 1840s and the entire costs of £3,881 were raised by public donation. The project began after Slade had requested that a public subscription raised to honour him, totalling over £500, be put towards the erection of a church and school in the most eligible part of Bolton.[44]

The highway surveyor carried a relatively low social status and, because of this, it was one of the least attractive of the offices of parochial administration in nineteenth-century English towns.[45] Nevertheless, as with the other parochial and township institutions reviewed here, his role in public expenditure via the levying of highway rates meant that the radicals used the office to highlight further instances of abuse, inefficiency and extravagance on the part of the Tory establishment, and in this way it was drawn into the all-embracing struggle for local control.

The radicals first began to return their own nominees to the office in 1831, when the magistrates agreed to make their appointments from lists of names adopted at township meetings (Great Bolton and Little Bolton had two surveyors each). Again, most interest was focused on Great Bolton. The list for Great Bolton for 1833–4, for instance, was reported as being adopted by a well-attended meeting, but only five people attended the corresponding meeting for Little Bolton.[46] In the two years following the election of radicals as highway surveyors for Great Bolton, public expenditure in this department was first reduced from over £2,200 per annum to £970 and then to £807.[47] As in the case of church rates and the other institutions of local government, however, the significance of this to the radicals went further than a concern for economy. It appears that these petit-bourgeois radicals were less concerned with altering the precise functions of the various institutions of local government than with opening up those bodies to public participation. Thus popular control of even the humblest of offices, in this case that of highway surveyor, was evidence for one radical source of 'the beneficial operation of the public voice in such appointments. In fact, popular elections afford the best, if not the only security, that the business of such offices will be conducted with the greatest regard to economy and general utility.' For the same source, the argument even extended to the institutions responsible for law and order, it being contended that a popular voice in the management of the police would also bring greater efficiency to that department. It was in this way that the surveyors were drawn into the struggle for control over local administration:

It is very probable that the next struggle, on the part of the inhabitants, will be for that proper voice in the appointment of the municipality they ought to enjoy, and for the sole appointment of the salaried officers connected with that body. These have hitherto been considered as places of patronage, and the town has been saddled with the persons filling them, and been obliged to pay them, without being at all consulted on the affair; and all their efforts to effect a change have been to no avail. The leypayers are, however, now determined that they will no longer defray the expense of these officers, unless the appointment is vested in them ... Institutions of such antiquity as court leets, which, according to their ancient form, are fast verging into insignificance, and becoming also obsolete in power, must give way, and be remodelled according to the spirit of the age. If they are not, their utility is gone; for being disowned by society they will no longer be obeyed. But if ... the appointments under them were determined by the public voice, they might yet be of utility ... We have solely been induced to refer to this subject again, from a fear that the town may be left without an efficient police, at a time when one may be needed ...[48]

The two main regulatory bodies for public health and improvement purposes were the Great Bolton and Little Bolton trustees. These were established by an Act of Parliament in 1792 which provided the Great Bolton trustees with an income from rents from the enclosure of Bolton Moor. The Little Bolton trustees had no such income from rents, but both trusts were given powers to levy a 'police rate' for paving, lighting and improving purposes.[49] Both bodies were at first oligarchic in character; the trustees, who had to hold property to the value of at least £1,000 in Great Bolton and £500 in Little Bolton, were appointed for life and vacancies were filled by co-option.

In 1830 an Act of Parliament reformed the Little Bolton trust, making it more open in character by providing for the annual election of at least ten out of the thirty trustees at a public meeting of ratepayers of only seven months' standing or more.[50] It became the usual practice for trustees to be elected by a show of hands and without any stringent checks as to the eligibility of the voters who made up the crowd. This meant that the Liberals, who had the support of the radicals, were able to establish a control which the Tories only challenged after municipal incorporation made it exigent to do so.[51]

The Great Bolton trustees, forty in number (commonly referred to by the radicals as the 'forty thieves') and Tory-dominated, resisted pressure to make that body also more open in character, though in 1831 they did agree to try a reformed method of appointment. Vacancies in the trust were now to be filled from lists of nominees elected at Great Bolton vestry meetings. Having been in operation for a period of nearly two years, however, the procedure was terminated after the radicals had successfully managed to insert seven of their nominees into the trust. In March 1833 the trustees went back to electing themselves when they rejected the ratepayers' list of nominees by fifteen votes to eleven and appointed a Tory instead. The pretext for this decision was that the trustees had not taxed the people for two years and therefore the ratepayers were considered no longer to have any material interest in the trust. The income from rents from Bolton Moor was worth £2,700 per annum to the trustees. When expenditure exceeded this limit, they had the authority to levy a police rate up to a maximum of 2s. 6d. in the pound. But the success of the highway surveyors in reducing public expenditure meant that the police rate had not been levied for two years and was now deemed effectively abolished, the trustees ignoring radical protests that they nevertheless retained this power if and when there was occasion for it.[52]

We have already seen how radical control of the highway surveyors was used to make a case for the benefits of a more open, but not necessarily remodelled, local government. And in 1833 the high-handedness of the Great Bolton trust brought forth calls for an Act of Parliament to open that body to greater public participation, whilst leaving its essential functions intact: 'because we believe the present police acts, if properly administered, are quite adequate to the purposes of the town, and the only bar to their being efficiently administered, is the want of representation we have laid down'.[53] The point is made here because it will be argued in Chapter Two that designs for a more sweeping reform of the institutional system were more representative of the perspective of the Liberal big bourgeoisie who entered the political arena in force in 1837.

The analysis presented so far has shown how a radical petite bourgeoisie opposed the Tory-Anglican oligarchy in the institutional network that constituted local government. The various posts surveyed carried their own intrinsic status and authority, but the emphasis here has been to show how they were all focal points in a wider struggle for supremacy in local affairs. Now it will be shown how this conflict was the foundation of the prominent role played by the town's petit-bourgeois radicals in national politics. Among the most persistent advocates of parliamentary reform over the period 1830–2 were those who had been pressing for greater parochial representation. For this social group in particular, the reform of both local and national political structures became almost inseparable issues, and some aspects of national politics are therefore considered here. The wealthy Liberal élite, although not altogether absent from the campaign for parliamentary reform, maintained a low profile, as indeed was the case in local politics. This left the way open for cooperation between petit-bourgeois and working-class radicals and an alliance was facilitated by a convergence of outlook on both economic and ideological grounds. These groups also brought important differences in perspective into the alliance, which subjected it to bouts of tension and disunity. The emergence of a more militant strand of working-class radicalism was instrumental in the eventual subsumption of the early petit-bourgeois radicalism described in this chapter into an all-embracing Liberalism. But the concept of the essential unity of the 'industrious classes' against an unproductive aristocracy and its allies was not subjected to quite the same stress as it was in the Chartist agitation, when the Liberal élite played a greater role in the reform movement.

The political outlook of the petite bourgeoisie in perspective: local campaigns and national politics

The campaign for parliamentary reform began in earnest in Bolton in April 1830, with the formation of the Bolton Political Union at a crowded public meeting addressed by petit-bourgeois and working-class radicals.[54] It was 'founded nearly upon the same principles as the Birmingham Union', though in an attempt to 'render it palatable to all parties' and attract the influential and wealthy, 'not on the broad basis of annual parliaments, universal suffrage, and vote by ballot'.[55] However, these demands were later adopted when the Political Union was relaunched at a public meeting in October. Although the wealthy were not altogether absent from the reform agitation, they remained aloof from the Political Union, whose moderate stance also apparently worked against it attracting a mass support.[56] However, its adoption of more radical policies marked an increase in the scale of political activity in the town. Over 1,000 people crammed into the theatre at its relaunch. Thereafter it successfully built up its support and by January 1832 it had more than 4,000 names on its books, about double the membership achieved by the Bolton Working Men's Association during the later Chartist agitation.[57] No less significant was the fact that working-class radicals were united under a single organisation with those petit-bourgeois radicals who were agitating for reforms in local government.

Those of the latter who supported radical causes appear to have done so willingly and not because of their alleged vulnerability to forms of organised working-class pressure. As argued earlier, little credence is given to Foster's account of exclusive dealing.[58] As far as the uncovered evidence goes, radicals did on occasion call for the adoption of the tactic. However, it does not appear to have been particularly effective or organised on any extensive scale. In fact, most references to it allude to a system of securing votes through a mixture of patronage and coercion exercised from above. The town-centre shopkeepers were subject to influence and intimidation from their wealthier clientele and Robert Heywood once withdrew his account from a Deansgate shopkeeper for voting Conservative in the 1847 parliamentary election.[59] Coercion of this type extended down the social scale to the few enfranchised operative spinners, who were generally regarded as captive voters by their employers. Those who did not display due deference were liable to dismissal, as was the case with fifteen of the spinners in the employ of William Bolling, Tory candidate in the 1841 parliamentary election. The spinners' leader, Samuel Howarth, claimed that the practice of exclusive dealing by Tories in that election was carried out to a 'frightful extent'.[60] The Tory party was also thought to have established an extensive system of patronage among the town's professional groups (especially legal and medical), which was attributed to their greater wealth.[61] In general, therefore, coercion was unlikely to have significantly affected the course of elections and does not satisfactorily explain political motivation and behaviour. Persuasion and not intimidation was the key to obtaining political allegiance.[62]

To understand why reformers could cooperate in the parliamentary reform campaign, it is important to understand that, whilst deteriorating industrial relations was an important factor in the development of a more militant political outlook among working-class radicals, this was not fundamental to relations between groups of reformers who were predominant in the Political Union; this tension emanated from outside the economic relationship between workers and shopkeepers/tradesmen, which differed significantly from that between the two major classes. There was much to unite the two groups. For instance, a squeeze on wages often meant a reduction in turnover for shopkeepers. In March 1827, for example, shopkeepers and owners of cottage property publicly bemoaned the deteriorating condition of the hand-loom weavers, which they said also adversely affected their own situation. The shopkeepers suffered from loss of custom, while the cottage owners experienced increasing difficulties in securing payment of rent.[63] Similarly, the widespread practice of 'truck' (which compelled workers to accept payment of wages in kind or to purchase goods from shops run by their employers) reduced the amount of potential working-class custom, which meant that many shopkeepers had little sympathy with millowners and, in this respect, they were able to cooperate with workers. The opening of the parliamentary reform agitation also coincided with an anti-truck campaign. Meetings were described as being attended by the likes of traders, shopkeepers, small property owners – whose petition to Parliament contained 7,000–8,000 signatures – and workers, whose petition amassed 14,000 signatures. Again, some familiar names played a leading role – Naisby, Cropp (proprietor and editor of the *Bolton Chronicle*) and Ormrod (currier), all of whom were original members of the Leypayers' Committee.[64] Shopkeepers also supported the more specifically working-class demands for shorter hours in cotton factories. In the 1833 campaign to secure the ten-hour day, for instance, all the local townships in and around Bolton petitioned Parliament, with the one from Great Bolton receiving the signatures of 702 tradesmen and shopkeepers.[65] In Manchester the situation was different, probably as a result of its variegated social structure and the greater presence of the 'shopocracy' there, as befitted its position as a major retail and servicing as well as manufacturing centre. The Manchester Political Union, formed in July 1830, was also ignored by the wealthy and its decision-making council was dominated by petit-bourgeois shopkeepers and small masters. These seem to have been confident enough to exclude working men, who formed their own rival and more radical 'low' Political Union.[66]

The terrain of political ideology also provided a basis for co-operation. The attack on 'Old Corruption' in State and Church was a stock-in-trade theme of the British radical press between 1800 and the 1830s.[67] It was of importance to local radicals not least because it was part of a wider attack against irrationality and unaccountability in all spheres of public life. Those social groups that were excluded from the benefits of Old Corruption were nevertheless taxed to maintain it and were further subjected to instances of abuse in the local political system whose origins were located in the unreformed constitution. One of the main reasons why radicals supported the agitation for parliamentary reform was because this promised to be a means not only of dismantling Old Corruption at Westminster, but also of reforming the closed municipal corporations and manorial courts which were seen as integral features of that system. In the attack on the unreformed constitution, the essentially petit-bourgeois radicalism surveyed here was able to cohere with a developing working-class politics because the centrality of Old Corruption in the radical analysis made possible an alliance based primarily on political rather than economic roles and analyses. Petit-bourgeois and working-class radicals were able to unite because both saw their problems as arising primarily from their exclusion from political power. Thus, although the reform agitation of 1830 to 1832 coincided with a phase of widespread industrial conflict, this was because the petite bourgeoisie played an insignificant role as employers in a time of structural economic change and economic distress. The concept underpinning the alliance of the essential unity of interests held by the 'industrious classes' against an idle and parasitic aristocracy was not subjected to the degree of stress it received in the Chartist agitation, when the Liberal big bourgeoisie played a greater role in reform movements. The radical analysis of society accorded the suffering of the 'industrious classes' to political causes and, as such, the emphasis was on parliamentary reform. The fundamental conflict in society was not seen as one between working class and middle class or labour and capital, but one between 'the industrious classes of every description' against an unproductive aristocracy and their parliamentary nominees, 'whose interest it is to serve the lords of the soil, at the expense of the industry of the nation'.[68] This was not an ideology of capitalist exploitation, but one that denounced oppression and parasitic wealth of a financial and speculative kind: the emphasis was on Old Corruption and taxation and not production relations and profits.

From the reports, addresses and resolutions passed at the meetings which saw the formation and subsequent relaunching of the Political Union, we can elaborate upon the general nature of the ideology under discussion. Pride of place in the radical analysis of society's ills was accorded to the crippling burdens imposed by excessive taxation, levied against the consent of the people to fight ruinous wars and enrich a parasitic and spendthrift aristocracy. The disproportionate tax burden imposed on the 'working classes' was 'fast levelling every poor man and tradesman to the ground':

> The lower orders are sunk into a state of distress, and the middle classes are descending, from the inability of the former body, into the same state; and upon a political axiom, unless the working classes be in a prosperous condition, because they comprise the great majority of consumers and producers, other classes must inevitably fall.[69]

As a corrupt Parliament was the means by which the aristocracy extracted the wealth produced by the industrious classes and legislated against their interests, a reform of Parliament would constitute the corrective to the burdens imposed by the direct acts of the legislature, and would also be the means of pushing through such measures as the abolition of the newspaper stamp duty and the removal of 'the enormous revenues which the Church extracts from the pockets of the people in the shape of Tythes, Dues, and other exactions'.[70] Furthermore, as petit-bourgeois radicals especially were 'convinced of the necessity of economy and retrenchment in parochial affairs, as well as in affairs of state' and angry at 'the manner in which the public money of this town has lately been appropriated to individual, illegal, and unjust purposes', parliamentary reform was further desirable as a means of effectively abolishing 'local abuses' by opening up those 'parochial aristocracies', the closed manorial courts and municipal corporations.[71]

The inter-connections made in the radical analysis between Old Corruption and the 'barbarism and feudal government, of Court Leets and Court Barons'[72] in Bolton and elsewhere, would have had some appeal to the minor as well as middling ranks of the ratepayers, though it is clear that this part of the Political Union's platform was formulated and articulated by the vestry radicals, a point further underlined by Naisby's belief that parliamentary reform would be the means of changing parochial representation; at a vestry meeting in October 1832, in moving an amendment to reject the constables' accounts, he was of the opinion that:

> after the present authorities were out of office the Magistracy would not pass the official accounts again; and as the holding of the Court

Leet was drawing very near, he trusted that some arrangement would be made, by which the Leypayers would be consulted in the appointment of the salaried officers; indeed, it was likely that the Court Leet would meet for the last time, as he expected the Reform Bill would be the means of putting into the hands of the Leypayers the power they ought to possess.[73]

There were no plans for social and economic levelling, but a better deal for the middling and minor ratepayers was envisaged and the avowed intention of the platform of the Political Union was 'the better protection of property belonging to all classes of the community'. The state of economic relations between the two major classes was not specifically discussed, but both shopkeepers and workers had reason to dislike those wealthy employers who 'amassed their fortune by the unrewarded industry of the labourer'. Many artisans were themselves small masters and property-owners, and labour power itself was seen by many workers as a form of property that ought to be accorded due protection. Thus, whilst there was to be no fundamental reform of property relations as such, parliamentary reform held out the prospect of making the labour market a politically regulated one.[74] This appealed especially to the hand-loom weavers, whose industrial weakness had been behind their periodic appeals to Parliament for some form of statutory regulation of wages. They were strongly represented on the council of the Political Union, as were the spinners, whose industrial position was now under serious technological threat, but it was the weavers who provided the major working-class presence in the reform agitation. Thus the weaver Thomas Smith, whilst seemingly aware of a relationship between capitalist relations of production and the exploitation of labour, nevertheless saw taxation rather than profits as the main source of his oppression:

The labouring man built the gorgeous palaces of the rich, and invented and manufactured all the machinery which puts the wealth into the pockets of the capitalist; still he is deemed one of the mob, one of the swinish multitude; and if he happens to meet one of those whom he clothes and feeds, he is shunned lest their fine broad cloth should come into contact with the filth and rags which their oppressions compel him to wear ... He was compelled to serve a government which he must naturally abhor, because they deprived him, of the means of earning his bread by the sweat of his brow; a government which rejoiced over their victims when writhing under the effects of their misrule ... He would therefore never consent to any but a real radical reform in the House of Commons, which once obtained, all our grievances would vanish like the dew before the morning sunbeams. (Cheers)[75]

Thus the view that the ills of society were attributable to the misrule of an aristocratic clique who, with their tail of sinecurists, placemen and priests, maintained a grip on the nation's resources was an analysis common to radicals from all social classes.

However, although reformers could agree that a radical reform of Parliament was necessary, there was much disagreement on strategy, tactics and principles, mostly attributable to important differences in the perspectives and conceptions of the aims of parliamentary reform between working-class radicals and the more moderate reformers. Only the wealthier and more influential sections of the middle class were likely to sway an aristocratic Parliament by rational persuasion, but we have already seen that the failure of the Political Union to attract these sections was a prime motive in the adoption of the popular radical platform of universal manhood suffrage, the ballot, and annual Parliaments. The tactics of the Catholic Association in Ireland had demonstrated an alternative strategy in the potential of carefully organised mass pressure, ostensibly peaceable, though hinting that force would be resorted to if suitable concessions were not forthcoming.[76] Reactions to the rejection of the second Reform Bill in October 1831 were quite different and highlighted latent differences of opinion about how far popular pressure ought to be taken if rational persuasion was ineffective in carrying through a measure of reform. Upon news of the rejection reaching town, the moderate reformers requisitioned the town's authorities to call a public meeting for the purpose of adopting an address to the King, asking him to stand by his ministry and exercise his royal prerogative to push the Bill through Parliament. At the same time, the more radical reformers issued a similar requisition, though they were in favour of an even more extensive measure of reform. They also formed a committee of twenty-five people, consisting chiefly of working men, to organise a public protest in case the authorities declined to sanction one. When this actually happened, the committee (not to be confused with the council of the Political Union) resolved to 'go the whole hog' and, declining to support any measure not founded upon universal manhood suffrage, the ballot and annual Parliaments, organised a meeting attended by over 6,000 people.[77] The *Bolton Chronicle*, now with a new editor though still the mouthpiece of the moderate reformers, considered this essentially to be a 'Bolton Radical Operative Meeting' and declined to publish a report on 'this ridiculous affair'.[78]

Towards the end of the year attitudes hardened even further as the reform crisis deepened. Early in November the Political Union, now in fact operating illegally after the King's proclamation banning political unions, moved further to the left and adopted the principles of the National Union of the Working Classes. This in itself did not alienate its petit-bourgeois supporters, but when, later in the month, the union organised a public meeting to support a Declaration of Rights, agreed upon at a delegate meeting in Manchester, and to appoint deputies to a National Convention (an 'anti-Parliament' representing the wishes of the people, but considered too extreme by many), this was all too much for the moderate reformers, and several shopkeepers and small masters resigned from the council: Naisby, J. Robinson (provision dealer), P. Staton (barber), J. Waring (tailor), W. Greenhalgh (jobbing carpenter), T. Black (boot and shoemaker), J. Brown (clogger), W. Hayhurst (publican) and others.[79]

Thus, although reformers had cooperated under a single organisation, facilitated by a degree of convergence on economic and ideological grounds, the different conceptions of parliamentary reform that each brought to the alliance subjected it to tensions that resulted in its rup-ture in 1831. But this did not prevent further cooperation, for tactical considerations were also important. It seems clear that the more radical reformers were quite prepared to accept a moderate measure of reform, but only as a first instalment. Thus, in February and March 1831 leading working-class radicals, including the weavers Thomas Smith, John Aston and John Cargon, spoke at public meetings along with moderate Liberals, petit-bourgeois radicals and Tories in support of resolutions calling for a moderate measure of parliamentary reform, equivalent to household suffrage.[80] In October at least four leading 'radical operatives' reacted to news of the rejection of the Bill by urging continuing cooperation with the middle class.[81] And it was not only the petit-bourgeois members of the council who were against the November demonstration, for three weavers and four spinners had also voted against it.[82] These meetings went ahead anyway and in the absence of the moderate reformers. Piecemeal reform was seen as a viable strategy, but ultimately only the full radical programme would suffice. At the February reform meeting, 'in the heat of the moment', Aston indicated that he believed that important differences in per-spective among reformers signified the limits to unity:

> There are three parties in the kingdom. The first are those who wish for no reform at all, the second for a moderate reform, and the last are the people – the radical reformers, who wish for a universal reform ... The first class wish to keep all the privileges to themselves; the second wish to share the privileges with the first, that is to divide the spoil; but I, as a radical, and belonging to the third class, claim no privilege which I would deny to another man. (Loud cheers)[83]

Cooperation returned during the 'Days of May' in 1832, which were designed to prevent the return of Wellington at the head of an anti-reform ministry. A petition to the House of Commons, urging it not to vote any more supplies to the King's government, was launched at a public meeting and within two days obtained 20,304 signatures, being 'more numerously and more respectably signed than any previous petition in the same time in this town'. And a new 'Political Union of all classes, not only for national purposes, but also to take cognizance of all local abuses' was formed.[84] In June a public meeting 'to consider the best means to be pursued to make the elections under the reform bill as effective as possible, in sending members to parliament who would forward the interests of the industrious classes' was addressed by many familiar petit-bourgeois and working-class radicals.[85] This cooperation was maintained throughout the 1832 parliamentary election campaign and showed that, while the experience of 1832 left something of a legacy of middle-class betrayal, it did not mean that class collaboration was now ruled completely out of court. When the Liberal big bourgeoisie appealed to working-class radicals to form an alliance in 1838, the inter-class vocabulary of political radicalism helped them to achieve some success.

This chapter has outlined the important role played by a radical petite bourgeoisie in Bolton politics from the late 1820s to the mid-1830s. Finally, some of the pressures accounting for its decline as an independent political force have been identified. When the Liberal élite adopted a higher political profile from 1837, the radical petite bourgeoisie provided impressive support for its causes (indeed, this support proved crucial), especially that of municipal incorporation, the prospect of which seemed particularly attractive after the failure of attempts to reform the old unrepresentative and unaccountable system. The consequence of this was the subsumption of much of its identity within an all-embracing Liberalism. This is not to suggest that the radical petite bourgeoisie ever became marginalised – far from it – but from about the mid-1830s it no longer provided quite the same leading role as it had in earlier national and local political agitation.

It has to be considered that the petite bourgeoisie was far from a unified whole and that there were marked differences in terms of market situation and consciousness. Those members of the petite bourgeoisie identified in this chapter mostly came from among the ranks of the more substantial retailers and traders, enjoying a higher status and greater economic standing than the typical small shopkeeper or trader. Their greater material security was always likely to give way to reaction whenever militant strands of working-class protest seemed seriously to threaten property. We saw earlier that many of them had become convinced of the need for extra police protection by 1836. When depression returned in 1837, even Naisby came round to this view; just three months after moving an amendment at a vestry meeting that no new constables be appointed until the town was incorporated, he was no longer prepared to oppose the constables' accounts, the reason being 'that the people were likely to be badly off, and ... hunger would break through a stone wall'.[86] These fears would seem to have been justified by events in the first phase of Chartism. In June 1839 an open-air meeting of Chartists voiced their approval of the recently issued Manifesto of the National Convention, including the sixth part, which called for the use of 'exclusive dealing' to intimidate politically unsympathetic shop-keepers into giving their support (though there is no evidence that the tactic was effective,[87] or that its adoption was widespread). Moreover, during Chartist rioting in the national holiday later in August: 'The shops of Little Bolton ... were first attacked by the populace; and some of them are said to be gutted.'[88]

This is not the whole picture, however, for the Chartists were careful to discriminate between the 'politically dishonest' shopkeepers and those who continued to support political reform movements.[89] Signifi-cant in this respect was the continuing support for political reform from the likes of Naisby and the timber-merchant Isaac Barrow (they chaired some of the early Chartist meetings, for instance), which was important in cementing links between reformers of all social classes at various times in the 1830s and 1840s. Moreover, it is not clear how many radical petits bourgeois joined the ranks of the 'shopocrats', or if their property was amongst that attacked in 1839. Furthermore, while there is less local evidence for the small masters than the shopkeepers and traders, this group's political differences with the working class do seem to have decreased after 1832. As structural economic change undermined their position, many were to support Chartism, displaying attitudes and values closer to the world of labour, to which artisans related, than to the economic liberalism often associated with petit-bourgeois producers.[90]

Notes

1.   For social structures in the north-west of England, see: D. S. Gadian, 'A Comparative Study of Popular Movements in North-West Industrial Towns 1830–1850', Lancaster University Ph.D. thesis (1976), ch. 1; N. Kirk, *The Growth of Working Class Reformism in Mid-Victorian England* (Beckenham, 1985), ch. 2.

2.   See the discussion by G. Crossick in his 'The Petite Bourgeoisie in Nineteenth-Century Britain: The Urban and Liberal Case', in G. Crossick and H.-G. Haupt (eds), *Shopkeepers and Master Artisans in Nineteenth-Century Europe* (London, 1984), pp. 71–81.

3. J. Foster, *Class Struggle and the Industrial Revolution: Early Industrial Capitalism in Three English Towns* (London, 1974).

4. D. S. Gadian, 'Class Consciousness in Oldham and Other North-West Industrial Towns 1830–1850', *The Historical Journal* 21, 1 (1978).

5. R. A. Sykes, 'Some Aspects of Working-Class Consciousness in Oldham, 1830–1842', *The Historical Journal* 23, 1 (1980). Sykes shows that, although the concentration of ownership and size of industrial unit in the Oldham cotton industry was not on average as large as in the other cotton towns, the great number of petty capitalists, who were observed by the correspondent of the *Morning Chronicle* during his visit to the town in 1849, were concentrated in the subsidiary sectors of yarn-doubling and the spinning and weaving of waste cotton. Despite comprising about three-quarters of all cotton masters, these petty capitalists employed only about a quarter of all the town's cotton operatives. Oldham's mainstream cotton industry employed the great majority of the rest and these did not work in particularly small-scale mills.

6. C. Behagg, 'An Alliance with the Middle Class: The Birmingham Political Union and Early Chartism', in J. Epstein and D. Thompson (eds), *The Chartist Experience: Studies in Working-Class Radicalism and Culture, 1830–60* (London, 1982).

7. Foster, *op. cit.*, pp. 169–70; M. J. Winstanley, *The Shopkeeper's World 1830–1914* (Manchester, 1983).

8. W. Brimelow, *Political and Parliamentary History of Bolton, Vol. 1* (Bolton, 1882), pp. 156–92, for the parliamentary election poll.

9. C. Behagg, *Politics and Production in the Early Nineteenth Century* (London, 1990).

10. V. A. C. Gatrell, 'Incorporation and the Pursuit of Liberal Hegemony in Manchester 1790–1839', in D. Fraser (ed.), *Municipal Reform and the Industrial City* (Leicester, 1982), p. 18. This is not to deny the primacy of local politics, especially for the petite bourgeoisie. Consider, for example, the view of Geoffrey Crossick: 'The universe of the British petite-bourgeoisie tended to remain enclosed within their own towns and localities, marking out their social and cultural localism in a way quite different from the trend within the more substantial middle class. Their politics, their organizations, one might say their their concerns, failed to take on a significant national character during this period': Crossick, *op. cit.* p. 63.

11. D. Fraser, *Urban Politics in Victorian England: The Structure of Politics in Victorian Cities* (Leicester, 1976); Foster, *op. cit.*, ch. 2.

12. *B.C.*, 3, 10 February 1827. The *Bolton Chronicle* was a radical newspaper until the mid-1830s and furthered the radicals' cause by publishing detailed reports and advertisements relating to their activities. To reach a mass audience, radical publicists disseminated over 1,000 copies of a pamphlet written by Naisby and there were plans for a second edition. As for the burden imposed by the unequal assessment, Naisby claimed that he owned seven shops worth £4,000, but that he paid more rates than some properties which had cost £60,000, and this was after a revision of the rates on more equitable terms (*B.C.*, 15 September 1827).

13. *B.C.*, 6 December 1828.
14. Foster, *op. cit.*, ch. 3.
15. *B.C.*, 3 March 1827.
16. *B.C.* 10 March 1827 (Select Vestry Act as explained by Naisby); Fraser, *Urban Politics*, pp. 27–8; Foster, *op. cit.* p. 62.
17. *B.C.*, 10 March 1827. It has to be noted that Naisby was no advocate of full democracy and a firm supporter of both of the Sturges Bourne Acts.
18. Foster, *op. cit.*, pp. 61–4.
19. *B.C.*, 7 April 1827.
20. *B.C.*, 28 April 1827.
21. B.C., 6 December 1828. Some of the overseers' reports for Great Bolton have survived. By way of comparison, these indicate that, from 1st May 1823 to 1st May 1824, a rate of 6s. in the pound was levied, while in 1831 a rate of 2s. in the pound was levied in May and a further 1s. in September (General Reports of the Overseers of the Poor of Great Bolton, B.R.L., extant for years 1820, 1823, 1831, 1832, 1833). In August Naisby still complained 'that there was a vast number of cottages empty in Great Bolton, the very reverse was the case in Little Bolton, and this was owing to the difference in taxation between the townships' (*B.C.*, 11 August 1827).
22. *B.C.*, 24 March 1827.
23. For a good example of this, see the September monthly meeting of the committee for regulating the affairs of the town. Here Naisby raised the otherwise seemingly petty issues of the liability of the ratepayers to an annual charge for a suit of clothes for the market regulator and a hat for the bellman (*B.C.*, 15 September 1827).
24. *B.C.*, 11 August 1827.
25. *B.C.*, 26 January, 19 July, 25 October 1828.
26. There may have been something of a compromise. After the January 1829 vestry meeting, 'Mr. Scowcroft [former boroughreeve] expressed his satisfaction at the conciliation which had taken place and he hoped it would continue' (*B.C.*, 17 January, 2 July, 17 October 1829).
27. For events in 1831, see *B.C.*, 9 April, 14 May 1831.
28. *B.C.*, 4 February 1832. The magistrate in question was the Tory bleacher Joseph Ridgway.
29. *B.C.*, 5 May, 21 July, 13 October 1832. Thus, after the vestry meeting of the second quarter had again disqualified the accounts, Naisby felt that when the accounts were subsequently submitted to the magistrates, 'we should hope that due deference in respect to this subject will be paid to the so oft expressed opinion of the leypayers'. But at the next such meeting he complained that 'They were treated like donkeys, and had to bear all the burden, but were not allowed to have anything to do with the chusing of new servants, or appointing the old ones.'
30. *B.C.*, 6 April 1833; Heywood Papers, correspondence 1833, B.A., ZHE/130/13/39.
31. B.A., ZZ/130/13/28, Miscellaneous Collection of Handbills – Local Government and Politics, 'To the Independent Leypayers of Great Bolton' from the Great Bolton Leypayers' Committee; *B.F.P.*, 26 March 1836.

The magistrates repeated the procedure of appointing a person who was not from an elected list in the case of nearby Horwich. After one of the deputation heard the decision, he observed in 'broad Lancashire dialect': 'Haw see its no use in us howding a vestry, we meet us weel whistle' (*B.F.P.*, 2 April 1836).

32. *B.C.*, 16 July, 29 October 1836; *B.F.P.*, 16 July, 29 October 1836. The question of appointing extra police had in fact been initially defeated in a Sturges Bourne poll by 74 votes to 70 (*B.F.P.*, 16 July 1836). After the eventual Tory victory, the *B.C.*, now a Tory newspaper following a change in ownership, observed that 'a well known *clique of interested patriots*' were not motivated primarily by concerns for frugality in municipal expenditure, but rather that 'the deeds of their friends and supporters should not have to brave any extra opposition of the law' (*B.C.*, 29 October 1836).

33. *B.F.P.*, 8 April 1837.

34. Fraser, *Urban Politics*, chs. 2, 12.

35. *B.C.*, 9 April 1831 (James Ormrod [currier], an original member of the Leypayers' Committee).

36. *B.C.*, 16 April 1831.

37. *B.C.*, 28 April 1832. There was to be no additional sidesman, however, to serve alongside the extra churchwarden.

38. *B.C.*, 13 April 1833.

39. *B.C.*, 9 April 1836. The Reverend Slade claimed, without contradiction, that although five years ago the ratepayers had been vested with the power to nominate one warden, their nominee of two years ago had failed to serve, and last year they had failed to nominate. Therefore 'the custom was broken' and Slade indicated that he would challenge the legality of Naisby's appointment in court. Thereafter the evidence is incomplete, but after 1836 the Tories clearly had overall control of the churchwardens, which they used to maintain control of the overseers until 1839.

40. *B.C.*, 14 July 1832.

41. *Ibid.* Naisby raised particular objection to a charge of £200 to defray the costs of building the walls around the grounds of Trinity Church. Trinity Church was to feature in the ending of church rates in Bolton, and had been involved in an earlier episode in 1827 when ratepayers from the semi-rural and rural townships of Bolton parish mustered to oppose the grants for completing it. Their main grievance was the unequal assessment which favoured urban Great and Little Bolton, land being taxed at a higher rate than other forms of property (*B.C.*, 31 March 1827).

42. *B.C.*, 14 July 1832.

43. *B.C.*, 7 December 1833.

44. B.A., ZZ/130/8/5, Testimonial of Respect to Reverend James Slade, Vicar of Bolton ... 30 November 1836; P. N. Dale, 'A Study of the Growth of Churches in Bolton during the Industrial Revolution', University College of North Wales Ph.D. thesis (1984), ch. 3. In 1860, in commenting on the raising of the question of church rates in the House of Commons, a Liberal source remarked that: 'Many years have passed away since any attempt has been made to exact church rates in this town. To the population of this

district they have passed into the pages of history' (*Bolton Guardian*, 11 February 1860).

45. Fraser, *Urban Politics*, p. 103.
46. *B.C.*, 28 September 1833.
47. *B.C.*, 29 September 1832, 28 September 1833. The linen-draper Joseph Skelton, whom we noted earlier playing a leading role in the agitation against church rates, was successively elected as highway surveyor for Great Bolton in 1832 and 1833.
48. *B.C.*, 29 September 1832.
49. J. C. Scholes, *History of Bolton: With Memorials of the Old Parish Church* (Bolton, 1892), pp. 464–9, for information on the trusts.
50. *B.C.*, 10, 17, 24 April 1830.
51. The newly formed town council had no powers to tax the people to defray its operating costs, neither did it automatically displace the functions of the older governing institutions. The Tories feared that the Liberals would use the rate-levying parts of the latter to collect their expenses, under the guise of a general poor rate in the case of the overseers, or a police rate in the case of the Little Bolton trust. The whole incorporation episode will come under focus in Chapter Two.
52. *B.C.*, 8 January, 19, 26 March 1831, 10 March, 28 April, 10 November 1832, 2, 9 February, 9 March 1833.
53. *B.C.*, 9 February 1833 (leader). For further comment, see *B.C.*, 16 February 1833.
54. *B.C.*, 17 April 1830. The popular reform campaign began in earnest in Lancashire in general in 1830. See J. K. Walton, *Lancashire, A Social History, 1558–1939* (Manchester, 1987), p. 158.
55. Subsequent comment by Naisby, *B.C.*, 25 September 1830.
56. *B.C.*, 25 September, 23 October 1830.
57. *B.C.*, 7 January 1832. Another major influence raising the aspirations of reformers were the French and Belgian revolutions of 1830. In November 1830, for instance, following the downfall of Wellington's administration, 'a large crowd of persons', headed by tricoloured flags, marched in procession from Bolton Moor to the centre of the town. Hand-loom weavers made up the bulk of the crowd – and it was about this time that the radical weavers of Bolton became known as the 'Bolton Moor Belgians' – who, after praising the actions of the French and Belgians, paraded through the principal streets, stopping outside Naisby's house en route to give three cheers (*B.C.*, 20 November 1830).
58. See below, pp. 26–27.
59. Heywood Papers, correspondence 1847, B.A., ZHE/43/28.
60. *B.F.P.*, 10 July 1841; B.A., ZZ/130/4/10, Miscellaneous Collection of Handbills – Parliamentary Election, July 1841, 'Electoral Intimidation' – pledge by 39 prominent supporters of free trade (mostly Liberal cotton masters) to recompense any workmen or tradespeople punished by their employers for supporting free trade, 19 June 1841: 'It having been stated that some of the Spinners, Manufacturers, and others, in this district, have attempted to intimidate their Tradespeople and Workmen, and thereby

influence their Votes at the ensuing Elections for Bolton and South Lancashire ...' The Liberals, however, were also guilty of this practice. Thus in 1841, for instance, the Liberal Unitarian cotton-spinner Thomas Thomasson was discovered to be 'vote manufacturing' when he raised the rents of the spinners who resided in his housing to 4s. per week (*B.C.*, 16 October 1841; *B.F.P.*, 23 October 1841). During his visit to Bolton in 1849 Reach noted that: 'The case of certain mills in Bolton has been brought under my notice, in which the charge of a complement of spinning mules ... is always clogged with the condition that the spinner shall live in a house belonging to the employer. In the workpeople's own phraseology, "a key goes to each set of mules"' (C. Aspin, *Manchester and the Textile Districts in 1849* (Helmshore, 1972), p. 67).

61. *B.F.P.*, 30 April 1836.
62. See the discussion on exclusive dealing, both from above and below, and the political motivation of shopkeepers, in Winstanley, *op. cit.*
63. *B.C.*, 10 March 1827.
64. *B.C.*, 13 March, 6, 13 November 1830.
65. *B.C.*, 16 February 1833.
66. D. G. Wright, *Democracy and Reform 1815–1885* (Harlow, 1970), p. 45; Gatrell, *op. cit.*, p. 38.
67. P. Hollis, *The Pauper Press: A Study in Working-Class Radicalism of the 1830s* (Oxford, 1970); W. D. Rubinstein, 'The End Of "Old Corruption" in Britain 1780–1860', *Past and Present* 101 (1983).
68. *B.C.*, 17 April, 23 October 1830.
69. *B.C.*, 23 October 1830.
70. *B.C.*, 17 April 1830.
71. *B.C.*, 17 April, 23 October 1830.
72. *B.C.*, 21 July 1832.
73. *B.C.*, 13 October 1832.
74. *B.C.*, 17 April, 23 October 1830.
75. *B.C.*, 12 February 1831.
76. N. Gash, *Aristocracy and People: Britain 1815–1865* (London, 1979), pp. 140–1.
77. *B.C.*, 15 October 1831; Brimelow, *op. cit.*, pp. 109–12.
78. *B.C.*, 22 October 1831. Some details can be found in Brimelow, *op. cit.*, pp. 109–13.
79. *B.C.*, 5 November, 3 December 1831 (see the latter edition for the Declaration of Rights). About 800 persons attended the November demonstration at which tricolours were in evidence. In 1837 Naisby told a public meeting that he had resigned from the council of the Political Union because it had advocated the calling of a National Convention, which he regarded as 'treasonable' (*B.F.P.*, 11 November 1837).
80. *B.C.*, 5, 12 February, 9 March 1831. The town's wealthy were more visible at these meetings than at any other time during the whole of the parliamentary reform agitation. Included among the speakers were the Tories Hardcastle (bleacher), Scowcroft (foremost opponent of the vestry radicals) and Stockdale (solicitor), and the Liberals P. Ainsworth

(bleacher), Darbishire (Unitarian manufacturer) and the Reverend Baker (Unitarian minister of Bank Street Chapel).

81. These included John Aston, weaver, and Finlay Frazer, a spinner at Ormrod's, who later became a beerseller before becoming a tobacconist.

82. *B.C.*, 3 December 1831.

83. *B.C.*, 12 February 1831.

84. *B.C.*, 19 May 1832.

85. *B.C.*, 2 June 1832; B.A., ZZ/130/1/1, Miscellaneous Collection of Handbills – Bolton Parliamentary Election 1832, 'Meeting of the Political Union'.

86. *B.F.P.*, 29 April, 12 August 1837.

87. In August Charles Darbishire, the first mayor of the newly incorporated borough, acknowledged a communication from the Home Office containing 'instructions to take immediate steps to bring to justice such persons as may attempt to obtain money from or injure in their business shopkeepers and others by intimidation', whilst indicating to Russell that the borough magistrates were completely in control of the situation in this respect: *H.O. 40/44*, Darbishire to Russell, 1 August 1839.

88. *Northern Star*, 17 August 1839.

89. *B.F.P.*, 22 June 1839. The Chartist distinction between the 'good' and the 'bad' shopkeeper was explained by Bronterre O'Brien to a correspondent in 1838: 'It is because we are not opposed to shopkeepers, merely as such, that we coined the term '*Shopocrats*', in order to distinguish the good from the bad, the politically honest from the politically dishonest, those to whom we are hostile and those to whom we are not. Under the present arrangements of society, Shopkeepers are almost as necessary as producers, but under no constitution of society ought there to exist the animal we call a '*Shopocrat*', which means a Shopkeeper or capitalist, who would keep all the powers of government in his own class *through a monopoly of the elective franchise*. Now as all Shopkeepers are not necessarily, nor in point of fact, enemies of Universal Suffrage, it follows that they are not what we call '*Shopocrats*', or shop-exclusives, who would monopolise all political power to themselves, like the base middle class National Guards of France' (cited in Sykes, *op. cit.*, p. 178).

90. The ideological content of Chartism will be discussed in Chapter Three. However, to illustrate the point made in the main text, in 1841 James Parkinson, a small master (brass-moulder) and Chartist, in correspondence with a 'cotton spinner' conducted through the medium of the *Bolton Free Press* (6, 17 November, 11, 18 December for the exchange of views), denied that the system of 'artisan' production was in any way comparable to the factory system. Not opposed to profit or capitalist relations of production *per se*, Parkinson nevertheless argued for a regulated system of employment relations and a more equitable division of rewards. His views reveal an essentially moral critique of intensified exploitation (the tyranny of employers being unnecessary in economic terms), which left the way open for cooperation between the economically productive within all strata: 'He wishes them to believe that I am opposed to capital honestly

employed to its proper use, having its legitimate rights and privileges. I entertain no such foolish opinion; on the contrary, I would do all that lies in my power to secure to capital … an honest and just remuneration for its use. All that I object to is, the capitalists of this country employing their capital on such principles as to give them princely mansions, splendid equipages, extensive territory, undue influence, false dignity, in a word, enables them to ride rough-shod over the operative millions … No, sir, I have no objections to the capitalists of this country getting rich, if I did not see, in the same ratio, those that labour and toil to accumulate those riches getting poorer and poorer every day. Let the capital be employed on scriptural principles, and then we should hear nothing of the Malthusian political economical mare's-nest of demand and supply. Let the first principles be, the well feeding, the well clothing, the well housing, with an honest provision for decrepitude and old age, not such as is practised at the present day, then I would allow the capitalists the use of the surplus remaining.'

CHAPTER THREE

Local Politics 1837–1850:
Middle-Class Social Formation and
Municipal Reform [1]

A central theme in the history of nineteenth-century social development relates to the claim variously expounded by Anderson, Rubinstein and Wiener that the northern industrial middle class failed to achieve its hegemonic ambitions within the British power bloc.[2] Accordingly, during the course of the century the industrial bourgeoisie is first seen as suffering political and cultural subordination to the landed governing class, with aristocratic political control at Westminster as the natural corollary to the supposed social, economic and ideological dominance of the landed governing class over the industrial bourgeoisie. Then, in the later part of the century, the commercial and financial élites of London – who, according to Rubinstein's calculations, far outstripped the northern industrial bourgeoisie in terms of wealth, influence, prestige and power – are seen to have drawn closer to the aristocracy in the creation of a new social bloc in which the city was predominant. However, as the city is only seen as emerging as the dominant sector of British capitalism from the 1880s, a consideration of city-industry relations lies beyond the temporal parameters of this book. In order to put municipal reform into historical perspective, it is the aristocratic hegemony thesis that concerns us here.

Critics of that thesis not only argue that Rubinstein has exaggerated his portrayal of the northern industrial bourgeoisie as the poor relations among British élites,[3] but also that aristocratic domination of Parliament did not block state receptivity to the needs of industrial capital.[4] From this perspective, despite the façade of apparent aristocratic hegemony, British society was progressively reordered to the needs of industrial capital. By 1850 the industrial bourgeoisie is seen as living in an economic world of its own making, in which no serious obstacles were faced in the pursuit of profit. Moreover, although the Reform Act of 1832 represented a strengthening rather than a weakening of the landed interest in the House of Commons, there was 'a middle-class side to the political compromise of 1832 in addition to the terms of the 1832 Act, and that was the Municipal Corporations Act of 1835, a measure which went quite a long way to qualify the landowning classes' domination at

Westminster'.⁵ Thus it is held that municipal reform left political power in the industrial centres firmly under the control of the owners of industrial capital.

An examination of local politics and the Victorian construction of power lends some support to the case for the 'triumph' rather than 'failure' of the Victorian middle class. While power resided in Parliament, it was devolved locally mainly by the non-compulsory or permissive Bill procedure, enabling the middle class firmly to imprint its identity over much of urban life. When the middle class voiced its disapproval of the prospect of central interference in local affairs – as, for instance, embodied in the terms of the Poor Law Amendment Act of 1834 and the Public Health Act of 1848 – Parliament could show a remarkable degree of sensitivity to the needs of industrial capital and local wishes. In this respect, the decentralised character of the British state served the main interests of the middle class well, conferring upon it a range of executive functions adaptable to local circumstances: control of law and order, regulation of the poor, sanitary and public health arrangements, and provision of an infrastructure for industry.

Local evidence does not, however, give unqualified support to the 'triumph' thesis. For while the focus of middle-class power clearly lay in its own towns and cities, in Bolton – especially up to 1850 – its rule was far from unproblematical. The creation of a smooth and efficient system of local government was only one of a number of serious problems that had to be overcome or significantly alleviated before the middle class could fully realise its hegemonic ambitions. Concerted extra-parliamentary pressure was usually sufficient to mitigate the worst excesses of interference by central government in local affairs, and the working class made only brief and limited forays into local politics on its own behalf. However, as was the case in other towns, the middle class was far from a monolithic whole⁶ and it is significant that intra-class relations were more important in defining the parameters of class action in local government than relations with either Parliament, the working class, or propertied groups lower down the social scale.

A radical petite bourgeoisie mounted a vigorous campaign for reforms in the institutional network that constituted Bolton's system of local government from the late 1820s to the mid-1830s. But it failed to shake the stranglehold exercised by the Tory-Anglican oligarchy. Within a middle class divided internally along political, denominational and kinship lines, only in the 1837–50 struggle for supremacy that followed was the process of decision-making in local government substantially affected. The depth of divisions was such that, even as south-east Lancashire became a hotbed of Chartism over 1838–42, the predominant endemic political rivalry in the town was that within the middle class, who viewed their own struggle as more important than the parallel Chartist agitation and conflict between capital and labour. The Liberals secured municipal incorporation in 1838, but this conferred little effective power upon the town council and did not automatically displace the functions of the older governing institutions. Until 1850 the rival élites used the power residing in these to counter many of the initiatives by the town council, bringing institutional paralysis to local government in a period of mounting social problems. All this qualifies the significance of 1835 in the local context. The local pattern of events supports Derek Fraser's view that the turning-point in the civic history of most towns was not 1835 or incorporation, but the date of the first Act granting extensive powers to the town council.[7] The Bolton Improvement Act of 1850, by removing those institutional points of power from which the rival élites had frustrated each other, facilitated the stabilisation of intra-class relations and signified the emergence of a consensus as to how the town was to be governed. Only then did the town council, as the sole multi-purpose institution of local government, possess the powers to provide the facilities and amenities to satisfy a growing sense of civic pride and to deal with the problems associated with economic growth and an expanding population.

Thus, middle-class social formation in Bolton at least was a process accompanied by a significant degree of fragmentation. Central to those divisions was the struggle between Church and Dissent, which paralleled similar religious tensions in other communities and was central to much of the political conflict in national and local political arenas for most of the nineteenth century. As Derek Fraser has said: 'Men who disagreed about the very nature and purpose of existence were natural enemies'[8] to begin with, and disputes and tensions which were often theological at heart were continually embittered by political disagreements and struggles. In 1838 the now Tory *Bolton Chronicle* defended 'our Church Establishment' as a model of social usefulness, the preserver of religious tolerance and high moral principles and worthy of its privileged position 'as a legal and visible representative of the national faith'.[9] But, for local Liberal political leaders, religious grievances were an important motivation for political action and the 'ecclesiastical monopolies' enjoyed by the Church were no less unjust than commercial and political monopolies and were 'so potent an obstacle to the intellectual and moral progress of England'.[10] It has already been shown how the successful campaign to abolish church rates boosted the confidence of local Dissenters. The attempt to end the injustice of their exclusion from decision-making in local government – through the campaign for municipal incorporation outlined below – further broadened their political and social outlook.

The backbone of the efforts of local Dissenters was provided by the families worshipping at Bank Street Unitarian Chapel, who exercised an influence out of all proportion to the modest size of the congregation. Asa Briggs has suggested that 'Where Unitarianism was weak in the nineteenth century Liberalism lacked a social cutting edge'[11] and other historians have similarly noted the importance of Unitarianism in the cultural, social and political life of Britain in the late eighteenth and nineteenth century.[12]

The divided middle class: Bolton Liberals

By the 1830s the Bank Street worshippers were in a similar ambiguous situation to their fellow Unitarian congregations at Cross Street and Mosley Street in Manchester. They too were wealthy and well-educated, but nonetheless systematically excluded from the higher offices of local political power that their economic and social roles would seem to have commanded.[13]

Among the congregation were many of the leading business families of the town, including the Darbishires, Heywoods, Crooks, Haslams and Barrows. It could also count among its members the Winders, who provided a succession of legal experts for Liberal organisations and administrations, as well as the Quaker Thomassons and the Quaker Ashworths of Turton. Beyond the 1830s the material solidarity of the Chapel community was strengthened with the accession of new wealth from the likes of the Scotts and Potters and the later business success of some of the long-established families, such as the Harwoods.[14]

The strong association between the congregation and Liberal causes owed much to the principles and heterodoxy of the Unitarian doctrine. Common traditions which put the emphasis upon the potential of man, the power of reason, and the merit of moral and civic duties as a foundation of faith[15] ensured that this rational form of Christianity embodied a concern to eliminate irrationality in all spheres of public life. From this came a detestation of the 'aristocratic ideal' and all that it implied in terms of the pursuit of a profligate lifestyle and the maintenance of social inequalities through nepotism and a corrupt Parliament. Moreover, its attachment to certain doctrinal points – such as that of the Trinity, over which it contested the Church of England – made its members pariahs in the eyes of many of their neighbours. Indeed, although the Toleration Act of 1689 had permitted worship by Dissenters, it had denied these benefits to any who did not accept the doctrine of the Trinity. It was not until the Trinity Act of 1813 that Unitarians were placed on the same legal footing as other Dissenters.[16]

These political implications of religious identity helped to reinforce the cohesiveness of Unitarian communities, a trait which was perhaps most sharply defined in those congregations which felt the worst effects of the traumas of the 1790s.[17] Gatrell, for example, has shown that although wealthy and respectable Unitarians had been able to hold local office in Manchester in the eighteenth century, the semi-persecution inflicted by rival Tories in the loyalist backlash of the 1790s did much to undermine their status, leaving those who professed Unitarianism with a political, social and doctrinal liability into the 1830s. Bolton's Unitarians were subjected to similar hostilities.

A Church and King Club was formed in December 1792, with a general committee of seventy-four 'gentlemen' which actively sought out and persecuted persons suspected of harbouring Republican principles, who were therefore considered seditious and enemies of the Crown and country. A combination of propaganda, repression and a mounting wave of patriotic fervour forced radicals and even moderate reformers to operate under cover. But, nevertheless, according to Brimelow, 'under the surface there was considerable activity. By varied means copies of the publications of Thomas Paine and other writers were obtained and circulated, exciting no small degree of uneasiness in the minds of the upper classes in the town.'[18] Thomas Cooper, a Bolton merchant and Unitarian who took an active part in the reform agitation of the 1790s, reacted enthusiastically to Part Two of Paine's *Rights of Man*: 'it has made me more politically mad than I ever was. It is choque full, crowded with good sense ... heightened also with a profusion of libellous matter. I regard it as the very jewel of a book ... Burke is done up for ever and ever by it.'[19]

The Conservative political philosopher Edmund Burke had considered that 'Unitarians were united for the express purpose of proselytism' and aimed 'to collect a multitude sufficient by force and violence to overturn the Church ... concurrent with a design to subvert the State'.[20] The authorities saw a connection between the religious heterodoxy of Unitarians and their political sympathy with the 'de-Christianising' revolution in France, and they therefore persecuted them both for their religious and political radicalism. On one occasion an effigy of the Reverend John Holland (minister from 1789 to 1820) was burnt in the town centre, and on another he was represented as chief mourner, riding a donkey to the burning of Tom Paine in effigy with copies of the *Rights of Man*. His successor Franklin Baker later recalled of Holland:

His intrepidity in persisting to preach the doctrines of Unitarianism, denounced on all sides as they were as destructive to Christianity and hostile to civil government, drew upon him the frequent remonstrances of many of the more timid of his own friends, besides an accumulation of odium from religious and political opponents. His utter disregard to all opposition, when truth and justice required him to speak and act, rendered him still further obnoxious to the cry of 'Church and King' which then echoed through the country.[21]

This freedom of conscience and sense of equality before God, which was typical in the outlook of many Dissenters, nurtured a strong sense of injustice towards civil inequalities suffered under laws designed to favour the established Church. Theological debate thus engendered political struggle.

If the principles and heterodoxy of Unitarian doctrine ensured its connections with Liberalism, then its religious-cultural preferences ensured the élitist and exclusive character of its congregations. It was perhaps the most persecuted sects which erected the firmest barriers to expansionism.[22] It was remarked in the Bampton lectures of 1818 that 'Unitarianism is not indeed calculated to become easily a favourite doctrine with the common people', and from an early period the wealthy were disproportionately represented among the congregation at Bank Street.[23] In common with the other sects that made up the 'Old Dissent', this congregation was concerned to maintain what it saw as the seriousness of religion, the preservation of regularity in matters of polity and liturgy, and high professional and intellectual standards among ministers.[24] For the historian of the growth of religion in Bolton, the 'profound views' held by Unitarians made them 'a select body based on serious discussion'.[25] Successive ministers at Bank Street maintained an excellent academy, with a library which contained no less than 1,500 volumes by 1854.[26] These traits, together with its lack of conversionist zeal and distrust of 'enthusiasm', clearly distinguished Unitarianism and Old Dissent in general from newer Dissenting movements such as Methodism, which characteristically maintained an evangelical preoccupation with expansion and a relative indifference towards denominational order and formal ministerial training.[27] Moreover, although many congregations may have attracted a tail of working-class followers, the ties of religious identity did not detract from their essentially middle-class character. As John Seed has argued, despite the rhetoric of community and brethren, the middle-class character of Unitarian communities was confirmed by informal networks of social contact which maintained and reproduced class divisions, cutting across the outward appearance of social association and mutual support.[28]

Thus Burke was incorrect when he insisted that the Unitarians were a proselytising denomination. Expansion was by secession and not conversion. The initial growth of Unitarianism had depended on the metamorphosis of existing congregations, in particular the heterodox remnants of English Presbyterian and general Baptist traditions. In 1825, of eighty chapels occupied by Unitarians in the north-west, only eight had been built specifically for members of that belief. Bank Street Chapel itself was founded as the first Dissenting chapel in Bolton in 1672 by Presbyterians, with the foundations of the conversion to Unitarianism being laid between 1729 and 1750, during the ministry of John Buck.[29] Expansion was hardly spectacular thereafter. In Lancashire, by 1851, only nine Unitarian chapels had been added to the twenty-six occupied by the denomination at the start of the century.[30] In Bolton itself in 1851, Unitarians only provided one place of worship, with 614 sittings out of a total accommodation of 36 places of worship with 20,976 sittings. There was a modest absolute increase to two places of worship, with 828 sittings, by 1881, though Unitarianism failed to maintain its proportion of a total accommodation in the town, which then stood at 85 places of worship with 45,017 sittings.[31] Moreover, minimal expansion meant that there was little social dilution of the Bank Street congregation. In 1820 the appointment of the Socinian Noah Jones as successor to Holland brought growing divisions to a head and a more theologically orthodox group seceded to form Moor Lane Chapel. At one time they could boast a congregation of more than 300, whereas Bank Street had only 120, but they got into financial difficulties and, as the original doctrinal differences disappeared, the secessionists gradually drifted back to Bank Street, with Moor Lane Chapel finally closing down in 1843. In 1868 Commission Street Chapel was founded, but even then there was little dilution of the parent congregation, and there was no further expansion until 1899, when Halliwell Road Free Church was established in the northern suburbs of the town.[32]

The sense of identity given to the Unitarian community by its business success and political and religious radicalism was further buttressed by a web of extraordinary kinship linkages. According to Gatrell, a similar network of ties was the source of the Manchester Unitarians' greatest strength,[33] and this was no less the case at Bolton. A firm impression of the sequences of familial linkages built up throughout the eighteenth and early nineteenth centuries has been reconstructed through a mixture of chapel records, biographical notes (mainly newspaper obituaries and pen-portraits) and Ramsden's survey of the major Chapel families.[34] Thus the Quaker Thomassons were connected to the Quaker Ashworths by marriage in 1793, the latter having a direct family connection to Unitarianism by its links with the Kays. The Andrews were a branch of a London family of Presbyterian stock whose roots in Bolton were established in the 1620s. The family maintained important connections with its Presbyterian relatives in London and built up family linkages in the eighteenth century with the local Unitarian Cromptons, Goodwins, Darbishires and Taylors. Another major sequence of kinship linkage ran through the Hollands, Pilkingtons, Barnes (of Cross Street Chapel in Manchester), Mangnalls, Kays and Ashworths. The leading families of Simpson, Harwood, Taylor and Haselden, among others, claimed direct descent from the marriage of James Smith to Mary Mason in 1776. A further major sequence centred around the Heywood family, which was connected to the Shawcross family of Manchester, to the Haslams, who established important business and marriage ties with the wealthy Scotts of Mosley Street Chapel in Manchester, to the Crooks, who were intermarried with the Bakers, and to the Harwoods. Moreover, there were connections linking all the major familial sequences together. Thus the Taylors were linked to the Harwoods, who were connected to the Barrows. The Taylors were also connected to the Darbishires through the Masons (in 1764 Samuel Darbishire married Mary, daughter of Robert and Elizabeth Taylor (née Mason), and their youngest daughter married Ashworth Clegg, a wealthy merchant of Cross Street Chapel). The Darbishires were intermarried with the Kays, the Haslams with the Crooks, and so on.

These alignments were not invariable, but there were few outcrosses to Anglicanism before 1880. The only Anglican-Unitarian connection of any note was formed from the marriage of Francis Dorning to the cotton employer William Gray in 1804. Their son, the Conservative Colonel William Gray, represented Bolton in Parliament from 1857 to 1874. The Dornings were one of the more substantial of the Chapel families, establishing family ties with the Rasbothams of Cross Street Chapel in 1719 and the Bayleys, also of Cross Street, in 1762.

From the 1850s there was a clear trend towards the development of a more unitary middle-class culture, but the distinction between Liberal-nonconformist and Tory-Anglican was only gradually eroded and the lines of denominational and political allegiance remained fairly intact until beyond the 1880s.[35] It was only by the end of the nineteenth century, for instance, that the Ashworths had all been converted to Anglicanism. In 1834 the Quaker Thomas Thomasson, who proved to be a leading figure in Bolton Liberalism, was converted to Anglicanism after his marriage to Sarah Pennington of Liverpool. The impact of the Crimean War, however, led him to sever his connection and he became a member of the Bolton Free Christian Church. His daughter married the Liberal-Anglican Stephen Winkworth, partner in the cotton giant Cross-Winkworth, but by the 1880s his son John Pennington Thomasson, hailed as one of the town's greatest benefactors, was among the congregation at Bank Street. George Harwood (1845–1912), elected Liberal MP for Bolton in 1895, left the Unitarians for the Church of England, but his cousin John Harwood was perhaps the leading personality in Chapel life from the 1870s. Another example of uneven and limited dilution was the Haslam family, one of the wealthiest and most philanthropic among the congregation. Ralph Marsden Haslam set up a cotton-spinning business with the Tory-Wesleyan William Cannon in 1849, but remained a Unitarian and Liberal in politics. His nephew John Percival Haslam also retained his denominational allegiance, and is the only Unitarian-Conservative listed among Thorpe's 'summary of political and religious affiliation of cotton spinning families in Bolton 1884–1910'.[36]

In Bolton, as in other places where Unitarianism was strong, it was this close-knit, wealthy, self-consciously intellectual and rational community that was to provide most of the energy and direction of the middle-class reform movement from 1837. Robert Heywood's biographer has neatly summed up many of their social attitudes:

> Lancashire Unitarians, conscious of their pedigree and traditions and their aloofness from the main stream of Anglican religious and social life, kowtowed to no one. Heywood had no difficulty in mixing on terms of equality with foreign aristocrats; he took it for granted that he should meet the President of the United States and the ruler of Egypt. He had an undisguised contempt for the idle and spendthrift, however aristocratic.[37]

The divided middle class: Bolton Tories

Bolton Toryism was an amalgam of landed and industrial interests, the Conservative nexus of county society being well integrated with a substantial semi-rural and urban industrial Toryism. At its head were the aristocratic Stanley, Bridgeman and Egerton families (the Earls of Derby and Bradford and the Duke of Bridgewater). Francis Egerton assumed the role of south-east Lancashire's most prestigious Conservative when he settled on his Worsley estate in 1837 after a long period of absence.[36] The Stanleys had coal-mining interests around Bolton and, with the landed Bridgemans, had a direct entry into local politics as two of the three co-lords of the manor of Great Bolton. It was these families, along with the lord of the manor of Little Bolton, who selected the invariably Conservative senior officials for the court leets which, backed by the authority of the county magistrates, controlled the local political system up to the end of the 1830s. Surviving transcripts of the deliberations of the Little Bolton Court Leet indicate that a few Liberals and Unitarians were sworn in, but that the senior officers, the boroughreeves and constables, were invariably Tory-Anglicans.[39] According to Robert Heywood, the Great Bolton Court Leet was even more partisan:

> I stated before the Privy Council that during the last thirty years only one liberal Dissenter has been appointed to the office of Bor-oughreeve of Great Bolton and he only because he happened to be a wealthy client of the Clerk to the Court Leet. This fact I believe is undeniable and for sometime past such office has been filled by ultra conservatives and hence we may readily suppose what must be the character and conduct of the constables and the rest of the underlings even down to the bellman; every individual will be found of the same order exercising his political influence through every channel more especially upon innkeepers and others during an election.[40]

Several of the Liberal Bank Street families claimed minor landed or humbler yeomanry origins, such as the Morts, Heywoods, Lomaxes, Haslams and Harwoods. Others could trace a considerable pedigree – the Cromptons tracing theirs back to 1190, for instance. With few exceptions, however, the higher-status local gentry were all Tory. Heywood advised the South Lancashire Election Committee of the Lancashire Reformers' Union (later the National Reform Union) in 1859 'that not much aid can be expected from this district, surrounded as we are by large landed proprietors nearly all extremely Conservative'.[41] In the second quarter of the nineteenth century the coal-owning Fletchers and Hultons were the spearhead of gentry penetration into urban affairs. Members of both families served on the Bolton division of the county magistrates and Ralph Fletcher and William Hulton were part of the Manchester bench that gave the order that led to the Peterloo incident. Fletcher's attitude remained implacable until his death in 1832. Hated by radicals for his zealous promotion of the spy system, he was revered by ultra-Tories and the anniversary of his death was one of the high points of their social calendar in the 1830s and 1840s.[42] Hulton went on to play a leading role in Conservative party reorganisation after 1832, and was equally revered as 'the father of Conservatism in South Lancashire'.[43] The Hulton family dominated the out-township of Little Hulton, which was considered a Tory stronghold until Liberals won all the seats at the inaugural elections to the newly created local board in 1877.[44]

For Bolton Toryism, the importance of industry in a semi-rural setting went further than the influence of the aristocratic and gentry coal-owners. For Bolton stood pre-eminent as a centre of textile bleaching and finishing, most of which was located in the less densely populated out-townships. According to one estimate, 3,500 operatives were employed in bleaching establishments in the neighbourhood of Bolton in 1837.[45] All the major employers were Anglican and, with the exception of the Liberal Ainsworths, Tory, though even the Ainsworths had been converted to Conservatism by the 1860s.[46] The Ridgways relocated the centre of their business operation from Bolton to the village of Wallsuches in 1777, thereafter dominating much of the political and social life of the township of Horwich. In 1836 the devotion of Joseph Ridgway to the Conservative cause was perhaps exaggeratedly described as 'without a single parallel in the Kingdom', though he was the major force behind the formation of Operative Conservative Associations in Blackrod and Horwich. The membership of the latter was apparently largely recruited from among the 400-strong workforce at Wallsuches.[47] In 1818 the Ridgway brothers brought in their nephew, Thomas Ridgway Bridson, as a partner. In 1833 the partnership was dissolved and Ridgway Bridson subsequently established T. R. Bridson and Sons as one of the giants of the industry. George Blair came to Bolton from Cumberland in 1804, having purchased part of the Mill Hill estate. He established a bleaching business which his son Stephen took over in 1826. Stephen Blair was an original trustee of Little Bolton, director of Bolton Gas Company and several turnpike trusts, the first Conservative mayor of the town council in 1846 and MP for Bolton from 1848 to 1852. The other major firms could trace older lineages. The Ainsworths, who became owners of the manor of Smithells and its hall in 1801, established the Halliwell bleachworks in 1739. The Bradshaw Works was established by James Hardcastle in 1784, while Thomas Hardcastle founded Firwood in 1803.[48]

Turning to industry in an urban location proper, it has proved difficult to trace sequences of business, family and denominational connections among the Tories for the late eighteenth and early nineteenth centuries – in other words, during the period when their conflict with the Liberals was at its most intense. However, from information taken from a survey of newspaper obituaries and pen-portraits, histories of individual firms, and other minor biographical sources,[49] it has been possible to form an impression of linkages that were established roughly from the late eighteenth century up to about the 1870s. The evidence firmly suggests that, although connections were not as dense as those in the Unitarian cousinhood, the Conservatives represented a cohesive social group and major linkages among even long-standing Anglican families were still being formed throughout our period.

The formation of the business partnership between the Anglicans James Ormrod and Thomas Hardcastle in 1798 linked cotton-spinning with bleaching, coal-mining and banking, the ties being further cemented by the later marriage of their offspring Peter Ormrod to Elisa

Hardcastle.[50] Further marriage and business ties extended the Hardcastle-Ormrod linkage to the cotton-spinning Crosses, Briggs, and Eckersleys, but it was not until 1868 that they established links with the engineering Hicks by the marriage of James Ormrod to Edith Hargreaves, and only in 1871 did they cement a more distant connection to the machine-making Dobsons through the marriage of the solicitor Thomas Rushton to Emily Ormrod.[51] All these families were Anglicans.

Ormrods was the largest cotton-spinning firm in Bolton in the second quarter of the nineteenth century, employing over 1,000 workers, a distinction shared by only one other Bolton cotton firm at that time. This was the Bollings, who were also coal-owners, Tory-Anglican, intermarried with the clerical Slades, and who also established marriage connections with leading bleaching interests when Edward Bolling married Henrietta Bridson in 1852.[52] Likewise, the Tory-Anglican cotton-spinning Heskeths, who dominated the Astley Bridge out-township, established concrete links with the bleaching Cottrills by marriage in 1877.

Throughout the period under consideration, Bolton's iron and engineering industry was largely concentrated under the ownership of Conservative employers. In 1866 it was estimated that about eleven-twelfths of the industry's 6,000 workers were employed by Tories.[53] Up to mid-century much of it was carved up between the three major firms of Dobson (textile machinery), Hick (stationary steam-engines), and Rothwell (locomotives). All three were Anglican and maintained close business and social ties. Isaac Dobson, the youngest son of a Westmorland yeoman family which could trace its pedigree back to the twelfth century, migrated to Bolton and set up in business in 1790. His machine-making establishment began on a relatively small scale, with thirty-five employees and a 'gin turned round by one horse' as the only source of motive power. Edward Barlow, the son of a partner in the banking firm of Hardcastle, Cross and Co. (in which the cotton-spinning Ormrods and Crosses and the bleaching Hardcastles were also major partners), was brought in as a partner in 1851. By 1860 Dobson and Barlow's were the largest employers in Bolton, with 1,600 workers, using steam power exceeding 350 horse-power. From 1797 until 1811 Dobson had been in partnership with Peter Rothwell, a wealthy timber-merchant (at this time textile machinery was mostly made of wood). Rothwell, an original trustee for Great Bolton, had important commercial connections throughout Lancashire and was related to many of the early cotton-spinners. He was also involved in establishing the Union Foundry in 1801. Rothwell's influence was instrumental in persuading both John Musgrave and Benjamin Hick to cross the Pennines and join him at the Union Foundry. Several other partners were involved in the enterprise at various times, including Dobson, but by 1821 Hick was described as the 'managing partner'. Hick, who had come to Bolton in 1810, became a prominent member of the Pitt Club and moved easily among the social circles of the leading gentlemen and business élite of the town and neighbourhood. He became a trustee for Great Bolton in the early 1820s, a post he shared with many of his business associates, who were altogether more successful in exploiting the position to further their private business interests than at improving the town's public facilities. By 1833 he had established his Soho Foundry as an independent venture. Musgrave was his first manager. In 1839 Musgrave, a Wesleyan who came to Bolton in 1805, set up in business on his own account in partnership with his son at the Globe Ironworks. The Musgrave family firm subsequently added another foundry and eight cotton mills to their business empire.[54]

Thus, the urban and industrial side of Bolton Toryism represented a distinctive social grouping held together by a solid core of business, political and denominational ties among families who predominantly married into local society rather than outside it. The Tory-Anglican oligarchy and the Liberal-Unitarian caucus represented the focal groups of middle-class political struggle from about the mid-1830s onwards. Both were small élitist groupings, but could usually draw upon support from lower down the social scale. The latter could sometimes gain the allegiance of other Dissenting groups, usually of a less elevated social standing, though perhaps better integrated into the surrounding community. This was not invariable, however, for – as with class – there was a marked tendency for religion to straddle party lines.[55] Moreover, the Tory-Anglicans could usually claim the allegiance of a substantial group of Tory-Wesleyan employers. The Musgraves have already been mentioned and further notables were the cotton-spinning Knowles, Cannon, Taylor, and Marsden families. The Liberals were successful in subsuming the radical petite bourgeoisie that had maintained such a high profile in the local and national political agitations of the late 1820s and early 1830s, but poll-books show that the Tories were also able to generate support among the same social stratum in parliamentary elections at least. Up to mid-century the Liberals' more populist approach to politics also brought them greater success in attracting a base of working-class support, though the Tories did begin to make ground in this respect from the late 1840s.

Bolton's manufacturing middle class was thus deeply divided by religion and party, and cultural differences and divisions in aspects of economic policy should also be considered. Many Tory employers shared some of the economic beliefs of their Liberal rivals, but this did not necessarily compromise what was essentially an independent

Conservative stance. It has already been shown that the largest employers in all the major industries were Tories. In this environment,
Conservatism was totally committed to industrial society and there was
little scope for the development of anything like the Tory radicalism
that was a feature of the West Riding, in which Tory paternalists and
clerics supported Oastler's anti-Poor Law and Factory Acts' agitations.
As shall be seen, the Conservative attitude to the New Poor Law was
equivocal and Tory millowners were among the firmest opponents of
factory legislation.[56] A peculiarity of local manufacturing Toryism,
however, was its support for the Corn Laws. The Liberal *Bolton Free
Press* was astounded by the protectionist stance of the cotton-spinner
William Bolling, which 'in this country means a man who does his
best to destroy the business of cotton spinning. Why Mr. Bolling
should manifest so strong an antipathy to the trade by which he lives, is
a problem we cannot solve.'[57] And Robert Heywood was of the opinion
'that the Corn Laws have proved very injurious' to trade, but 'With
regard to W. Bolling, I have little hopes that he will be induced to break
from his party though he is perhaps a greater sufferer than any other
person being a very large spinner and not upon the most improved
principle.'[58]

    Bolling's intractability is not necessarily attributable to any deep-
rooted loyalty to the national Conservative party. It can also be put
down to their material situation. Local Tory manufacturers were just as
middle class as the Liberals they opposed, but in economic matters they
were generally of the view that the home market was the most important
one, that it ought to be protected to ensure social stability, and that it
was best supplied by a small number of stable and large producers. Many
of them felt that, if the Corn Laws were repealed, an already fiercely
competitive cotton industry would become subjected to cut-throat
competition, because 'hundreds of grocers, drapers, druggists etc. who
had no right in the cotton business at all, would enter it'.[59] This outlook
was, in large part, clearly a reflection of the substantial material situation
of local Tory entrepreneurs. Moreover, the fact that Bolton was pre-
eminent in the bleaching trade goes some way to account further for
Tory attitudes. For this industry viewed the home production of manufactured cloth as essential to its well-being. In 1831 bleaching employers
joined with local cotton manufacturers, hand-loom weavers, and the
'most extensive and respectable spinners' in memorialising Parliament
to transfer the duty on raw cotton to export yarns as a means of boosting
the home trade. In 1833 all the town's major officers (boroughreeves,
constables, overseers, churchwardens), who were predominantly Tory,
lent their support to the campaign, along with local clergy, magistrates,
gentry and Bolling in his capacity as MP.[60]

Deep divisions were manifested at the cultural level too. Robert Poole has suggested that 'Bolton Conservative society was little more than an urban extension of the hunting, shooting and cockfighting world of county society.'[61] This was opposed by a rational reforming culture, influenced by nonconformist religion and a concern for self-improvement and strongly repelled by wasteful indulgence in unproductive pursuits. In the long term, the Conservatives were to benefit from their endorsement of such forms of popular recreation, though a culture which found room for beer, blood sports and bonhomie often offended the rational sensibilities of Dissenters. In the mid-1830s, for instance, Heywood, complaining that 'certain bleachers' enticed their workers to Conservative party meetings with gifts of alcohol, bemoaned the fact that teetotalism did not prevail among the working class.[62]

The rival élites inhabited their own distinct social and cultural orbits. A string of loyalist clubs, established in the town from the 1790s, served as a focal point for the leisure activities of leading Tories. Prominent among these were the Church and King Club (formed 1790) and the Pitt Club (1809). Among the membership of both were the town's senior officers, leading industrialists, gentry and magistrates. By 1827 the Pitt Club was in decline, much to the delight of radicals, but the Church and King Club remained in existence until 1837.[63] The latter ran a library which, in theory at least, was inter-denominational until Dissenters were banned in 1829.[64] This was typical of divisions which split a whole range of new institutions which emerged in the town from the mid-1820s. The *Exchange Newsroom* was established in 1827 as a general library and newsroom on avowedly non-political terms. Among the eighty shareholders were many leading industrialists of all political and religious complexions, including Ainsworth, Ashworth, Barlow, Bridson, Crook, Darbishire, Heywood, Hardcastle, Hick, Ormrod, and Ridgway. The venture was dogged by problems from the start and, after suffering from Conservative defections, folded in the early 1830s. Similar divisions delayed a project to build some public baths – a Tory faction first bringing about the dismissal of the radical architect Greenhalgh and replacing him with their own man, the Liberals then reinstating Greenhalgh after regaining the ascendancy – and scotched two early attempts to establish a park. A 'whole string of choral societies and glee clubs were split and destroyed by political argument'.[65] Robert Heywood resigned from the Bolton Cattle Fair Society in 1832 because of its alleged subservience to the Tory party.[66] Between 1839 and 1842 both the court leets and the newly created town council claimed the right to preside over official celebrations to commemorate the Queen's birthday. As both sides refused to recognise the legitimacy of the other, entirely separate ceremonies were held.[67] Soon after its foundation in 1825, the Mechanics'

Institute was boycotted by many Tories, allegedly because it was the haunt of radicals. They continued to stay away even when the Conservative T. R. Bridson served as chairman in the 1840s.[68] Much of this was attributed to the influence of the vicar of Bolton, William Slade, who also led a Tory faction that sabotaged a plan for an Athenaeum in 1846, after refusing to accept any form of education that was not based on Anglican doctrine.[69]

In terms of political differences, it is clear that, despite the relatively low profile maintained by the Liberal élite in Bolton's political life up to 1837, tensions within the internally divided middle class were never far from the surface. Demands made on the Canning and Wellington administrations, from both Protestants and Catholics, marked the beginning of a new phase of conflict. In 1827 the Bolton District Association of Protestant Unitarian Dissenters forwarded a strongly worded petition to Parliament against 'those degrading laws', the Test and Corporation Acts. Early in 1828 a meeting of the Church and King Club decided to petition against their repeal. Doubts about the likelihood of strong popular support meant that the idea of launching the petition at a public meeting was rejected. It was sent round a succession of selected mills, foundries and factories, but met with a cool reception and apparently received little working-class support.[70] A Church and King 'mob' could not be raised in the present political climate, though the question of Catholic emancipation aroused greater passions.[71] But with a hostile source gleefully proclaiming the decline of Orangeism in the town, this time the Church and King Club was careful to operate under the guise of the town's officers and leading magistrates, and a more vigorous petitioning movement claimed 12,000 signatures.[72]

In 1837 the Liberal élite abandoned its low profile in local and national politics. By that date it was becoming increasingly clear that the 1832 Reform Act had done little to satisfy the aspirations of all classes of reformers. From then until 1850 the political perspective of the Liberal élite was clearly focused on national as well as local developments. Dissenters had expected parliamentary reform to increase their political power, but very few had been returned to the Commons. As Gash has argued, what they wanted was not just relief from any penal legislation, but from the bias of the law and the constitution, and they had assumed that a reformed Parliament would be the means to guarantee the removal of their remaining marks of historic inferiority. Some progress towards this object was achieved in 1836, after the Whigs had returned to office under Lord Melbourne, but the withdrawal of the Bill to abolish church rates in 1837 signified that the limits of Whig concession to their erstwhile Dissenter allies was nearing exhaustion.[73] As has already been seen in the previous chapter, church rates in Bolton were effectively abolished in 1833, without any member of the Liberal élite playing a prominent role in the agitation. As such, they were no longer a matter of contention in local politics. Nevertheless, there was strong local support for the Bill, and this issue marked the beginning of a period of sustained political agitation on the part of the Liberal big bourgeoisie. A requisition notice to the town's officers, urging them to call a public meeting, was signed by eighty notable persons, including Unitarians such as the minister Franklin Baker and the cotton employers Joseph Crook and Charles Darbishire, though the Tory-Wesleyan cotton-spinner Thomas Taylor was also among the signatories. Permission to hold the meeting was refused, but it went ahead regardless and, chaired by the Unitarian Robert Heywood, adopted a petition eventually signed by no less than 7,000 ratepayers.[74] In holding aloof from the Bolton Political Union and in failing to display any independent initiative, the Liberal élite had not taken a prominent role in the earlier Reform Bill agitation. But it was their agitations that opened a new phase of popular political activity, including the campaign for further parliamentary reform.

Municipal incorporation and the emergence of a middle-class consensus

The internal social and cultural divisions within the middle class were confirmed by political allegiance. In the pre-reform period and in the contest for the parliamentary seats of 1832, the terms 'Whig', 'Tory', 'Liberal' and 'radical' already denoted meaningful and specific positions, notwithstanding the pronouncements of historians as to the imprecision of the latter.[75] It was only in the period from the mid-1830s to 1850, however, through the campaign for further parliamentary reform and the struggles for free trade and municipal incorporation, that a new and popular Liberalism was established. A significant development in this direction was the formation of the Bolton Reform Association in August 1837. During the first year of its existence the association petitioned Parliament for household suffrage, triennial Parliaments, the ballot, national education, and a charter of incorporation.[76] All these issues were important in giving the Liberals a significant degree of popular political credibility in the town. Aspects of national politics are considered in the next chapter. Municipal incorporation and its aftermath provides the focus of what follows.[77]

The Reform Association had a committee of electors and non-electors, and among its stated objectives was the aim to 'better the condition of all classes of society'. The congregation at Bank Street Chapel was particularly well represented. Henry Ashworth was the association's first president, and Thomasson, Crook, Darbishire and Barrow were on the committee. But with the proportion of electors to non-electors on the committee initially fixed at twenty-four to twelve, the association failed to attract significant working-class support and was always a distinctly middle-class organisation (a point which is elaborated in the next chapter). In February 1838 the number of non-electors was increased to equal the number of electors, but this move was too late to have any impact, and later in the same month the Bolton Democratic Association (the forerunner of the Bolton Working Men's Association) was formed.[78] However, the association had more success in accommodating the radical petite bourgeoisie. They had played an important role in uniting radicals under a single organisation in the earlier Reform Bill agitation and, although that pattern of development was not repeated in the Chartist period, they nevertheless gave support to both Liberal and Chartist causes, thereby playing a significant role in establishing links between reformers of all social classes. Among the enfranchised on the committee were an assortment of small producers and retailers, including the boot- and shoemaker John Brown, the clogger James Brown, and the drapers Skelton and Naisby (all of whom had been members of the council of the Political Union). Their influence should not be exaggerated, however, and it has to be noted that they did not figure in the initial decision to apply for a charter of incorporation. This was not made under the auspices of the association, but by a small clique of Manchester and Bolton Liberal notables at a 'private tea party', held at the residence of John Dean (another Bank Street Unitarian who succeeded Ashworth as president of the Reform Association in 1838) and attended by Henry and Edmund Ashworth, Heywood, Darbishire, Thomasson, and Winder, along with Thomas Potter, George Wilson, J. C. Dyer, and W. R. Callender from Manchester.[79]

In part, the decision was conceived as a means of building Liberal influence at the national level. The parliamentary Whigs and radicals had regarded the old unreformed corporate boroughs as strongholds of Tory-Anglican power and had hoped that the Municipal Corporations Act would strengthen their cause at Westminster through a parallel transfer of power at the local level. Joseph Parkes, secretary of the radical-dominated commission of inquiry that prefaced the legislation of 1835, predicted that the measure would mean the eclipse of Tory power in the Commons and declared that 'Municipal Reform is the steam engine built by the Mill for "Parliamentary Reform"'.[80] As the Act of 1835 automatically reformed the government of only 178 named corporate boroughs, it is hardly surprising that there appears to have been some collusion between local Liberals and the Whig administration.

Ashworth was a friend of Joseph Parkes and during the campaign he wrote to him for advice. Moreover, after the charter was granted in August 1838, there was suspicion among the Tory anti-incorporators that the whole thing had been secretly fixed by the Whig government and the Liberal incorporators.[81]

As a means of securing reforms of benefit to the middle class, a shift in the balance of power at Westminster also appealed to local Liberals and radicals. Thus, for local Liberals, who were also agitating for parliamentary reform, incorporation was seen as a means of strengthening a more general cause. For Thomas Thomasson, Bolton was 'thoroughly a Reform town' and the 'common cause' would be served through incorporation, which was part of the wider battle 'between the people and their oppressors – between the tax-payers and the tax-eaters – between the lazy, useless drones of society and the patient, industrious producers of all wealth'.[82] The same was probably true elsewhere. Derek Fraser remarks that, for the great Manchester radical Richard Cobden, 'the great political issue of his day was the class struggle between bourgeoisie and aristocracy, between town and county, for the soul of England, and his cause would be served by asserting urban authority through incorporation.'[83] Henry Ashworth noted that the Act 'appeared to Mr. Cobden a most suitable provision for Manchester, Bolton, and others of the large towns of Lancashire'. In other words, those towns not automatically incorporated by the Municipal Corporations Act were to pursue incorporation as a means of building Liberal influence generally. Bolton and Manchester were chosen as test cases, with the Manchester men at John Dean's considering 'the case of Bolton to be more promising for reform than Manchester'.[84]

Securing increased influence at Westminster was an important consideration, but the replacement of the county-orientated nexus of manorial and magisterial authority with a more rational, representative and efficient system of local government was a desirable object in itself. For this promised to provide a means of dealing more effectively and fairly with issues directly relating to middle-class economic and social interests, including the conferment of status, rate-fixing, control of municipal expenditure, regulation of transport, law and order, and the provision of infrastructure for industry. Thus the clique that met at John Dean's considered the continuing rule of the court leets to be 'inappropriate and unworthy of the population, wealth, and commercial character of the place'.[85] Heywood informed the government commissioner appointed to consider the case for incorporation that the oligarchical domination of the court leets and Great Bolton trust by 'ultra Conservatives' had 'at length roused the people to seek through a Charter for the recovery of their rights and privileges so long withheld'.[86]

Despite the fact that the decision to initiate a movement for incorporation was neither a public nor a consultative one, the Liberal cause could only be carried with the support of the wider middle- and lower middle-class community. Thus the clique at John Dean's advised Ashworth to 'put in motion the best means for obtaining a decision of the inhabitants upon the matter'. The popular support of the ratepayers was required to confirm the legitimacy of the Liberal cause as that of a *'democratic* case' against a *'baronial* one'. The Liberal notables thus requisitioned the overseers to call a joint public meeting of the two Bolton townships as a platform from which to persuade ratepayers to lend their support to the petitioning campaign about to be launched.[87]

The meeting was held in a 'densely crowded' town hall in January 1838. The Liberals based their case on the alleged inefficiency, corruption and unrepresentative nature of the existing system. Charles Darbishire's arguments were reminiscent of those put forward by petit-bourgeois radicals in earlier campaigns. Public expenditure in Little Bolton, as far as lighting, paving, and sanitation was concerned, was in the hands of the ratepayers, who had the right to vote in elections for the township's trustees. But the householders were forced to pay the salaries of the boroughreeves and constables, whose management was not vested in the trustees and who 'were chosen by a power irresponsible to the people'. As for Great Bolton, the ratepayers exercised no control over public expenditure at all. The contests which had taken place over the constables' accounts had 'so much disturbed the harmony of the town … Irresponsible power was tyranny, and could never command willing obedience.' However, the system – which, in earlier agitations, the petit-bourgeois radicals had aimed only to modify – was to be replaced. Thus, for Henry Ashworth:

> The present mode of appointing the local authorities in this town was so completely absurd that no person would attempt seriously to defend it. The power which the lords of the manor exercised, had its origin in times when Bolton was an insignificant village. Now that the wealth and population of the town had so greatly increased, no one could suppose that the old, imperfect system was at all fitted for the present altered state of things.[88]

The meeting enthusiastically endorsed the Liberal proposals and a parliamentary petition was organised. But the Tories showed a determined opposition to the scheme and reacted with their own counter-petition. By the time Captain Jebb, the government commissioner, arrived in Bolton to examine the authenticity of the petitions, both sides were claiming majority support. The Liberal petition complained of the constant overriding of decisions made by the ratepayers in vestry by a Tory oligarchy – an oligarchy operating through the agency of a largely non-resident and unrepresentative county magistracy, since the power to appoint magistrates was vested solely in the Duchy of Lancaster. Moreover, not only did political bias prevail in the selection of boroughreeves and constables, but the mosaic of separate manorial and parochial authority was inherently inefficient because the separate authorities did not always communicate or cooperate with each other; the Bolton townships were practically a single urban entity and should be administered as such. The Tory petition implausibly countered that the local institutional network *was* representative, in that it was staffed by local inhabitants. More convincing was their claim that many vestry decisions had in fact been secured illegally by 'majorities not entirely composed of Ratepayers'. When a poll was taken, these show-of-hands decisions were often overturned. Moreover, the present system was inexpensive and more efficient than alleged by the incorporators.[89] Nonetheless, a charter of incorporation was granted early in August. According to Jebb's final report, 3,213 ratepayers assessed at £40,530 had been in favour, whereas only 1,886 worth £33,681 were opposed.[90]

The Liberal 'victory', however, was far from conclusive. The Tories refused to accept the legitimacy of the newly formed town council and subjected it to a four-year legal challenge, during which time they boycotted council elections. The only compulsory functions imposed on the council were judicial and public order ones, the maintenance of borough magistrates and police. But incorporation did not automatically displace the functions of the older governing institutions. The court leets continued to appoint boroughreeves and constables who maintained the old police force (dressed in brown uniforms) in opposition to the new (whose uniforms were blue). The county magistrates competed with the borough ones for jurisdiction within the borough,[91] and for a while even went so far as to refuse to allow the use of the county gaol to detain persons committed by the borough court. Even the county coroner refused to give up his rights, and, until he was compensated for the loss three years later, each corpse was subjected to two inquests. A further problem for the Liberals was that the charter did not bestow the corporation with the power to tax the people to defray its operating costs. In practical terms, law and order aside, it was an impotent body with few functions to perform. This meant that the more open parts of the old institutional network not only retained their intrinsic status and authority, but actually became the object of intensified party rivalry as the Liberals attempted to use their rate-levying powers to defray corporation expenses.

The Liberals' attempts to raise a borough rate under the guise of a general poor rate drew the overseers into the struggle over the validity of incorporation. Late in March 1838 a Great Bolton township meeting elected a Liberal list from which the magistrates were expected to appoint overseers for the forthcoming year. But, as shown in the previous chapter, the county magistrates had a habit of rejecting township nominations and replacing them with Tories whenever they saw fit to do so. Now two Liberals were appointed to serve alongside two from the rejected Tory list, the Conservatives retaining overall authority through their control of the churchwardens.[92] In 1839 the new borough magistrates contested the right to appoint the overseers and, at a joint meeting of magistrates, sanctioned the list adopted by the Great Bolton township meeting. The Tory JPs present were prepared for the 'emergency' and tried to cheat the Liberals by immediately dispatching a signed form of appointment to the appropriate quarter, before the proper one had been completed. This manoeuvring was subsequently overturned at the Salford Intermediate Sessions, which confirmed four township nominees as the rightful overseers.[93] But the Conservatives continued to resist and many refused to pay their poor rates. By May 1840, despite the threat of prosecution against many leading Tories (including Ormrod, Hardcastle, Bolling, Hick, Rothwell and others), between £4,000 and £5,000 was owing. In the meantime, with expenditure on policing far exceeding income, the Liberals had been forced to make up a deficit of nearly £2,000 out of their own pockets.[94] To make matters worse, since its inception in 1837, the rural-dominated Bolton Union (for which, see the map opposite and Tables 3.1, 3.2) had been in the control of the opponents of incorporation. Liberals were in the majority in the two Boltons, but these represented only two out of the twenty-six townships or eight out of a total of thirty-three guardians. In the out-townships, landowners still exercised a firm control and in most of them Tories were usually returned unopposed. In 1840 the Tories summonsed the overseers for their share of the rates, which apparently forced the Liberals to concede defeat, the town clerk, Winder, pledging that no part of the poor rate would be used to defray corporation expenses. Yet poor rates were reportedly still being withheld pending the validity of the charter in February 1842. In July it was calculated that the overseers of Great and Little Bolton were over £6,000 in arrears, £3,000 of it owing to the guardians, who again summonsed them for non-payment of their share. Conservative anger stemmed from the fact that, despite Winder's assurances, resources were nevertheless being diverted from their stipulated use; between 1838 and 1842 only 60 per cent of all money collected for poor relief was used as such, the figures for the last year being a mere £6,400 out of £15,894.[95]

**Bolton Poor Law Union
1837–1930**

ANGLEZARKE

EDGEWORTH

ENTWISTLE

LONGWORTH

RIVINGTON

TURTON

QUARLTON

SHARPLES

LB

BRADSHAW

BLACKROD

LITTLE BOLTON

HORWICH

SHARPLES

LB

HARWOOD

HALLIWELL

LITTLE
BOLTON

TONGE
WITH
HAULGH

HEATON

BREIGHT-
MET

LOSTOCK

GREAT
BOLTON

RUMWORTH

DARCY
LEVER

GREAT LEVER

WESTHOUGHTON

LITTLE
LEVER

OVER
HULTON

MIDDLE
HULTON

FARNWORTH

KEARSLEY

LITTLE
HULTON

——— Township Boundaries

- - - Parish Boundaries

Townships not in
Bolton Union

Table 3.1

Population Levels in the Townships Comprising the Bolton Poor Law Union, 1841

Township	Males	Females	Total	Increase on 1831	Decrease on 1831
Great Bolton	16,551	17,058	33,609	5,310	—
Little Bolton	7,882	8,262	16,144	3,248	—
Bradshaw	428	399	827	54	—
Breightmet	643	666	1,309	283	—
Edgeworth	873	824	1,697	—	471
Entwistle	301	254	555	—	146
Harwood	1,051	945	1,996	—	15
Darcy Lever	848	853	1,701	582	—
Little Lever	1,261	1,319	2,580	349	—
Great Lever	318	339	657	20	—
Longworth	80	69	149	—	30
Lostock	331	294	625	19	—
Quarlton	193	177	370	—	6
Sharples	1,447	1,432	2,879	290	—
Tonge-with-Haulgh	1,308	1,319	2,627	426	—
Turton	1,787	1,790	3,577	1,014	—
Farnworth	2,331	2,498	4,829	1,910	—
Heaton	368	345	713	—	6
Little Hulton	1,534	1,518	3,052	71	—
Middle Hulton	485	417	902	—	32
Over Hulton	240	205	445	—	93
Horwich	1,902	1,872	3,774	212	—
Halliwell	1,607	1,635	3,242	279	—
Kearsley	1,636	1,799	3,435	730	—
Rumworth	683	615	1,298	134	—
Westhoughton	2,262	2,265	4,527	27	—
Total	48,350	49,169	97,519	14,949	799

Source: *Bolton Free Press*, 31 July 1841.

Table 3.2

Population Levels in the Townships Comprising the Bolton Poor Law Union, 1851

Township	Males	Females	Total	Increase on 1841	Decrease on 1841
Great Bolton	19,525	20,398	39,923	6,314	—
Little Bolton	9,902	10,567	20,469	4,325	—
Bradshaw	412	441	853	26	—
Breightmet	736	804	1,540	239	—
Edgeworth	626	604	1,230	—	467
Entwistle	267	219	486	—	69
Farnworth	3,072	3,302	374	1,545	—
Halliwell	1,869	2,070	3,959	717	—
Harwood	1,046	1,010	2,056	60	—
Heaton	402	424	826	113	—
Horwich	1,946	1,996	3,942	168	—
Little Hulton	1,613	1,571	3,184	132	—
Middle Hulton	485	403	888	—	14
Over Hulton	249	203	452	7	—
Kearsley	2,041	2,194	4,235	800	—
Darcy Lever	1,096	994	2,090	389	—
Little Lever	356	357	713	56	—
Great Lever	1,732	1,780	3,542	932	—
Longworth	79	73	152	3	—
Lostock	331	289	620	—	5
Quarlton	186	175	361	—	9
Rumworth	720	666	1,386	88	—
Sharples	1,889	2,015	3,904	1,025	—
Tonge-with-Haulgh	1,383	1,443	2,826	199	—
Turton	1,956	2,202	4,158	581	—
Westhoughton	2,267	2,282	4,549	22	—
Totals	56,206	58,482	114,688	17,733	564

Source: *Bolton Chronicle*, 3 May 1851.

The Liberals were also prevented from collecting a borough rate under the guise of the Little Bolton police rate, for between 1838 and 1841 the Little Bolton trust was heavily influenced by the Tories. In October 1838 a 'small knot' of twenty-two 'respectable and wealthy' Tories caught the election meeting by surprise and invoked the Sturges Bourne clause to produce 122 votes to elect ten Conservative trustees. In October 1840 the Tory boroughreeve of the township again exercised his right to chair the election meeting and insist upon a poll. This threatened to weaken Liberal influence further, but no poll was taken after the boroughreeve was forced to adjourn the disorderly proceedings. The Liberals reconvened the meeting and filled the fourteen vacancies, but this action was subsequently declared void and the trust functioned with only sixteen trustees throughout the year. This left the Tories firmly in control until the 1841 election, when the reformers' list of twenty-one persons was adopted, in opposition to a Tory list, to fill the vacancies of seven retiring trustees and those left unfilled from the previous year.[96]

The council had formally attempted to absorb the powers of the trusts in November 1838, but had withdrawn its parliamentary application after the Tories had used their recently acquired influence within the Little Bolton trust to mount a united front in opposition.[97] An attempt by the Liberals to wrest control of the old police from the two sets of boroughreeves and constables, by using the vestry to try and withhold its finance, was similarly unsuccessful. The county magistrates simply reinstated the constables' accounts.[98] During Chartist rioting in August 1839 the problems of dual policing were exposed to a wider audience, and Parliament passed the Bolton Police Bill. This established a singular police force, modelled on the Metropolitan Police and, under a commissioner appointed by the Home Office, to be paid for out of the local rates. It was to remain in operation while the legal case against incorporation was pending. The Liberal *Bolton Free Press* considered it an expensive Tory measure against self-government in local affairs, but the Unitarian Charles Darbishire, in his capacity as the first mayor of Bolton, had in fact made a request to central government early in August to include the town in legislation originally designed to cover Birmingham and Manchester (whose new charters were subject to similar legal challenges).[99]

From 1839 the Liberals made conciliatory gestures in an attempt to persuade their opponents to accept the council. It was no mere coincidence that Robert Heywood was chosen as the second mayor of the new corporation. He had been a Great Bolton trustee since 1826 and in 1835 was the first Bolton Liberal to be appointed county magistrate. At the meeting which saw his appointment, James Arrowsmith, in proposing him, said he was 'of so much moderation he could scarcely be called a partisan'. Henry Ashworth was informed that the Tories were desirous of a settlement and was optimistic that Heywood would 'be the means of restoring order betwixt the Corporation and the Anti-Corporation'.[100] But neither Heywood's appointment nor the offer of twelve unopposed seats in 1841 could persuade the Tories to accept the council.[101] The struggle over incorporation was not settled until the Boroughs Incorporation Act of August 1842.

This finally confirmed the legality of the council and conferred the powers to levy rates for purposes of law and order. It was complemented by the Parish Constables' Act, also passed in August 1842, which effectively put an end to the policing functions of the court leets.[102] But while the institutional system was no longer subject to the near paralysis of 1838 to 1842, a smooth-running system of local government was delayed until 1850, despite developments towards consensus in many areas. For although the appalling sanitary condition of the town had been the object of greater publicity, attention and middle-class concern since 1842, the council did not possess the necessary powers to cope satisfactorily with problems of public health. In attempting to deal with the situation, it encountered determined resistance by vested interests. The two sets of trustees remained as the main bodies for improvement purposes, and the domination of each by a separate party negated plans for a co-ordinated and effective sanitary and public health service. In trying to improve and extend urban facilities, the council also came into conflict with the privately owned and Tory-dominated gas and water companies, both of which had supported the Tory petition against incorporation.

Municipal reform enabled men who had made their mark in the local economy, but who had previously been excluded from the pursuit of the higher echelons of local office, to achieve a position of social leadership appropriate to their economic standing. If the achievement of incorporation was envisaged in terms of Liberal domination of local government, however, then it was the fragility of Liberal hegemony which soon became apparent. Now that the full legality of the charter had been confirmed, the Conservatives were left with little choice other than to participate in council elections and here they achieved immediate success. The council was composed of twelve aldermen and thirty-six councillors. The latter normally served for a period of three years and elections were organised on the basis that twelve seats became available by rotation in the annual elections. The aldermen were selected by the councillors. This meant that the Conservatives would have to contest a number of elections to gain overall control. The first council elections along party lines took place in November 1842, with nine Conservatives and only four Liberals being returned (the early retirement of a Liberal councillor made thirteen seats available). This heralded a period of strong Conservative revival, and Conservatives had only to wait until 1844 for their first majority.

The elections of 1843 and 1844 were perhaps the most fiercely contested until the late 1860s. The contest in 1843 was embittered by the notorious 'Fifteen Plot', hatched by fifteen leading Liberals, including the mayor, alarmed by the rapid Conservative ascendancy. Municipal electors had to have paid rates continuously for three years to qualify for the vote, and were disfranchised if rates were in arrears. Pending the confirmation of the legality of the charter, several rates had been laid by the council which the Conservatives consistently resisted as unlawful. Some of these were subsequently abandoned, while others were paid solely by the Liberals. One of the rates laid but never collected, and therefore regarded as forsaken, was resurrected and paid on the very last day of the qualifying period. If successful, this manoeuvre threatened to disqualify all but the fifteen of the registered electors of Little Bolton. The Conservatives responded by challenging the legality of all 1,980 electors at the revision court. This had to conduct its business during a specified period (between 1 and 15 October), but as the Liberals themselves objected to the qualification of 1,000 voters, a long revision, extending over ten days, took place. As planned, this worked in favour of the Conservatives; the previous year's list had to be used for the elections, as no new list had been prepared in time.[103]

With the struggle for supremacy in the balance, the 1844 elections were fought with all the passion of a parliamentary contest, the Conservatives gaining control only after the aldermanic elections tipped the balance.[104] With Tory dominance now seemingly confirmed, and with little prospect of any immediate Liberal recovery (by 1848 they held only six of the forty-eight council and aldermanic seats), there was a reduction in the bitterness of party rivalry from the mid-1840s. Nevertheless, the town council continued to serve as a focus of the ongoing power struggle between rival élites within the middle class, a struggle fought out in the annual revision courts and municipal elections. Moreover, in the allocation of the prestigious aldermanic robes and mayoral chain, party considerations nearly always prevailed over mere social and economic standing. Party also played a major role in the distribution of other spoils, as James Winder, the town clerk, found out to his cost in 1844, when the new Tory council dismissed him from his post because of the leading advisory role he had taken in the struggle for the charter of incorporation.[105]

While party rivalry in council politics may have declined in intensity after 1844, this was less true of some other parts of the institutional system. The publication of Chadwick's report on the appalling sanitary condition of the towns prompted much documentation on conditions in Bolton, which, in turn, promoted general agreement among the middle class of the need for improvement.[106] But the council did not itself possess the requisite powers to supply the necessary improved public facilities or to deal with the pressing problems of sanitation associated with largely unregulated urban expansion. An effective improvement policy required suitable council regulation of the private gas and water companies and the absorption of the powers of the two sets of trustees. The latter, however, continued to be controlled by the rival parties and refused willingly to surrender their powers to the council. All this was a serious obstacle to effective practical action.

The first moves to change this situation were made during 1843, when a Liberal council decided to oppose two local private Bills before Parliament as a means of securing greater control over the town's gas and water supply. Opposition to the Bolton Gas Bill gained the inclusion of a clause allowing the council to contract with the gas company to supply lighting for all or any part of the borough. The water company's private Bill was originally intended to empower the company to let its works to whoever it chose, but negotiations led to restricted use by the council alone. Since many Liberals had long been of the opinion that the company's charges were excessive, which dissuaded many of the poorer ratepayers from obtaining a water supply, a clause limiting profits to 10 per cent was inserted into the Bill. Further plans to obtain a municipal water supply, however, which emerged while negotiations with the company were still in progress, came to nothing. In October, with the backing of some popular support from the ratepayers, the council submitted its own Bill to municipalise the water company and to take over the powers of the Great and Little Bolton trustees, including the recently acquired water supply of the former trust.[107] However, the water company's 'reputation for power' was sufficient to cause the withdrawal of the plans to municipalise its waterworks, and the formidable opposition of the Tory-controlled Great Bolton trustees, who contended that the council's still shaky financial powers did not entitle it to cover any of the Bill's parliamentary costs out of the borough fund, was enough to see off the rest of the Bill, and a plan to defray expenses through public subscription failed even to get off the ground.[108]

Thus, the Liberal council's determination to expand municipal facilities was thwarted by the opposition of party and private vested interests, but the Conservatives found themselves in a similar position after they came to power in 1844. They were soon in dispute with the water company, with the council again opposing a private Bill to increase the capacity of company water supplies. This time there was a more amicable settlement, the council negotiating to lease the waterworks in 1846 with an option to purchase. According to one source, the reason for this was clearly evident in the terms on which that option was settled in October 1847. It was alleged that many of the Tory councillors who voted for the purchase were also shareholders in the water company and therefore stood to gain substantially from a purchase price which, at £170,000, was estimated to have been about £50,000 above the real value of the waterworks.[109] The council then sought to ratify the purchase in a Bill which also applied for the acquisition of certain improvement powers and the absorption of the trusts. There was some protest against the water take-over, but it was not sustained.[110] However, the plan to take over the trusts was thwarted by the Liberal-dominated Little Bolton trustees, who, after first submitting the question to a township meeting, steadfastly refused incorporation with the council. The refusal was enough to frustrate the Tories, who found the situation of 1844 reversed when the Liberals questioned the legality of attempting to defray the parliamentary expenses of the Bill through the borough fund. Thus this part of the project became prohibitively expensive and it was dropped. The Bolton Improvement Act of 1847 increased the improvement powers of the council, but once again an attempt to create a unified and more efficient improvement body had been checked by party rivalry.[111]

In 1849 the Tory council made another attempt to absorb the trusts. In part, this was prompted by an influx of the Irish (who mainly resided in the notorious Newtown area of the town) and outbreaks of typhus and cholera in 1847 and 1848, which exposed the inadequacy of a system by then strained to the limits in the face of major threats to public health. In 1849 a Tory source contemplated another cholera outbreak and the resistance of the Little Bolton trustees to a further attempt at absorption:

> The more the incongruous position of the *several* managing author-
> ities is considered, the more singular it appears that the expense,
> inefficiency, and inconvenience of such a divided government should
> have been endured so long ... it will require very little ingenuity to
> understand how it is that with the number of local bodies appointed
> by law to promote the welfare of the borough of Bolton, that welfare
> is almost as far from being really promoted as if none of those bodies
> existed ... No one acquainted with the unwholesome condition of the
> town ... the terrible want of cleanliness, sewerage, broad and open
> thoroughfares, and control over those dens of immorality and filth,
> the lodging-houses ... must perceive at once that with the whole
> posse of Councillors, Trustees, and Guardians at the service of the
> inhabitants, they are very nearly as inadequately tended as if they
> were left to their own unregulated resources ... A divided authority

weakens power, shifts responsibility, and leaves that which can only
be partly done by each not at all.[112]

The later 1840s saw further documentation on the state of public
health. Much of it was propagandist in nature, designed to support the
Tory case, though it also reflected a degree of genuine middle-class
concern. Despite the persistence of party squabbling, there was general
agreement that something needed to be done. Thomasson, for example,
although leading the resistance of the Little Bolton trustees to absorption, considered 'it necessary to preserve the health of this town'. In his
opinion: 'no man's health was safe in the presence of such filth as was to
be found in the borough'.[113] In 1848 the mayor obtained and published
a detailed report on the condition of Bolton from the secretary of the
Mechanics' Institute, whose revelations on the prevalence of 'abundant
dirt', 'lack of drainage', 'crowded and disgusting homes', 'noxious airs',
'poisonous gases', 'pestilential nuisances', 'defective sewerage' and
'complete absence of all sanitary arrangements', were given wider
publicity in a series of articles published by the Tory *Bolton Chronicle*.[114]

No less significant than humanitarian concerns was the threat of state
intervention in local affairs via the provisions of the Public Health Act
of 1848. Middle-class reactions to the Act have to be understood in the
context of the significance of the urban and local as the focus of middle-
class power. Local autonomy in relation to central authority was a sacred
principle to both sections of the middle class. Both Liberals and Tories
had opposed the centralising tenets of the New Poor Law and now
unanimously condemned the idea of supervision in matters of sanitation
by a central board of health modelled provocatively on the Poor Law
Commission. In describing Morpeth's Bill as 'one vast Political
Inclosure Bill', the *Bolton Chronicle* spoke for the sentiments of the
middle class in general:

> It is ... a bill to suppress ... those rights and privileges of self-
> government which have always been recognised as the root and firm
> basis of English liberties ... It is a proposal to take away from every
> municipal corporation and local jurisdiction in England and Wales
> the principle part of its powers of managing its own affairs, and
> regulating its local taxation and expenditure.[115]

Under the terms of the Act, the option of its adoption in municipal
boroughs fell to the town council, which would then operate as the local
board of health. Other places could set up a board elected by the ratepayers, modelled on the board of guardians. While the Bill was in progress,

the combined pressure of parliamentary deputations from many towns, including Bolton, had been successful in ensuring that the Act deferred to local wishes in significant respects.[116] However, in places where the Act was not adopted, if 10 per cent of the local inhabitants asked for it, or if the death-rate was twenty-three per thousand or higher p.a. (as in Bolton), the central board was empowered to compel local authorities to implement sanitary measures. This seemed all the more likely to be Bolton's fate after investigations by the council's inspector of nuisances supported the findings of a Poor Law inspector on the 'filthy state of Newtown, and other localities', especially the condition of the town's unregulated lodging-houses. In rooms measuring as little as 100 feet square, anything up to thirteen persons, of both sexes, were found sleeping 'together indiscriminately, without any clothing whatever', in damp and dirty conditions. Altogether, the lodging-houses accommodated over 700 persons in this fashion, but 'there was no power under any of the local acts to remedy the evil'.[117]

The state of the lodging-houses – the communal sleeping habits to be found therein, which offended the 'respectable' sensibilities of the middle class no less than the squalid conditions – featured prominently in the discussion at the council meeting in August which made the initial decision to attempt to absorb the trusts. As the mayor argued, it would be pointless for the council to absorb one trust without the other, 'because then the natural effect of keeping persons from thronging into lodging houses in Great Bolton would be that such persons would go to Little Bolton, and as a necessary consequence Little Bolton would have to go for a further act, for a similar purpose'.[118] The Tory majority planned to realise its ambitions in a local improvement Act, the details of which were revealed in October. While threatening to adopt the Public Health Act if the Liberals attempted to thwart them once again, the Tory majority argued that this course would be more advantageous for the town, the council thereby pre-empting any move on the part of the central board to enforce its own set of more stringent, intrusive and expensive measures. Besides absorbing the trusts, the proposed Bill included powers to erect a prestigious market hall and to incorporate a wide range of sanitary functions contained in existing legislation.[119]

Nevertheless, the Little Bolton trustees were unwilling to surrender their privileges, and, led by the Liberal councillors Thomasson and Stockdale, they organised an immediate and sustained opposition to Tory plans. In arguing that the present arrangements were adequate for that township's own particular purposes, they were labelled the 'anti-improvers', the 'filth interest' and 'the enemies of cleanliness, comfort, and good local government'.[120] Further opposition to the Bill emerged after it was submitted to the Commons in January 1850. In conjunction with a petition from the Little Bolton trustees, the Liberals also organised petitions against the Bill from the inhabitants of Little Bolton and Haulgh. And there were further opposition petitions from the Lancashire and Yorkshire Railway Company, the trustees of the Bridgewater Estate, the Earl of Bradford, and various other private interests and individuals. But the Tories also organised their own petitions of ratepayers in favour of the Bill, representing a majority of the rateable value of the borough.[121] Moreover, the Little Bolton trustees were unable to scupper the main provisions of the Bill by raising technical or legal obstacles, as had happened previously. Thus they had to appeal to the ratepayers of that township, claiming that they would be charged with the cost of improving Great Bolton. But their case was undermined when the Tories appeased the ratepayers by agreeing to strengthen a clause that stipulated that improvements applying to only one township could be charged to the ratepayers from that township alone. A few minor concessions were needed to neutralise remaining opposition, but the Tories got most of what they wanted and the Bill went through Parliament with its main provisions intact.[122] The town council was now an effective governing body, with control over the most important functions of local government.

The Bolton Improvement Act of 1850 represented a major landmark in local municipal history. Locally, the network of local governing institutions and their rate-levying functions had been rationalised and made more democratically accountable to the ratepayers through municipal elections. Thus, the establishment of the town council as the major multi-purpose institution of local government by 1850 did much to resolve internal tension within the middle class. But the removal of institutional paralysis does not solely account for the increase in middle-class unity by 1850. While cultural, religious and political differences continued to be important until at least 1880, the impulses to greater class cohesion were nevertheless evident by the early 1840s. The real significance of 1850 was the confirmation of a growing consensus as to *how* the town should be governed.

Of the first encounters in the council chamber, the mouthpiece of the Liberals noted how Tory recognition of the full legitimacy of the council came immediately after its full legal status was confirmed in 1842:

The conflict has commenced ... But what a change has come over the spirit of some of the Tory Councillors. They who were the abettors of irresponsible power, of secrecy, of partizanship, now talk loudly of responsibility, of publicity, of the desirableness of uniting men of all grades of political and religious opinion, in the working out of good local government.[123]

In 1843 the same source commented on the lack of significant ideological differences in the conduct of municipal affairs:

> Should there be a continuance of the same tone and spirit which were evinced by the Town Council on Wednesday, we shall shortly be looking out for the Millennium. The lion now lies down with the lamb; the Ethiop has changed his skin, the black has become white. The Reformers are Reformers still, but they can scarcely lay claim to that title as a distinctive characteristic in the business of the council, for the Tories, when there, are Reformers too ... Had the grant of the Charter of Incorporation done little else than work these reformations, and draw forth these declarations, we should say it had worked wonders.[124]

Thus, after their accession to power in 1844, the task of uniting the major functions of local government under the council fell to the Tories, who completed it in the face of resistance from those who had initiated the process. It was now the Liberals who, in defence of vested interests, raised the main obstacles to progress and efficiency. The pattern was established whereby the improvement programmes of the party in power were defended against opposition charges of extravagance. The theme of municipal pride was embraced by successive Liberal and Tory administrations alike, and was not the specific ideological property of either.

All this did not end party conflict within the town council, or bridge the wider political and cultural gulf in the middle class. The developing middle-class consensus had its limits. Nevertheless, municipal reform had removed the institutional paralysis from local government and laid down new rules which the opposing power blocs could agree to, thus eliminating a major source of tension.

Further impulses to class cohesion, aspects of which will receive greater attention in subsequent chapters, will now be briefly considered. Early elections to the board of guardians in the Great and Little Bolton sections of the Bolton Union were characterised by bitter party rivalry. However, there was little ideological divergence in attitudes to the poor and both sides shared a common hostility to the meddling of the Poor Law Commission in local affairs. Early meetings of the guardians were characterised by conflict over the application of the notion of less eligibility, while the intrusion of such questions as the relationship between poverty and the Corn Laws, brought further tension. However, charges of administrative incompetence and extravagance declined in frequency from the early 1840s. By April 1846 neither of the rival élites seems to have considered control of the union to be important to the ongoing struggle within the middle class. In a spirit of conciliation, the Conservatives gave up their majority on the board, forming an electoral pact with the Liberals to avoid the expense of elections and allow an equal number of Tories and Liberals to sit as guardians. This action came soon after a similar gesture in March 1846, when the Liberal-controlled borough magistrates appointed an equal number of Tory and Liberal overseers for the townships of Great Bolton and Little Bolton, thereby ending their previous practice of appointing a majority of Liberals to the office.[125]

The town council, borough bench, Bolton Union, Poor Protection Society, and Benevolent Society were all important examples of institutions that emerged between 1837 and 1842 which gave the middle class a greater sense of shared identity, buttressing the common ideological, economic, social, and political determinants of class power and eroding cultural differences. At the same time, the more extreme string of Tory loyalist and patriotic clubs that had sprung into existence during the wars with France finally passed away with the folding of the Church and King Club in 1837.

Religious divisions continued to be important, and until about 1850 they served to disrupt the spread of cultural provision for the working class. Party conflict was less disruptive in the areas of charity and philanthropy, however, and social relations with the working class indicate the underlying essential unity of interests in the perpetuation of class rule. The cooperation of all the town's leaders was needed to cope with the Chartist crises of 1839 and 1842. Most of the major cotton-factory owners were members of the Associated Master Cotton-Spinners of Bolton by no later than 1840.[126]

Also important was a growing Tory accommodation of financial reform, though it has to be stressed that this was far less evident nationally than it was in the arena of municipal politics. The *Bolton Chronicle* and *Bolton Free Press* welcomed the plans for tariff reform outlined in Peel's budget of 1842, which proposed the reduction of duties on a wide range of articles (though the latter continued to insist on the necessity of the repeal, rather than reform, of the Corn Laws). Both the Bolton newspapers made some criticism of the reintroduction of income tax which was coupled with the programme of tariff reduction, but, significantly, this was really limited to the details of its form, for the way in which hard-earned salaries were taxed at the same rate as fixed incomes – especially those deriving from landed capital.[127] Peel's budget of 1845, and the repeal of the Corn Laws in 1846, continued the Peelite evolution from moderate protectionists to free traders,[128] and because these financial reforms were passed by a Conservative government, it was very difficult for local Tories to oppose them. The *Bolton Chronicle*, earlier intransigent in its support of the Corn Laws, cited suffering in

Ireland when, late in March 1846, it called for a speedy passage of the Corn Importation Bill into law. A town council comprised of thirty-two Tories and sixteen Liberals petitioned the House of Lords to pass the same Bill 'and other commercial measures' later in May.

As suggested above, however, the extent and pace of Tory changes in attitude in this area should not be exaggerated. Only eighteen councillors attended the council meeting that adopted the petition to the Lords, ten of whom were Tories, the rest being Liberals. The eight Liberals voted solidly for the petition, but only three Tories were in favour, three being against and the other four abstaining.[129] Moreover, when the issue of the propriety of restoring the Corn Laws was debated during the 1852 parliamentary election campaign, the Tory candidate Stephen Blair, while maintaining that a return to protection was 'very unwise' in the present 'most prosperous condition', appeared less than convinced that advances in prosperity were linked to free trade.[130] The Peelite initiatives reduced the gulf between the rival sections of the local middle class, but remaining differences over the question of further financial reform continued to constitute a source of division. After 1846 the Liberals soon regrouped under the Parliamentary and Financial Reform Association, which called for an extension of the suffrage as the best means of obtaining drastic cuts in civil and defence expenditure.[131] This plan was anathema to Tories on both counts, and in the 1850s, notwithstanding the enlightened civic improvement policy of the Tory-controlled town council in the late 1840s and early 1850s and the actions of the Peelites in Parliament, the Liberals became firmly identified as the party of social progress, parliamentary reform, peace and stringent retrenchment, while the Tories continued to oppose suffrage extension and provided impressive support for a Volunteer movement which remained the preserve of Tories until at least the 1880s. Nevertheless, despite these qualifications, by the end of the 1840s the free trade issue was no longer a source of major division within the middle class and it is significant that the Parliamentary and Financial Reform Association did not match the vigour of the earlier anti-Corn Law agitation.

The reform of local government, outlined in this and the previous chapter was part of the reordering of society to the needs of industrial capitalism, a process begun long before 1832, but only largely completed by 1850. Further aspects of this are covered in subsequent chapters. Middle-class rule was predicated on its claims to social leadership in its own communities. By the early 1840s it had gained the allegiance of the petite bourgeoisie, numerically more important than the middle class 'proper' in the early and mid-Victorian municipal and parliamentary electorates. As we have seen, the radical section of the petite bourgeoisie, the leading group in early radicalism, was largely subsumed by an all-embracing Liberalism, and from the mid-1830s many of its leaders firmly supported Liberal political causes and organisations.[132] A level of support among this stratum was achieved by the Tories too. Before the middle class could lay claim to the social leadership of the whole community, however, two further problems had to be alleviated – working-class political insurgency and the appalling state of industrial relations.

Notes

1. This chapter deals with some of the social factors that played a role in middle-class formation. The main economic processes of middle-class formation in Bolton have received attention from Katrina Honeyman. In documenting the displacement of the town's once pre-eminent hand-loom weaving industry by an economic base dominated by production in cotton factories, Honeyman has shown the important continuities in business leadership and capital formation: K. Honeyman, *Origins of Enterprise: Business Leadership in the Industrial Revolution* (Manchester, 1982).

2. P. Anderson, 'Origins of the Present Crisis', *New Left Review* 23 (1964); P. Anderson, 'The Figures of Descent', *New Left Review* 161 (1987); W. D. Rubinstein, 'Wealth, Elites and the Class Structure of Modern Britain', *Past and Present* 76 (1977); M. Wiener, *English Culture and the Decline of the Industrial Spirit* (Cambridge, 1981).

3. S. Gunn, 'The "Failure" of the Victorian Middle Class: A Critique', in J. Wolff and J. Seed (eds), *The Culture of Capital: Art, Power and the Nineteenth-Century Middle Class* (Manchester, 1988).

4. For example, see C. Barker and D. Nicholls (eds), *The Development of British Capitalist Society: A Marxist Debate* (Manchester, 1988).

5. J. Saville, 'Some Notes on Perry Anderson's "Figures of Descent"', in Barker and Nicholls, *op. cit.*, p. 37.

6. D. Fraser, *Urban Politics in Victorian England: The Structure of Politics in Victorian Cities* (Leicester, 1976), ch. 6; V. A. C. Gatrell, 'Incorporation and the Pursuit of Liberal Hegemony in Manchester 1790–1839', in D. Fraser (ed.), *Municipal Reform and the Industrial City* (Leicester, 1982).

7. D. Fraser, 'Municipal Reform in Historical Perspective', in Fraser (ed.), *op. cit.*, pp. 7–8.

8. Fraser, *Urban Politics*, p. 265.

9. *B.C.*, 7 April 1838.

10. *B.F.P.*, 18 December 1847.

11. Cited in J. Seed, 'Theologies of Power: Unitarianism and the Social Relations of Religious Discourse, 1800–50', in R. J. Morris (ed.), *Class, Power and Social Structure in British Nineteenth-Century Towns* (Leicester, 1986), p. 108.

12. For example, Gatrell, *op. cit.*; Seed, *op. cit.*

13. Gatrell, *op. cit.*, pp. 24–9, for the Unitarian community in Manchester.

14. Bolton Biographical Notes (B.R.L., arranged in seven bound volumes, the first two being the most extensively used in this chapter); G. M. Ramsden, *A Responsible Society: The Life and Times of the Congregation of Bank Street Chapel, Bolton, Lancashire* (Horsham, 1985).

15. For example, see *Bank Street Chapel Bolton, Bi-Centenary Commemoration 1696–1896* (Manchester, 1896), pp. 23–4 (Rev. F. Baker, confession of faith at his ordination service).

16. Seed, *op. cit.*, p. 112.

17. *Bank Street Chapel Bi-Centenary*, p. 147; Gatrell, *op. cit.*, p. 28; Seed, *op. cit.*, pp. 131–2.

18. W. Brimelow, *History of Bolton, Vol. 1* (Bolton, 1882), pp. 6–10.

19. Cited in E. P. Thompson, *The Making of the English Working Class* (Harmondsworth, 1968), p. 121. Cooper is to be found among the 1833 roll of trustees for Bank Street Chapel (see Ramsden, *op. cit.*, pp. 15, 83).

20. Cited in Gatrell, *op. cit.*, p. 28.

21. F. Baker, *The Rise and Progress of Nonconformity in Bolton* (London, 1854), pp. 67–8.

22. Thompson, *op. cit.*, p. 29.

23. P. N. Dale, 'A Study of the Growth of Churches in Bolton during the Industrial Revolution', University College of North Wales Ph.D thesis (1984).

24. A. D. Gilbert, *Religion and Society in Industrial England: Church, Chapel and Social Change 1740–1914* (London, 1976), p. 40; Dale, *op. cit.*, p. 35.

25. Dale, *op. cit.*, pp. 32, 35; Ramsden, *op. cit.*, p. 68.

26. Dale, *op. cit.*, p. 35; Ramsden, *op. cit.*, p. 68.

27. Gilbert, *op. cit.*, pp. 40, 51–7.

28. Seed, *op. cit.*, p. 153.

29. Gilbert, *op. cit.*, p. 41; Dale, *op. cit.*, p. 32; Ramsden, *op. cit.*, pp. 7, 11–12.

30. Gatrell, *op. cit.*, p. 25.

31. *Bolton Journal*, 10 December 1881 (Religious Census of 1881, including comparison with the Religious Census of 1851).

32. Dale, *op. cit.*, p. 32; Ramsden, *op. cit.*, pp. 56–59, 68.

33. Gatrell, *op. cit.*, pp. 25–7. And according to Seed, *op. cit.*, pp. 130–1: 'In the case of the Unitarians ... probably the most important factor in the strength of sectarian identity was its integration with kinship ties. In many of the largest and most influential Unitarian congregations in this period a network of interconnected families over several generations provided a central grouping within the membership ... To be a Unitarian was not just an individual and private avocation. It was a shared commitment, an affirmation of one's loyalty not just to a particular creed or congregation but to an extended family network and to a family tradition.'

34. Ramsden, *op. cit.*, ch. 8 (this is a book aimed at the general reader rather than the academic market, but it is a useful source nonetheless); Bolton Biographical Notes, *op. cit.*; W. H. Haslam and F. E. Morris, *John Haslam and Co. Ltd, 1816–1920* (B.R.L., n.d.); material relating to Bank Street Chapel deposited at John Ryland's Library, Manchester.

35. Bolton Biographical Notes, *op. cit.*

36. E. Thorpe, 'Industrial Relations and the Social Structure: A Case Study of Bolton Cotton Mule-Spinners, 1884–1910', Salford University M.Sc. thesis (1969), Table 30.

37. W. E. Brown, *Robert Heywood of Bolton 1786–1868* (Wakefield, 1970), p. 12. Seed, *op. cit.*, p. 108, also notes the importance of Unitarianism in the political and intellectual life of Britain in the first half of the nineteenth century.

38. F. C. Mather, *After the Canal Duke: A Study of the Industrial Estates Administered by the Trustees of the Third Duke of Bridgewater in the Age of Railway Building, 1825–1872* (Oxford, 1972), pp. 320–3.

39. B.A., MLB/2, Transcript of the Proceedings of the Court Leet of Little Bolton, 1797–1841.

40. Heywood Papers, Correspondence 1838, ZHE/34/4, R. Heywood to Captain Jebb, 24 March 1838.

41. Heywood Papers, Correspondence 1859, B.A., ZHE/55/4, R. Heywood to George Wilson, 24 April 1859.

42. According to Thompson, *op. cit.*, p. 536, Bolton appears to have suffered 'from two unusually zealous magistrates – the Rev. Thomas Bancroft and Colonel Fletcher – both of whom employed spies (or "missionaries") on an exceptional scale'. In any case, Thompson notes that: 'From the Public Record Office, Bolton appears to have been the most insurrectionary centre in England, from the late 1790s until 1820.' For examples of the celebrations held in honour of the late Colonel Fletcher, see *B.C.*, 21 November 1841; *B.F.P.*, 23 November 1844.

43. *Bolton Operative Conservative Association: Report of the Proceedings at the Meeting of the Bolton Operative Conservative Association Held in the Little Bolton Town Hall, June 1st 1836* (Bolton, 1836); *B.C.*, 4 June 1836.

44. *Bolton Journal*, 14 April 1877.

45. J. Black, 'A Medico-Topographical, Geological, and Statistical Sketch of Bolton and its Neighbourhood', *Transactions of the Provincial Medical and Surgical Association* V (1837), p. 177. By way of contrast, one estimate for the numbers employed in bleaching in the borough of Bolton gives 793 working in 8 bleach-crofts in 1847; 1,035 in 1848; 937 in 1849. See B.R.L., Reports of the Superintendent of Police, 1847–9.

46. It seems that the Liberalism of the Ainsworths was due primarily to political opportunism rather than ideological conviction. Peter Ainsworth was elected Liberal MP for Bolton in 1835, 1837 and 1841, though on many occasions his actions in Parliament met with the disapproval of influential Liberals. The Liberals suffered Ainsworth only because they hoped to build support among Anglican electors. Before the 1841 election, Liberal electors remonstrated with Ainsworth, expressing their dissatisfaction with his opposition to Morpeth's Irish Registration Bill to extend the suffrage in Ireland. He had also failed to live up to his pledges on the free trade question, and was forced to explain his past conduct and give assurances for the future on that issue before securing the candidacy in 1841. However, by August 1842 local Liberals were once again angry at Ainsworth's 'lukewarm' interest in the cause of reform, and in 1843 322

electors requisitioned him to resign after he refused to support a motion calling for the total and immediate repeal of the Corn Laws. Moreover, Ainsworth had been a member of the Church and King Club in the 1820s, would not support a petition from his own Liberal constituents calling for the suppression of Orangeism in 1837, supported Stanley's Bill to confirm Orange supremacy in Ireland, and from the late 1840s was at the head of an aggressive Anglican Protestantism given renewed vitality by Irish Roman Catholic immigration. In 1840, on more than one occasion, Thomas Thornley wrote to Heywood complaining of Ainsworth's parliamentary conduct. For example: 'Like many other weak men ... he has a great leaning to the Aristocracy and I understand Lord Stanley is the individual to whom he especially looks up ... I can only regret that a population such as yours ... cannot steadily send up two Liberal members': *B.F.P.*, 13 March, 3 April 1841, 6 August 1842, 21, 28 January, 11 February 1843; Heywood Papers, Correspondence 1837, B.A., ZHE/33/9, P. Ainsworth to R. Heywood, n.d., Correspondence 1840, B.A., ZHE/36/34, letters between Ainsworth and Heywood regarding Ainsworth's support for Stanley's Irish Registration Bill to reduce the Irish franchise, B.A., ZHE/36/37, T. Thornley to R. Heywood, 29 July 1840, Correspondence 1847, B.A., ZHE/43/13, R. Heywood to Dr Bowring, n.d.).

47.   *Horwich Operative Conservative Association First Anniversary Dinner, 1836* (Bolton, 1836).

48.   Bolton Biographical Notes, *op. cit.* The largest firms in the industry have been considered here. A table showing the dates of establishment of those firms from Bolton and district that survived to join the Bleachers' Association Ltd. in 1900 can be found in James H. Longworth, *The Cotton Mills of Bolton 1780–1985* (Bolton, 1986), p. 106. A table of the 'Number of Hands Employed by each Bleacher in the Neighbourhoods of Bolton, Bury, and Manchester, 8th July 1854' can be found in B.P.P. 1854–5, XVIII, Commission for Inquiring into the Expediency of Extending the Acts Relative to Factories to Bleaching Works, &c., p. 19.

49.   Bolton Biographical Notes, *op. cit.*, comprise largely of obituaries and pen-portraits taken from newspapers, especially runs of articles taken from the *Bolton Journal and Guardian*, 1933, and *Bolton Guardian*, 1933. These have been supplemented by obituaries and pen-portraits collected from newspapers in the course of research, and histories of individual firms available in Bolton Reference Library.

50.   For the Ormrod family history, see *B.C.*, 1 July 1871.

51.   Bolton Biographical Notes, *op. cit.*

52.   B.P.P. 1840, X, Select Committee on Mills and Factories, 1567 – list of the number of hands employed in the cotton mills of Bolton, supplied by the secretary of the Associated Master Cotton-Spinners of Bolton (Bollings employed 1,200 workers, Ormrod and Hardcastle's 1,089, the largest Liberal firm 420); *B.C.*, 24 January 1852.

53.   *B.C.*, 7 April 1866; *Bolton Guardian*, 7 April 1866.

54.   Bolton Biographical Notes, *op. cit.*; *B.C.*, 10 March 1860 (history of Dobson and Barlow); 'Short Histories of Famous Firms, V, Messrs. Rothwell and

Co., Bolton', *The Engineer*, January–June 1920; P. W. Pilling, 'Hick Hargreaves and Co.: The History of an Engineering Firm c.1833–1939. A Study with Special Reference to Technological Change and Markets', Liverpool University Ph.D thesis (1985), pp. 10–12, 27–30.

55. *B.C.*, 14 August 1847: 'Religious Opinions of the Electors of Bolton. The following is as correct an analysis as can be formed of the religious opinions of those who voted at the late election:

    95 Churchmen voted for .... Bowring (Liberal)
    97 Ditto .... Brooks (Liberal)
  376 Ditto .... Bolling (Conservative)

    71 Wesleyan Methodists voted for ... Bowring
    79 Ditto .... Brooks
    82 Ditto .... Bolling

    92 Independents voted for .... Bowring
    93 Ditto .... Brooks
    19 Ditto .... Bolling

    55 Unitarians voted for .... Bowring
    55 Ditto .... Brooks
     2 Ditto .... Bolling

     7 Independents and other Methodists voted for ... Bowring
     7 Ditto .... for Brooks

     6 Baptists voted for .... Bowring
     6 Ditto .... Brooks

    31 Catholics voted for .... Bowring
    25 Ditto .... Brooks
     7 Ditto .... Bolling

    12 Friends voted for .... Bowring
    13 Ditto .... Brooks

     1 Cowardite voted for .... Bowring and Brooks

     7 Swedenborgians voted for Bowring
     9 Ditto .... Brooks
     2 Ditto .... Bolling

     9 Scotch Kirk voted for .... Bowring
     9 Ditto .... Brooks
     1 Ditto .... Bolling

There are 421 individuals on the list whose religious opinions cannot be ascertained, or who have no religious opinions at all. Of these, 265 voted for Bowring, 241 for Brooks, 222 for Bolling.'

56.	B.P.P. 1847, XLVI, Memorials of the Master Manufacturers and Mill-owners in the County of Lancaster, with respect to the Ten Hours Bill of 1847.

57.	*B.F.P.*, 2 January 1841.

58.	Heywood Papers, Correspondence 1839, B.A., ZHE/35/34, R. Heywood to Thomas Thornley, n.d.

59.	*North Cheshire Reformer* (speech of Mr Thornley), cited in *B.F.P.*, 13 April 1839.

60.	*B.C.*, 12 February, 5, 26 March 1831, 13, 20 April 1833.

61.	R. Poole, *Popular Leisure and the Music Hall in 19th-Century Bolton* (Centre for North-West Regional Studies, University of Lancaster, Occasional Paper 12, 1982), p. 17; P. Bailey, *Leisure and Class in Victorian England: Rational Recreation and the Contest for Control, 1830–1885* (London, 1987) chs. 1 and 2.

62.	Heywood Papers, Letter-Book 1830s, B.A., ZHE/26/3/125, R. Heywood to the editor of the *B.F.P.*, n.d.

63.	*B.C.*, 9 June 1827, 31 May, 7 June 1828, 30 May 1829.

64.	Heywood Papers, Correspondence 1829, B.A., ZHE/24/3, ZHE/24/4, drafts of letters from R. Heywood to various newspapers.

65.	Poole, *op. cit.*, p. 17; R. Poole, 'Leisure in Bolton, 1750–1900' (typescript in B.R.L., a study undertaken for the Bolton Research Award in 1980–81), pp. 198–200; Brown, *op. cit.*, pp. 47–8.

66.	Heywood Papers, Correspondence 1832, B.A., ZHE/28/33, R. Heywood to the editor of the *Bolton Chronicle*, n.d. The Liberal *Bolton Free Press*, 7 May 1836, attributed great covert electoral power to the Cattle Fair Society.

67.	*B.F.P.*, 18 May 1839, 30 May 1840.

68.	Annual Reports for the Bolton Mechanics' Institute, 1825–1877 (B.R.L., incomplete); reports of annual meetings of the Mechanics' Institute in *B.C.* and *B.F.P.*

69.	Heywood Papers, Correspondence 1846, B.A., ZHE/42/50, R. Heywood to Noah Jones, regarding the opposition of vicar of Bolton to the proposed Athenaeum: 'From the very first he slighted the Mechanics' Institution and again with the Exchange Rooms, though admitting the "Church and King" to be only a reading library, he has done his utmost to destroy their usefulness and at the same time rendered the other still more exclusive by refusing to allow any consistent dissenter to be placed on the committee. He has fostered bigotry in every form and exhibited such feelings more particularly on each 5 of November by furiously denouncing the Catholics, encouraging the ringing of bells, shooting, &c., &c.'

70.	*B.C.*, 9 June 1827, 8 March, 12 April 1828.

71.	As Gash notes, while Dissenters could be charitably regarded as seceded members of the Church of England, Roman Catholicism was the ancient enemy with whom there could be no compromise if the essentially

Protestant character of the state and constitution was to be maintained (N. Gash, *Aristocracy and People: Britain 1815–1865*, pp. 138–9).

72. *B.C.*, 6 December 1828, 14 February, 21 March, 11 April 1829. The radical editor of this source claimed that the Tories had resorted to coercion to obtain signatures and had strenuously hawked the petition from door to door and around the neighbouring out-townships, assiduously visiting public houses and certain Sunday schools, to obtain the signatures of 'numberless little boys'. For Bolton Orangeism (of which Colonel Fletcher was a leading figure) at this period, see *B.C.*, 8 November 1828, 7 November 1829.

73. Gash, *op. cit.*, pp. 169–70; H. Perkin, *Origins of Modern English Society* (London, 1985), pp. 348–50. By mid-1839 Liberals considered that the Reform Bill was proving to be a complete failure, with the Tories its only defenders: e.g. *B.F.P.*, 15 June 1839 (editorial).

74. *B.F.P.*, 11, 18, 25 March, 1 April 1837; *B.C.*, 8 April 1837. The petition gave occupation and residency of the signatories and no person was allowed to sign unless they were a ratepayer.

75. For example, see D. Nicholls, 'The Personnel, Methods, and Policies of English Middle-Class Radicalism, 1760–1924', *The International Journal of Social Education* 3, 1 (Spring 1988).

76. *B.F.P.*, 30 December 1837, 17 February, 10 March, 18 August 1838.

77. The struggle for municipal incorporation and its aftermath to 1850 has been covered by other writers, though the account here considers it in a specific historical context that makes for some differences in interpretation. It can be traced in H. Hamer, *Bolton 1838–1938: A Centenary Record of Municipal Progress* (Bolton, 1938), pp. 3–44, and J. Garrard, *Leadership and Power in Victorian Industrial Towns 1830–80* (Manchester, 1983), pp. 187–94.

78. *B.F.P.*, 12, 26 August 1837, 18 August 1838; *B.C.*, 1 September 1838; Brimelow, *op. cit.*, p. 333.

79. H. Ashworth, *Recollections of Richard Cobden, MP, and the Anti-Corn Law League* (London, 1876), p. 28. The first committee of electors of the Reform Association comprised of 5 cotton-spinners, 4 manufacturers, 3 tea-dealers, 2 drapers, 1 joiner and builder, 1 boot- and shoemaker, 1 corn- and flour-dealer, 1 manufacturing chemist, 1 shuttle-maker, 1 wine and spirit merchant, 1 grocer, 1 beer-retailer, 1 clog- and pattern-maker, 1 timber-merchant.

80. Gash, *op. cit.*, pp. 166–8.

81. *B.C.*, 10 November 1838, argued that the charter had been granted secretly on 5 March 1838, fourteen days before Jebb's visit.

82. *B.F.P.*, 20 January 1838.

83. Fraser, *Urban Politics*, p. 22.

84. Ashworth, *op. cit.*, p. 28.

85. *Ibid.*

86. Heywood Papers, Correspondence 1838, B.A., ZHE/34/4, R. Heywood to Captain Jebb, 24 March 1838.

87. Ashworth, *op. cit.*, pp. 28–9.

88. *B.F.P.*, 20 January 1838.
89. *B.F.P.*, 17 March 1838. The Tories also plausibly argued that incorporation would be more expensive for the inhabitants of Little Bolton. Great Bolton's policing bill was four times that of Little Bolton's, though it had only twice the population. Moreover, Great Bolton had a marked absence of public buildings, while Little Bolton already had a town hall and other 'buildings suitable for its purposes'. Great Bolton was bereft of these and they would need to be erected in the near future.
90. B.P.P. 1841, XX, Municipal Corporations: Report of Captain Jebb on the Bolton Corporation; Ashworth, *op. cit.*, p. 30.
91. In 1839 the Bolton division of the county magistrates applied to the Home Office for confirmation of their current powers. When it was received, they printed the following placard: 'Borough of Bolton: Whereas a number of would-be gentlemen, presumptuously calling themselves Borough Magistrates, are in the habit of holding a Court over the Tap Room and Stables in Bowker's Row, and at such Court they are granting *Summonses* and *Warrants*, by those means obtaining Funds to support their so-called Corporation: THIS IS TO GIVE NOTICE, to the inhabitants of the Borough of Bolton, that by applying at the said Court for Summonses and Warrants they are assisting the so-called Corporation to keep up their expensive farce of Mayor, Aldermen, and Council-men. The inhabitants of the Borough are therefore requested to apply at the OLD POLICE OFFICE, for all Summonses and Warrants as heretofore, it having been decided by the highest Legal Authority that the COUNTY MAGISTRATES have jurisdiction within the Borough' (placard enclosed in *H.O. 40/44*, n.d.).
92. *B.F.P.*, 7 April 1838 (the number of overseers appointed in the two Boltons had now increased to four).
93. *B.F.P.*, 30 March 1839, 9 May 1840.
94. *B.F.P.*, 21 December 1839, 7 March 1840; B.P.P. 1840, XXXIX, Bolton Police: Account of Monies Received and Expended for Police Purposes in the Borough of Bolton … and Return of all Persons Appointed as Members of the Police Force etc.; *H.O. 40/44*, Darbishire (Mayor) to Russell, 29 July 1839.
95. *B.C.*, 16 November 1839; *B.F.P.*, 30 March 1839, 9, 16, 30 May, 20 June 1840, 26 February, 30 July, 3 December 1842.
96. *B.C.*, 27 October 1838, 21 March 1840; *B.F.P.*, 24 October 1840, 23 October 1841.
97. *B.C.*, 24 November, 8 December 1839; *B.F.P.*, 17 November 1838. The election of ten Tories to the Little Bolton trust in 1838 still left Liberals in the majority in that body for the time being, but Tories nevertheless attributed the failure of the council to absorb the powers of the trusts in 1838 to the changing balance of power within the trusts as a whole.
98. *B.C.*, 27 April 1839; *B.F.P.*, 18 May 1839 (the radical draper William Naisby, a veteran of vestry politics, led the Liberals in this part of the campaign).
99. *H.O. 40/44*, Darbishire to Russell, 4, 16 August 1839; *B.F.P.*, 24 August 1839, 16, 23 July 1842 (the Bolton Police Bill was subsequently extended

to 1 October 1843, the borough police then coming under the control of the town council).

100. Brown, *op. cit.*, p. 39; Heywood Papers, Correspondence 1839, B.A., ZHE/35/25, Henry Ashworth to R. Heywood, n.d.

101. *B.C.*, 17 April 1841.

102. *B.F.P.*, 27 August 1842.

103. J. Clegg, *Annals of Bolton* (Bolton, 1888), pp. 62–3.

104. *Ibid.*, pp. 64–5.

105. *B.C.*, 16 November 1844.

106. J. Entwistle, *A Report of the Sanitary Condition of the Borough of Bolton* (Bolton, 1848); newspaper articles (such as *B.F.P.*, 19 November 1842, for example, which actually welcomed Chadwick's findings as evidence that the general unhealthiness of the population of the towns was not primarily caused by the nature of their occupations).

107. Many of the Great Bolton trustees were also directors of the Bolton Waterworks Company. In 1842 they had taken advantage of a grant from the Manufacturing Districts Relief Fund to provide employment for the poor; £2,600 was obtained to employ 300 men in the construction of a reservoir on Bolton Moor which subsequently came under the control of the Great Bolton trustees (Brown, *op. cit.*, p. 47). According to one source, only 7,065 houses in Bolton had a water supply by 1847, out of a potential 13,075 (B.P.P. 1847, XXI, Bolton Improvement: Report of the Commissioners Appointed to Make Preliminary Inquiries Respecting the Bolton Improvement Bill, with Minutes of Evidence, p. 31).

108. *B.F.P.*, 28 October 1843, 19 October 1844.

109. *B.F.P.*, 23 October 1847 (remarks made at the inaugural meeting of the Reform Ratepayers' Association. The membership of this organisation was predominantly petit bourgeois, hit hard by a rise in water rates, and on this occasion made complaints about working-class apathy on this question).

110. *B.C.*, 20 March 1847; B.P.P. 1847, XXI, Bolton Improvement, *op. cit.*, p. 31.

111. *B.C.*, 19 September, 17, 24 October 1846, 23 January, 6, 13 February, 20, 27 March, 15 May 1847.

112. *B.C.*, 22 September 1849 (editorial: 'Improvement of the Borough').

113. *B.C.*, 14 November 1846.

114. Entwistle, *op. cit.*

115. *B.C.*, 18 March 1848.

116. *B.C.*, 25 March, 13 May 1848 (for interview between Morpeth and deputations from the two trusts and the town council, and parliamentary lobbying of MPs by the mayor and town clerk and conferences with other deputations from large towns).

117. *B.C.*, 11, 18 August 1849.

118. *B.C.*, 11 August 1849.

119. *B.C.*, 18 August, 20 October 1849. The council decided to incorporate some or all of the clauses of the following legislation, all of it of recent origin: the Public Health Act of 1848, the Towns Improvement Act of

1847, the Towns Police Clauses Act of 1847, the Markets and Fairs Clauses Act 1847, the Gas Works Clauses Act of 1847, the Water Works Clauses Act of 1847, the Cemetery Clauses Act of 1847.

120. *B.C.*, 27 October 1849, 2 March 1850. Not all Liberals were opposed to the Conservative plans and not all Tories were in favour. The Conservative Alderman George Piggot (land surveyor and land agent) was one such opposed, basing his case on what he argued to be 'the excellent condition of the sewerage of Bolton!' (*B.C.*, 27 October 1849). Robert Heywood was one of the Liberals in favour, having long been an advocate of improved water supplies and now desiring the town council to acquire control of the Great Bolton trust's water supply. Heywood was himself a Great Bolton trustee and had collaborated closely with Burton, a Conservative Little Bolton trustee, on plans for the take-over of the trusts. In 1846 this cooperation even extended as far as an electoral pact in the municipal election. Burton and Heywood were both nominated for the two vacancies in East Ward, and hoped to avoid a contest. But some Liberals denounced the pact and fielded their own candidates who won the two seats (Brown, *op. cit.*, p. 50).

121. *B.C.*, 2, 16 February, 2, 9 March 1850. Haulgh was part of the semi-rural township of Tonge-with-Haulgh, though also included within the municipal and parliamentary borders. Leading ratepayers of the township were aggrieved because inclusion within the municipal borough had meant a steep increase in rates (Haulgh had to pay a borough rate of £170 after incorporation, but had only paid a county rate of £25 beforehand) and the 1850 Act would bring a further rise. The Bill also proposed to supply water to the neighbouring townships of Farnworth, Kearsley, Darcy Lever, Great Lever and Little Lever, and the Tories organised petitions in favour from the ratepayers of these townships.

122. *B.C.*, 11, 25 May, 10, 17, 24 August 1850.

123. *B.F.P.*, 12 November 1842.

124. *B.F.P.*, 25 February 1843.

125. *B.C.*, 18 April 1846.

126. B.P.P. 1840, X, Select Committee on Mills and Factories, *op. cit.*

127. *B.C.*, 19 March 1842; *B.F.P.*, 19 March 1842. The income tax was reintroduced in what could be termed an 'undifferentiated' form. As Matthew explains: 'A graduated tax is one in which, ordinarily, the rate increases with the amount taxed, large incomes paying at a higher rate than small; in a differentiated tax, different schedules pay at different rates, profits from land, for instance, paying at a higher rate than salaries' (H. C. G. Matthew, 'Disraeli, Gladstone, and the Politics of Mid-Victorian Budgets', *The Historical Journal* 22, 3 (1979), p. 618). The *Bolton Chronicle* and *Bolton Free Press* could be considered to belong to the school which advocated a 'differentiated' and 'graduated' tax, on the ground – as Matthew puts it – 'that equality of sacrifice required different levels of tax on different levels of income'. Thus the *Bolton Free Press* complained that it was unjust to put those salaried professionals and small businessmen with moderate incomes on the same footing 'with men whose incomes are

permanent and derived from fixed property', while the *Bolton Chronicle* admitted that it was 'unreasonable that a man should pay from his hard earned labour – from the sweat of his brow – a sum equal to a man whose income was fixed by his ancestors'.

128. P. Adleman, *Peel and the Conservative Party 1830–1850* (London, 1989), pp. 36–8; Gash, *op. cit.*, pp. 220–4, 233–4, 237–8; Matthew, *op. cit.*, pp. 616–17.

129. *B.C.*, 28 March, 23, 30 May 1846.

130. *B.C.*, 27 March 1852.

131. *B.C.*, 16 February, 30 March 1850. See Matthew, *op. cit.*, p. 633, for the percentage of total central-government gross expenditure taken up by defence and civil government spending between the years 1836–1913.

132. See n. 72 above; see also the composition of the first town council in *B.F.P.*, 1, 8 December 1838.

CHAPTER FOUR

Popular Politics 1837–1850:
The Ideological Origins of the
Mid-Victorian Consensus

It has already been suggested that the stabilisation of bourgeois intra-class relations by 1850 was an important element in the consolidation of middle-class hegemony by mid-century. The middle class thus overcame the worst excesses of its own internal contradictions, but this development represented the removal of only one of the major obstacles to the establishment of a smooth-running middle-class social leadership in the local community. Another problem requiring significant alleviation was a militant working-class opposition engendered in the changing forms of social relations that accompanied industrialisation. Technological change and capitalist innovation threatened the stability of society. Industrial relations are covered in the following chapter, whilst this chapter is primarily concerned with political developments. Discussion will centre around a consideration of the nature, social composition and ideological content of essentially popular forms of political protest, together with an examination of the attempts of Tories and Liberals especially to build a mass base of support among the working class.

The organisation of national political parties around distinct sets of political beliefs and principles only developed gradually after the 1832 Reform Act.[1] The label 'Conservative' was soon being applied to those who wished to preserve the institutions of the state against further radical change, but it was not until the 1841 general election that a Liberal party was recognised as being in existence.[2] In terms of the local pattern of events, this development was reflected in the fact that it was not until the mid-1830s that party politics really began to crystallise around the already existing networks of local allegiances outlined in previous chapters. Thus the Liberal campaign to secure municipal, parliamentary, and other reforms did not begin in earnest until the formation of the Bolton Reform Association in 1837. Then, as in earlier phases of agitation, the elevation of locally defined antagonisms into the arena of national politics was facilitated by a Liberal-radical analysis of society which viewed the political system as a comprehensive one in which there was no essential separation of local and national politics; all the ills of society were attributed to the rule of Old Corruption and therefore most local grievances were seen as ultimately emanating from corrupt and unrepresentative national power structures.

It was in this context that an all-embracing Liberalism emerged to subsume the radical section of the petite bourgeoisie which had been the major force in earlier radicalism. However, as this chapter aims to demonstrate, the consolidation of a base of support among the working class proved to be a more protracted and conflict-ridden process. From what we know of Chartism in Lancashire, Bolton seems to have been the only town where the middle class played any role in that movement.[3] But the alliance with working-class radicals was fraught with class tensions and suffered bouts of disunity. The middle-class role in influencing Parliament strained the credibility of its self-portrayal as part of a politically exploited 'people', while the appalling state of industrial relations exposed the contradictions between varying conceptions of the notion of the 'industrious classes'.

The middle-class concept of a unity of interests between employers and workers was designed to relieve the shoulders of manufacturing capitalists of the worst excesses of orthodox political economy. Unemployment, wage cuts, and the adverse effects of technological change were not ascribed to any inherent contradictions within capitalist relations of production, but to the injurious effects of the Corn Laws and the depredations wrought upon the 'natural' mechanisms of market forces by aristocratic privilege and political monopoly. The central emphasis on political explanations of misery and oppression in the radical analysis of society meant that working-class radicals supported the attack on the aristocracy. However, they also held alternative conceptions of how labour-capital relations ought to be regulated. These embraced traditional notions of a 'moral economy', informed by customary notions of fairness, expectation and mutual duties, firmly opposed to the developing classical political economy and now under threat from unrestricted economic competition and unregulated capitalist market relations.

Radicalism and popular political economy thus contained conflictual as well as consensual elements. In the long term, however, the latter held the balance and helped to pave the way for the consolidation of a Liberalism which, like radicalism, owed much of its success to its essentially inter-class appeal. Thus, whilst the Liberals failed to build significant supporting organisations among the working class, they nevertheless enjoyed the support of most labour leaders, some of whom never became Chartists, and overwhelming working-class support in the parliamentary election campaigns of the 1830s and early 1840s. Moreover, working-class radicals never dismissed the feasibility and desirability of class cooperation; although Chartists and Liberals drew apart in the periods leading up to the 'Sacred Month' and 'Plug Strikes' agitations, the essentially hybrid nature of radicalism facilitated reconciliation first in 1841 and then again after 1842, when affiliations of ideas between Chartism and Liberalism were brought into sharper focus. The understanding of the whole experience of intensified exploitation in the 1830s and 1840s was conditioned by the predominance of Old Corruption in the radical analysis of society. Working-class misery was consistently explained in terms of the exclusion of that class from political power. The emphasis was on political power and taxation rather than production relations and profits. The critique of employers did not reveal desires for an alternative social and economic order, but, informed by customary notions of fairness and expectation, was couched essentially in moral terms and expressed desires for the restoration of threatened reciprocities between employers and labour. This left room for class manoeuvre and compromise and, when capitalism stabilised after 1842 in circumstances encouraging greater class reconciliation on a number of interrelated levels, the middle class was able to move beyond its narrow economic interests to renegotiate the basis of its hegemony.

Middle-class Liberals and popular reform movements

The founding of the Bolton Reform Association in 1837 marked the emergence of a powerful middle-class reform movement. It is important to understand that, right from the start, the association was motivated by distinctly middle-class interests. As has been seen in the agitation leading up to the Reform Act, working-class radicals generally held conceptions of the aims of parliamentary reform which differed in important respects from those held by the more moderate middle-class and petit-bourgeois reformers. For the former, only universal suffrage and the conditions without which it would be illusory would ultimately suffice. But for the middle-class reformers, as the following episode illustrates, such far-reaching reform was usually considered unnecessary, if not undesirable.[4] In February 1838 the Reform Association petitioned Parliament for household suffrage, triennial Parliaments and the ballot. But these reforms were not presented as a package. Thus, at the prior meeting of the Reform Association to consider the propriety of petitioning Parliament, Edmund Ashworth declared his support for the idea of separate petitions, one for household suffrage and one for the ballot, either of which, he argued, would shift the balance of political power away from land to 'industry, which was true wealth'. An operative put forward the argument that, as the working class was able to exert a degree of popular pressure over the electors at the hustings, the ballot without an extension of the suffrage would take away 'the only particle of liberty which the non-electors possessed'. But although this argument found some sympathy with a few electors, it was resolved to present two petitions to Parliament, one in favour of household suffrage and short Parliaments (which received 4,800 signatures) and one in favour of the ballot (which significantly received a greater number of signatures – 6,850).[5]

Despite the Reform Association's somewhat half-hearted attempt to accommodate the interests of the non-electors,[6] the middle-class reformers were nevertheless aware of the potential of the mass platform – the fundamental radical tactic from Peterloo until the last great platform agitation in 1848 – as a means of achieving their aims. Relying upon open-constitutional agitation to carry its programme, the mass platform employed the likes of demonstrations, remonstrances, petitions and memorials, all of which provided the opportunity to demonstrate the legality and support of the radical cause. But in so doing, radicals often found themselves operating on the fringe of legality. Functioning beyond the communal framework and direct action of the 'pre-industrial' crowd, such as food riots, the mass platform was more protracted and its pressure more cumulative: activities designed to intimidate the authorities into concessions included torchlight demonstrations, incitements to arm (established by constitutional precedent in the Magna Carta), the formation of a National Convention (a familiar Painite element of radical ideology) and an anti-Parliament deemed to represent the true interests of the people in the face of the corrupt and unrepresentative institutions of the ruling aristocratic Parliament, and the call for a Sacred Month (an idea originating among French revolutionary writers and given its characteristic English expression by William Benbow in 1832). The tactics of the Catholic Association in Ireland were instrumental in securing Catholic emancipation in 1829, and had already demonstrated the potential value of carefully organised mass pressure, ostensibly peaceable, though hinting at force should concessions not be forthcoming. The reform agitation of 1830–2 provided a further lesson along this line, the Reform Bill having seemed to have been carried by quasi-insurrectionary violence following an ineffective period of peaceful demonstration. Thus the 'moral force' of the crowd warned of the 'physical force' that would come if peaceful demands were ignored – hence the Chartist slogan, 'peaceably if we may, forcibly if we must'.[7]

Along this line of reasoning, many middle-class reformers, while not in favour of some of the more extreme aspects of the mass platform, nevertheless took the view that the best hope for obtaining reform lay in the use of intimidation to squeeze concessions from an aristocratic

Parliament not normally given over to rational persuasion. Peter Rothwell Arrowsmith, a Unitarian cotton-spinner, made his views public on this subject early in 1839:

> He differed with those who said the passing of the Reform Bill had not done any good. It had taught people the great lesson they would never forget, that whenever the majority were firmly banded together, with a fixed determination to change the form of government, no power on earth could withstand them (cheers) ... He was no advocate of physical force, until every other means had failed; but he looked in vain to the history of this country, to find that any concession had ever been made by the ruling power except under the influence of fear.[8]

The middle class would achieve its ends by assuming leadership of popular agitation. As the Liberal *Bolton Free Press* made explicit in 1841:

> We are convinced that nothing but fear will convince the legislature that the Corn Laws ought to be repealed ... The 'Physical force' of the masses under the control and guidance of the middle class, is the power which has gained every great measure of reform that has been wrested from the aristocracy ...[9]

The means of obtaining such a mass base of support, however, was the main problem confronting middle-class reformers. Both Liberals and Tories failed to build significant supporting organisations among the working class. The Reform Association did not attract substantial working-class support, and the fact that its committee of non-electors was originally composed entirely of weavers, indicating the narrow base of that support, was a further cause of some concern; two spinners were eventually induced to accept office, but similar efforts to persuade 'several mechanics' came to nothing.[10] Moreover, as seen in Chapter One, Bolton was one of the towns where middle-class reformers had raised the hope that they might assist working people to obtain a more democratic franchise if they would support the Reform Bill as a first step. But the middle-class procrastination which followed left something of a legacy of distrust that was still strong in the late 1830s.[11] Furthermore, as will be seen in the next chapter, the appalling state of workplace relations between labour and capital meant that, up to the mid-1840s at least, neither Liberals nor Tories could generate significant working-class loyalty via the employment relation. Therefore, when, in September 1838, the movement for the 'People's Charter' began to gather support in the town around the Working Men's

Association, the middle-class reformers decided to support it as the best means of gaining the allegiance of the working class.

At the meeting to consider the propriety of supporting the People's Charter, Arrowsmith, Darbishire, Naisby and Thomasson were among the speakers and three resolutions (including the approval of the People's Charter and the national petition) were moved jointly by middle- and working-class speakers.[12] There was some hostility expressed to the middle-class reformers when John Warden, a gardener and leading Bolton Chartist, attacked their gradualist policies. But after Joseph Lomax, a weaver, reminded the audience of the experience of 1832 and called on the middle-class reformers to redeem their pledge, Darbishire (soon to be the first mayor of the newly incorporated borough) said 'he was one of those who made that promise, and he was exceedingly happy to have the present opportunity of redeeming that pledge'. When Joseph Wood (tea-dealer) of the Reform Association was chosen as one of Bolton's two delegates to the National Convention, it may have seemed to some that this time the middle class did intend to keep their promises.

But Chartism proved to be an unsuitable vehicle for middle-class interests, and over the winter of 1838 the allies pulled apart over the question of torchlight meetings. A shared political critique never completely eradicated class tensions and considerations. It seems that the middle-class reformers were less prepared to embrace elements of the mass platform when events threatened to go too far. After they had deserted it the Chartist movement came to function virtually as a vehicle for independent working-class political mobilisation. The Liberal *Bolton Free Press* regularly urged 'union among reformers' during the winter of 1838 and the early months of 1839, and a dinner sponsored by the Reform Association in honour of Joseph Wood, held in February 1839, was an attempt at reconciliation.[13] By April, however, most Chartists were completely dissatisfied with Wood and he was replaced with Warden at the National Convention. The middle-class experiment of close cooperation with working-class radicals had, for the time being, come to an end. Wood had angered Chartists by his moderate politics, typical of which was his refusal to attend the Convention until the presentation of the national petition. At the same time, Chartist language grew more violent in tone. Take, for instance, the speech of Duncan Robinson (hand-loom weaver) at the meeting to appoint Wood's successor:

The people were now preparing to 'work out their own salvation', not with 'fear and trembling', but with short prayers and long pikes. They had waited patiently and long; but they had now determined to enjoy political freedom or die; and they were taking the only way to accomplish their object, by concentrating on their friends in the Convention ... For himself, he should never think the cause in its proper position until every man was in possession of a pike or a gun.[14]

The problem facing middle-class reformers was how to turn such intrinsically powerful rhetoric into the kind of pressure that would intimidate an aristocratic state into making concessions. Middle-class and working-class radicals were divided on this question. The latter were usually prepared to push popular pressure much further than the former. For to the middle-class reformers, actual violence, with its inherent threat to property, was out of the question. But during the build up to the Chartist 'national holiday' in August 1839, which saw serious rioting in the town and attacks on property such as cotton mills and the major iron and engineering establishments,[15] working-class leaders had increasingly advocated recourse to 'physical force' measures. This factor contributed to the growth of a deep divide between the classes.

On the first day of the national holiday 2,000 Chartists assembled in the New Market Place and formed a procession which passed by all the major manufacturing establishments. In order to appreciate the provocative nature of what was declared a 'grand moral demonstration', some attention to Chartist strategy is appropriate here. The background to the national holiday was the increasing advocacy of a confrontationalist strategy by Chartist leaders. This involved incitements to arm, 'open talk of insurrection' at regularly held Chartist meetings, mass Chartist demonstrations and processions, the disruption of church services, reports of arming and drilling, and other similar intimidatory activity.[16] Sykes may well be correct to suggest that the Chartists were forced to move towards positive action amidst growing tactical confusion and uncertainty,[17] but most Bolton leaders were clearly intent on forcing the issue and apparently favoured Benbow's formula of a month-long general strike, designed to precipitate a decisive confrontation between the people and their rulers. Thus, for Warden, constitutional-style agitation was to be pushed to its limits:

He believed that measures would be taken to crush the Convention when it re-assembled. If the government drew the sword of war, the Convention would draw the sword of justice. If the government resorted to the 'last argument of kings', the people must resort to the last argument of free men. The present state of the country was alarming and must be altered. He had no desire to invoke the demon of revolution, but, if after exhausting every moral and peaceable means they still failed to obtain justice, then he would say 'Welcome revolution', and not shrink from the contest ... He would either live with universal suffrage or die by universal suffrage.[18]

Warden favoured Benbow's formula precisely because it was 'tantamount to a national insurrection', and John Gillespie (weaver and leading Bolton Chartist) commented that 'Dr. Taylor said a sacred month meant a physical revolution, and he always understood the same.' When delegates reported that few districts were fully prepared for such a course of action, however, the National Convention compromised and replaced it with a token three-day withdrawal of labour, during which time the localities were instructed to hold meetings and petition the Queen to dismiss her ministers.[19] Bolton leaders attributed the decision of the Convention to draw back from a nationwide confrontation to the personal policy and influence of O'Connor rather than to the mood or state of preparedness of the country. They always intended their demonstration to be more than token.[20] This would explain the otherwise apparently contradictory speeches of Gillespie, George Lloyd (joiner) and Warden on the first day of the national holiday. Lloyd, for instance, whilst urging the crowd to be peaceable, also spoke of 'dying for the cause' and reminded the crowd of the role of the Bristol riots in the passing of the Reform Act.[21]

There was no violence committed on that day, but on the following day warrants were procured for Warden, Lloyd and Gillespie and the arrest of the former two induced serious rioting, including attacks on property, the stoning of troops, running battles between Chartists and special constables, and an attack on Little Bolton Town Hall. The actual details need not concern us here.[22] What is important for the purposes of this study is the role of the middle class in the affair.

The middle-class claim for the leadership of the radical movement was necessarily dependent upon self-portrayal as part of a politically exploited people, possessing only a limited capacity to influence the legislature and, despite the Reform Act, still prey to the actions of a corrupt Parliament. With the granting of the charter of incorporation, this position had been compromised. On the one hand, the middle class invoked the right of physical resistance to unconstitutional government. On the other hand, incorporation now meant that they became locally responsible for the suppression of such resistance. Given this situation, all the town's leaders cooperated to maintain order. Darbishire, in his capacity as mayor, subsequently informed Russell that the riots were 'the first time that I had the opportunity of conferring with a single county magistrate on the subject of the peace with the exception of Mr. Heywood'.[23] Thus, the arrested Chartist leaders pleaded 'that they had done nothing more than the Mayor himself and other gentlemen on the bench had done aforetime … The agitation had originated with the persons in power.' Warden said: 'If these magistrates do commit us, it will be for that which they themselves have advocated – for acting up to their example.'[24] Some parallels can be drawn with Birmingham here, where a struggle for municipal incorporation was being conducted along similar lines and at the same time as that in Bolton. For in Bolton, as in Birmingham, incorporation transposed a number of middle-class radicals from anti-establishment to establishment figures. However, while we can agree to some extent with Behagg that the Municipal Corporations Act went some way to accommodating middle-class interests,[25] this process was far from complete and, despite the experience of 1839, political radicalism continued to be a theme around which middle- and working-class radicals could cooperate beyond 1850.

The middle-class reformers had thus achieved little concrete gain in their involvement with early Chartism, and in December 1838 they formed the Bolton Anti-Corn Law Association.[26] From now on they increasingly turned their attention towards the repeal movement, the cause being given further momentum with the formation of the Anti-Corn Law League in March 1839 to coordinate and focus the various provincial middle-class radical pressures. As Gadian has shown, Bolton took an early lead in the anti-Corn Law movement and maintained a prominent position in the agitation of the 1840s, with few other Lancashire towns rivalling the vigorousness of its activity.[27] However, the development of the superior pressure group tactics associated with the League lay beyond 1842.[28] To reiterate, until then working-class support was viewed as an integral element in the attainment of middle-class aspirations. As a Bolton middle-class reformer made clear: 'There is nothing so much dreaded by the aristocrats and the monopolists as a union of the middle and working classes. So long as they can keep them divided, so long are they secure in their monopoly.'[29] The main thrust of the League's approach to gain support among the working class was persuasion. Literature poured forth from Manchester 'on a massive scale' and lecture tours were organised. The usual message was that Corn Law repeal was the panacea to benefit the 'industrious classes' – the economically productive of all strata – at the expense of the privileged aristocracy and its unproductive allies.[30]

The context of middle-class overtures to the working class and the revival of middle- and working-class radicalism was the depression of 1837 to 1842, arguably the most profound depression of the nineteenth century (certainly in the case for Bolton).[31] For the working class in general, it was a period of rising food prices, high unemployment levels and wage cuts. Thus, although the workmen in the employ of the late Benjamin Dobson, machine-maker, were in a position to donate £40 to the Poor Relief Fund in March 1840, in February of the same year it was reported that the destitution of the labouring classes was more appalling week by week, with moulders, machine-makers (notwithstanding the position of the Dobson workers), spinners, carders, 'all sorts of factory hands', painters, stonemasons, brick-setters, crofters, power-loom weavers, and hand-loom weavers amongst the applicants for poor relief.[32] Statistics published annually by the Poor Protection Society and Benevolent Society confirm that the depression affected a wide range of trades.[33]

The depression of 1837 to 1842 was in fact part of a more general pattern in the development of industrial capitalism, the period between 1825 and 1848 being remarkable for the frequency and acuteness of commercial depressions, as a declining rate of profit in textile manufacture was not matched by a corresponding fall in the price of machinery and food.[34] In cotton-spinning, employers sought to cut costs by the introduction of labour-saving machinery such as long and coupled mules and repeated wage cuts. In weaving, the power loom was only slowly adopted in Bolton, but the trajectory of economic development nevertheless saw the displacement of many hand-loom weavers and, amid cut-throat economic competition, the debasement of those remaining. Capitalist practices and structures now extended to all industries. The workplace relations between labour and capital deteriorated amid bitterness and violence following workers' attempts to preserve their position.

Yet the middle-class reformers of Bolton were at pains to convince workers that their distress did not originate from any inherent contradictions or structured antagonisms within capitalist relations of production. Rather, the plight of both labour and capital was ascribed to political causes, in the form of aristocratic privilege and political monopoly. As such, it was argued that the interests of the middle and working classes were identical, in that they shared a 'common enemy' or, as Thomas Thomasson, the radical manufacturer put it:

> ... employers and workmen had a common interest. They sailed in the same boat, and they would sink or swim together. They must either put down the Corn Laws or the Corn Laws would put them down ... They were not to sit down quietly and starve because the landowners had hitherto had a monopoly of legislative power ... he thought the landowners formed only one link in the chain of monopolists who had so long ground down to the dust the noble energies of the wealth producers of this country ...[35]

The League thus attributed the depression of 1837 to 1842 to the injurious effects of the Corn Laws, which restricted commerce with grain-exporting countries. Deprived of the chance to export grain and raw materials in exchange for British manufactured goods, so the argument went, foreign countries were forced to turn to the development of their home industries. This meant higher food prices for home workers and reduced prosperity for British manufacturing industry. From this line of argument, it followed that technological change was not necessarily intrinsically productive of conflict between capital and labour. Poor labour-capital relations and the adverse effects associated with technological innovation were ascribed to political causes. Dear food restricted the purchasing power of home consumers and the Corn Laws and high rents restricted access to foreign markets, thereby reducing the competitiveness of British manufacturing industry. Therefore, the working-class notion of over-production was fallacious, goods only being surplus in terms of the unnecessary reduction of the purchasing power of workers and other injurious effects of the Corn Laws. As such, the blame for the widening breach between masters and men was said to originate from the privileges of the unproductive members of society and the machinations of the Tory press.[36]

In fact, the argument that, but for the obstacles to the free play of market forces, improvements in machinery would be naturally beneficial was a persistent theme in middle-class overtures to the working class. At the September 1838 meeting to consider the propriety of the People's Charter, Peter Rothwell Arrowsmith, in reference to Tory claims of a supposed lack of intelligence on the part of the working class, said:

> If the working classes were not so well educated as they ought to be, they might blame those for it who made bread dear and labour cheap, and who by their corn laws prevented the people from reaping those benefits which in a healthy state of things, would have resulted from improvements in machinery.[37]

At the attempted reconciliation between middle-class reformers and Chartists in February 1839 Thomas Thomasson spoke in support of the resolution 'may the middle and working classes learn that their true interests are identical':

> There was some who imagined that machinery was an evil to society, or at least, to the workingmen. Now, he was quite prepared to grant that, as things were ordered at present, it had not produced those benefits to the working classes of this country which it might have done. But surely this evil was not essential to the use of machinery. Surely it was not an evil in itself, that, in spinning, the productive power should, by successive inventions, have been increased ...

The evil was that a small class had interfered to prevent the benefit from being properly distributed.[38]

In short, according to the middle-class reformers, the negative effects associated with technological change, including low wages and high unemployment levels, were consequent upon the artificial restriction of market forces and the reduction of profit levels as a result of the Corn Laws. Therefore, the existing poor state of relations between labour and capital was not a natural state of affairs.

This was the message of the middle-class reformers to the working class. But the attempt to build a popular movement under the aegis of the Anti-Corn Law League was not entirely successful up to 1842. For, in adopting a populist approach, they came into conflict with the Chartists, with whom they competed for working-class attention. Early in 1839, just one week after the reconciliation dinner in honour of Joseph Wood, a meeting of Bolton Chartists resolved, by a majority of twenty to one, that it was inexpedient to petition for a repeal of the Corn Laws.[39] Chartists interrupted – and successfully carried their amendments – at all the main Bolton League meetings from 1839 to 1841.[40] In general, relations between Chartists and Leaguers followed the same pattern of mutual suspicion and tension as in other towns.[41]

One argument which held widespread support among Bolton Chartists maintained that, as wheat prices and wage rates rose and fell together, repeal would mean extensive wage-cutting as manufacturers sought to reduce their costs.[42] However, the Chartist attitude to repeal was not one of unqualified hostility. Opposition stemmed mainly from the prospect of facing repeal *unaccompanied* by the Charter. From the Chartist analysis of political power, the Corn Laws were not seen as the primary cause of working-class suffering, but as the effects of a cause, and that cause was legislative monopoly.[43] From this view, the solution to society's problems lay in the extension of political representation as maintained in the principles of the People's Charter; piecemeal reforms, such as the ballot or the repeal of the Corn Laws, could even worsen the position of the working class in power relations with other social groups. Thus, despite the fact that some Chartists favoured the development of the home market, most of them, apparently, were not opposed to Corn Law repeal if it was linked to far-reaching parliamentary reform. This attitude was demonstrated in the Chartist response to the 'complete suffrage' initiative. In February 1842, following the introduction of Peel's Bill to reform the Corn Laws, the question of formulating such a reform programme was canvassed at a public meeting held in the Temperance Hall. The meeting, which was said to be 'densely crowded, principally by the working classes', drew up a memorial to the

Queen which eventually received about 17,000 signatures, asking for all the 'six points' of the People's Charter and the 'total repeal' of the Corn Laws.[44] Despite the Plug Strikes, relations remained fairly cordial until December 1842, when the reformers again divided – significantly, not over the question of the Corn Laws, but over the issue of whether the name of the People's Charter should be dropped even though all its six points were to be retained. Dorothy Thompson suggests that the issue was important because Chartists 'sensed clearly that the name stood for a whole cluster of values and experience which could not be expressed only in a political programme, and that any movement which dropped the name would lose the following in the country'.[45] Thus, a meeting held to appoint Bolton's delegates to a forthcoming complete suffrage conference in Birmingham, attended mostly by working men, passed a resolution, 'almost unanimously', instructing the appointed delegates 'to adhere to the charter name and all, as the best means of relieving the industrious people of this country'.[46]

Moreover, an evaluation of the relationship between the League and the working class must go beyond the League's relations with the Chartists. The high points of Chartist activity, such as the sheer size of the torchlight demonstration addressed by O'Connor in November 1838,[47] for instance, indicate that at times Chartism undoubtedly attracted the support of large numbers of the Bolton working class. However, it is also clear that not all Bolton's workers were Chartists and that the success of the League's efforts in attracting support for Corn Law repeal must not be unduly discounted. The scale of anti-Corn Law petitioning, for instance, suggests that the League did have some influence among the working class. In 1840 an anti-Corn Law circular claimed that the working class had now found their '*real friends*', in that they were being won over by the League's lecturers. A petition was organised under the auspices of the Bolton Liberal guardians, who argued that the Corn Laws were reducing the resources of the working class and forcing them to apply for relief. 'Not one in twenty of the labouring classes refuses to sign it', it was claimed, and eventually the petition received the signatures of no less than 26,815 inhabitants of the Bolton Poor Law Union.[48] In 1841 the Bolton Anti-Corn Law Association forwarded another petition, containing 18,053 signatures from the borough of Bolton, to Parliament. An additional forty-five workpeople's petitions were also sent, with 3,155 signatures attached to them.[49] This scale of support compares favourably with the local level of support for the Chartist national petitions of 1839 and 1842.[50]

Further evidence of working-class support for the policies of the repealers can be found in the campaign activity leading up to the 1841 parliamentary election. After Richard Cobden had declined to stand as a Liberal candidate for Bolton, the Leaguers produced Dr Bowring as the second candidate to run alongside Ainsworth. Before large open-air meetings, Bowring pledged his support for the six points of the Charter before predominantly working-class audiences, and the populist tone of the Liberal campaign produced results. All the open-air meetings endorsed Bowring and during the campaign the Liberals received the support of a committee of several trades, including the spinners' union and organisations of hand-loom and power-loom weavers.[51]

Bowring's support for the six points was clearly important in gaining the allegiance of large numbers of workers, but he stressed that the issue of parliamentary reform should not be considered separately from that of Corn Law repeal, which, to his mind, was the principal cause of working-class distress. Moreover, the surviving election placards of the trades reveal quite different arguments from those prevailing among the Chartists. Repeal appears to have been considered the most appropriate panacea in their minds also. Thus the spinners argued that free trade would relieve the distress of the working class and dismissed outright the view that there was a correlation between wage movements and the price of food.[52] In 1840, 2,976 hand-loom weavers out of an estimated 4,000 resident in the town signed the guardians' anti-Corn Law petition. Therefore, the election petition of the hand-loom weavers, which dismissed as '*clap-traps*' arguments that cheap food would mean low wages, probably had the support of most of that body.[53] The power-loom weavers also declared their support for the principles of free trade.[54]

This is not to say that League policies met with unqualified approval from those trades. The chairman and secretary of the spinners' union, Samuel Howarth and Henry Rothwell, were firm advocates of free trade and took a leading organisational role on behalf of the committee of trades in the 1841 election. Neither became Chartists. In December 1839 Rothwell complained of general working-class apathy on the issue of free trade when he spoke at a Bolton League dinner held in honour of League lecturer A. W. Paulton.[55] This might only suggest that demands for repeal were slow to gain acceptance among significant numbers of the working class and support undoubtedly grew in the early 1840s. But the support of the spinners must be qualified. In September 1841 Howarth chaired a trades' meeting of the operative cotton-spinners, power-loom weavers, and 'other factory workers', together with their employers, 'to take into consideration the depressed state of trade, the consequent distress, and the means to be adopted to procure a remedy'. The effort was clearly staged by the League. Henry Ashworth, Thomasson and another millowner, Joseph Lum, were all on the platform, while Paulton was there by invitation. The meeting was prematurely adjourned, however, after the Chartists interrupted it and successfully carried their amendment. Later in September, at a meeting at the Red Lion, the spinners formed a Free Trade and Anti-Bread Tax Society. But everyone present was said to have held the principles of the People's Charter and not everyone agreed to join the new society.[56] Moreover, Corn Law repeal appears to have been low on the spinners' list of priorities when Chartism revived strongly in 1842, while the Plug Strikes and the collapse of the complete suffrage campaign exposed the limits of the ground made by middle-class reformers in attempting to build a middle-class-led popular movement. The existence of the Free Trade and Anti-Bread Tax Society is not firm evidence of any close involvement between the spinners and the League, which failed to build any significant supporting organisations among the working class. A Bolton Operative Anti-Corn Law Association was in existence from about early 1840,[57] but appears to have enjoyed little support. Furthermore, the spinners and Leaguers clashed over the question of factory reform, and even Rothwell and Howarth believed that they would not fully benefit from free trade without an efficient Ten Hours Act. The spinners were the backbone of the factory movement, which functioned essentially as an independent working-class movement between 1829–42, receiving little active support from any section of the middle class.[58]

On the other hand, however, the support of the hand-loom weavers for free trade and Liberal politics in general was less equivocal. It will be recalled that the non-electors' committee of the Reform Association was initially entirely composed of weavers. Despite the fact that some weavers became prominent Chartists, weaver commitment to Liberalism remained strong. In May 1842, for instance, only a few months before the Plug Strikes, the Chartists interrupted a public meeting of weavers that had been called to inaugurate a weavers' petition asking Parliament for the total and immediate repeal of the Corn and Provision Laws and all other duties affecting trade and commerce. However, the Chartists did not succeed in moving their amendment.[59]

Thus, while Chartism in Bolton contained an aggressive and sometimes independent vein of working-class consciousness, enjoying high levels of popular support during 1838–9, 1842 and, to a lesser extent, 1848, an acknowledgement of its strength and influence must not be allowed to disguise the significance of Liberal achievements. The Chartist insistence that permanent improvement would only be achieved following the securing of the Charter certainly commanded widespread support among the working class, and such perspectives were noticeably absent in the mid-Victorian period. But Chartism did not gain the allegiance of all workers, and significant elements among the working class were always willing to accept piecemeal reforms, even if these might be viewed as constituting a partial remedy. As the hand-loom weavers' address stated in the 1841 parliamentary election campaign, for instance: 'we would not wish to imply that a REPEAL OF THE CORN LAWS will cure all the evils under which this country labours; but we consider it a great step.'[60]

Moreover, Liberals enjoyed overwhelming popular support in the parliamentary elections of the 1830s and early 1840s. The popular endorsement of Bowring as Liberal candidate in 1841 was repeated at the hustings. The pattern followed earlier campaigns. About 12,000 persons were estimated to have been at the hustings in 1835, when the Liberal Ainsworth secured an 'immense majority' in the showing of hands. In 1837 the Liberal candidates were first endorsed at a meeting of 5,000–6,000 electors and non-electors, and then at the hustings by a crowd of 20,000 persons 'greatly in favour' of Ainsworth and Knowles.[61]

Toryism and the working class

Liberal success was further highlighted by the relationship between the working class and the Conservatives, who failed to attract a significant popular base of support before the late 1840s. As shown in the previous chapter, a preponderance of the manufacturing interest was probably Tory. In this environment, Conservatism was totally committed to industrial society, and events showed clearly that a common hostility to the factory system and the New Poor Law, along the lines of the Tory-radical agitations of the West Riding, could provide no basis for a Conservative-working-class rapprochement in Bolton. In the ten hours campaign of 1833, for example, when Richard Oastler lectured in the town on the question, he was well received by local workers and was presented with a silver cup from the operatives for his 'fearless advocacy of the cause'.[62] However, when William Bolling, Tory MP for Bolton, met with a deputation representing nearly all the mills in Bolton, he refused to lend his support to the campaign.[63]

There was some Tory opposition to the Poor Law Amendment Act, but this has to be qualified. In September 1837 William Bolling spoke at a meeting of the 'Bolton Operative Conservative Association And Friends', convened for the purpose of inaugurating a petition to Parliament for the repeal of 'The Starvation Act'. The petition eventually received over 8,500 signatures. The resolutions passed at the meeting reflected both middle-class and working-class anxieties over the Act. Namely, both would be the victims of interference by central government in local affairs:

> That this meeting feels the utmost alarm and apprehension that tyranny and oppression will inevitably result from the powers placed in the hands of the Poor Law Commissioners ...

That the industrious classes view with dismay the unparalleled and unconstitutional power given to the Poor Law Commissioners, in excluding all rate-payers from having a voice (general as well as local) in the building, altering, or enlarging of poor-houses; in the buying or selling of land; in the raising or borrowing of money; in the feeding, clothing, or employing the poor, or in any way relating to or connected with parochial relief; but shall in future be exercised by the persons authorised by law, to the total exclusion of all the usual local authorities.

As expressed in the above and further resolutions, it was considered that the New Poor Law was inappropriate to the requirements of the northern manufacturing districts. The building and maintenance of suitable workhouses would be impractical and expensive; they could not possibly accommodate the thousands of workers who could be thrown out of employment in an economic downturn. In addition, in threatening to mix the 'deserving' with the 'undeserving' poor in workhouses, while separating husbands from wives and parents from children, the Act was considered both indiscriminate and inhumane. It was believed that the 'usual local authorities' were well placed to determine who was deserving and undeserving, thereby keeping the costs of relief down and avoiding any unnecessary and distressful break-up of families. But under the new system their hands would be tied, the commissioners being vested with 'the power, at their discretion, to suspend, alter, or rescind all such rules, orders, and regulations made for the relief of the poor, as they in their tender mercy may see good'.[64]

Further Tory opposition to the Poor Law Amendment Act came from the Tory *Bolton Chronicle*, edited by John Foster. In one editorial, for instance, Foster referred to the Act as 'The Poor Law *Destruction* Act' and 'the unhallowed Starvation Act'.[65] Yet Foster only became an opponent of the Act after he had applied unsuccessfully for a position as an assistant Poor Law commissioner.[66] In the opinion of the *Bolton Free Press*, Bolling was equally guilty of hypocrisy, having voted in favour of the 1834 Act and abstained from voting against the 1840 Poor Law Continuance Bill only because 'it might have lost him him a few votes at the next election'.[67]

Despite the hostility expressed by the *Bolton Chronicle*, it is apparent from an examination of the proceedings of the board of guardians that many leading Conservative citizens were less equivocal in their support for the Poor Law Amendment Act. These included such notables as the gentry coal-owners John Fletcher and William Hulton and the bleacher Joseph Ridgway. In the early years following the inception of the board in 1837, Great Bolton and Little Bolton returned Liberals and radicals as guardians. However, the two Boltons comprised only two out of twenty-six townships, with eight out of thirty-three guardians in the Bolton Union. The predominance of Tory landed and industrial interests in the over-represented out-townships ensured that the Tories gained overall control of the board. The majority of Tory guardians, whilst showing some resentment to interference from the commissioners, were nevertheless generally in favour of some of the central tenets of the New Poor Law. The majority of Tory out-township guardians supported the principle of a workhouse test for relief, which may explain the less densely populated and rural and semi-rural character of those areas.[68]

In fact, Tories were altogether less successful than Liberals in appeasing working-class opinion on the question of the New Poor Law. Liberal hostility to the prospect of central interference matched that of the Tories. It is important to understand that hostility to the Act cut across class divisions. The most vociferous protest actually came from ratepayer groups.[69] Some leading Liberals, such as the Ashworths, Bowring and Darbishire, while generally in favour of the Act, were careful to relieve working-class anxieties.[70] In any case, there was no distinct working-class-based anti-Poor Law movement worth speaking of in the town. Early in 1838 it was reported that only eight or nine persons, from a population of about 60,000, bothered to attend a meeting of the local Anti-Poor Law Association to elect delegates for an anti-Poor Law conference at Manchester. Needless to say, Bolton was the only major community in south-east Lancashire not to present a petition at those proceedings.[71]

By this time it was becoming obvious to the middle class that the threat of central interference was less real than they had feared. In this situation, the conflict between central and local authority gave way to a localised struggle over how the Act should be administered in detail. Conflict between rival sections of the guardians thus became an extension of the ongoing power struggle within the middle class. Whilst also broadly sympathetic to the notion of less eligibility, Liberal guardians advocated the continuance of outdoor relief, and in the late 1830s and early 1840s actually led opposition to the full rigours of the new regime. The different attitudes were demonstrated at a guardians' meeting in April 1839 at which Hulton declared that 'he felt that a workhouse was necessary' and that he was in favour of the classification of paupers on moral grounds. To this, the Liberal P. R. Arrowsmith responded that 'He would not compel any pauper to go into the workhouse where it could be avoided. As for the power of the commissioners to withdraw out-door relief, he believed that it was a power they would never attempt to exercise. Should they do so, he would at once resign.'

And the Liberal Thomasson similarly remarked that 'When they with-draw the power of granting out-door relief, I shall resign.'[72] Moreover, Tory out-township guardians opposed the resolve of their Liberal counterparts to petition for amendments to the Act. In December 1838 they refused to sign a guardians' petition advising against the imple-mentation of the Act amid the present hostility. In March 1839 they refused to sanction another petition, asking for the commission's order permitting outdoor relief to be extended to the whole country.[73] There was much personal abuse at guardians' meetings. In February 1840, for instance, Thomasson put forward a motion that the guardians should petition against the Corn Laws on the grounds that they were reducing the resources of the working class and forcing them to apply for relief.[74] This, however, did not meet with the approval of the Tory chairman, who attempted to quash all discussion on the question by the 'barbarous expedient' of banging loudly on the table with his stick.[75]

In further consideration of the relationship between Conservative organisation and the working class, the only significant tail of working-class support established by the Conservatives before 1842 was among the hand-loom weavers, but the extent and significance of even this should not be overstated. For, as suggested above in the discussion on free trade politics and the working class, by the mid-1830s most weavers were probably Liberals. Bolton had long taken a leading role in weavers' extra-parliamentary agitations to halt their deteriorating situation, usually involving petitioning and memorialising Parliament with proposals for a legally enforceable system of wage regulation. In the early 1830s, with the support of leading Conservative citizens, the town's weavers again took a prominent role. In 1830 several Lancashire towns petitioned Parliament against the exportation of cotton yarns. The whole campaign – which aimed to provide more work for home weavers – was launched and co-ordinated by a Bolton weavers' committee.[76] In 1831 William Radcliffe and the Bolton weaver Richard Needham – who had long been active in agitation against the export of yarns – presented a memorial to the Board of Trade suggesting the transfer of a proposed duty on raw cotton to export yarn.[77] The issue was revived early in 1833 by a weavers' committee and was allied with demands for a minimum wage and a government inquiry into their conditions.[78] As noted in Chapter Two, the weavers were able to secure considerable support for these campaigns from Tory manufacturing interests and leading Tory citizens in their capacity as the town's major officers.

Of significance for our purposes, however, was the emergence of strong political disagreements among weavers. For Richard Needham and Philip Halliwell, two weavers, and John Makin, a manufacturer with whom they cooperated, were all Tories adept at acting as self-representatives of the weavers. But in 1833 the 'Junta' of 'Needham and Co'. was attacked by a rival committee of weavers endorsed by a public meeting of weavers. The issue ended in compromise when the Liberal weaver William Pilling was selected, along with Needham, to give evidence before the Select Committee on Manufactures.[79] When, in 1834, Bolton weavers followed those from Preston and Glasgow in agitating for the establishment of boards of trade to regulate wages, however, there was a repeat performance which had a different outcome. A weavers' committee organised petitions, was supported by weavers of all shades of political opinion, and secured influential support from manufacturers (who formed a manufacturers' committee), the local authorities and the town's MPs.[80] After the House of Commons responded with the appointment of a select committee, however, the weavers' committee attempted to ensure that all the witnesses from Bolton were Tories. This was done without public consultation, and a stormy public meeting of weavers followed, which first passed a resolution condemning the activities of the Tory 'self-elected few'. The meeting then endorsed a rival committee of weavers, out of which two were to be selected to go before the select committee, and the whole boards of trade scheme was denounced as 'humbug'. Following this pressure, the Tory committee now agreed that one of the representatives should be chosen by a public meeting. The rival committee did not vigorously contest the election, however, and Halliwell was elected, which meant that the four representatives who gave evidence from Bolton *were* all Tories.[81]

In 1835 there were further developments. In January a committee of weavers made a public declaration of support for the Tories Egerton and Bootle-Wilbraham in the South Lancashire parliamentary election. This was made on behalf of all weavers, but was in fact the work of the Tory faction. Later in the year, public meetings again witnessed the dismissal of Needham and his associates as unrepresentative of weavers' opinion. At a meeting in August which had been called to pass a vote of thanks to those MPs who had supported the weavers in the 1834 campaign, Needham and his associates were finally disowned by the majority of weavers. The Tory faction organised another public meeting the following week, arguing that the last one had been 'interrupted by a party of intruders for factious purposes'. This time the original motions were passed.[82] By now, however, the changing mood among the weavers was clear.

From 1835 Liberalism consolidated its hold among the weavers. In June 1837 a meeting of weavers resolved to petition Parliament to either repeal the Corn Laws or give protection to home manufacturers, but a weaver who advocated universal suffrage and the ballot was heard 'with mingled symptoms of applause and disapprobation'.[83] Later in July

Maxwell's motion for a commission of inquiry into the conditions of the hand-loom weavers received parliamentary assent.[84] A weavers' committee – appointed by a public meeting in September 1837 to give evidence to the commission – was dominated by Liberals in favour of free trade, and was easily able to resist Tory claims that it was not representative of the opinion of the majority of weavers.[85] When the representative of the royal commission visited Bolton to collect evidence in April 1838, six out of the seven weavers he examined were reformers and advocated the repeal of the Corn Laws. They included James McConnell and William Pilling, who were later to become members of the Reform Association but not Chartists.[86] When the Chartist movement gained ground in the town the following year, things began to change and some weavers became Chartists. But an assertion made in 1840 that 'the radicals ... are chiefly of that poor despised class called weavers'[87] is wide of the mark, since at the very least it did not reflect the wide occupational base of support that Chartism received in the town. The weavers' committee continued to act as the representative of weavers' opinion, competing quite successfully with the Chartists for the attention of the weavers over the period 1838–42.

At the same time, an attempt by the Conservatives to build a formal working-class supporting organisation, based around Needham and his associates, produced less satisfactory results. The decision to form an Operative Conservative Association in Bolton was made at a meeting of 'gentlemen' in November 1835. The committee was to be composed exclusively of upper- and middle-class Tories; the only worker to be offered a position was Halliwell, who deferentially turned the offer down, 'as he had come to the meeting for instructions to enable him to serve the cause effectually'.[88] The split in the ranks of the hand-loom weavers may only have been coincidental to Tory plans, given that several O.C.A.s were formed in imitation of the original Leeds model. However, the Bolton O.C.A. was the only one to attract any workers, with two ex-radicals, Charles Rothwell and John Cargon, both weavers, joining with those two longer-term Conservatives Needham and Halliwell.[89] To some Tories, the Bolton O.C.A. may have seemed to offer prospects for the establishment of a significant working-class base of support. At the end of 1835 branch societies were being formed in neighbouring townships, and by July 1836 the O.C.A. claimed a membership of 600.[90] But the O.C.A. held no political demonstrations, only 'public' and annual dinners heralding the 'Triumph of Conservatism', typically all-ticket affairs attended mostly by upper- and middle-class Tories.[91] It is not surprising that Liberal sources did not consider the O.C.A. to be a threat and treated it with scorn and contempt.[92]

The ideological content of political protest movements

In further consideration of the fundamental reasons for Liberal gains up to and beyond 1842, there follows an examination of the content and role of ideology within social relations. The claim is made here that, within the radical analysis of society, political analyses of oppression continued to hold sway over economic explanations of exploitation, notwithstanding the greater economic understanding of the nature of social relations demonstrated by Chartists between 1840–2. This meant that, whilst relations between Liberals and the working class had been strained at times, the former were nevertheless able to gain support among the latter in the assault upon Old Corruption. Despite the deteriorating state of class relations and the organisational strides that Chartism had made for working-class politics, political radicalism remained an area around which the classes could cooperate. Once Chartism declined after the Plug Strikes, the way was open for even greater class cooperation, the affiliations between Chartism and Liberalism helping the latter to consolidate further its hold among the working class.

To argue in this fashion is not to advocate a form of reductionist idealism, or to exaggerate the determining role of ideology, but rather to locate the significance of ideological factors and their relation to economic and structural factors in patterns of social relations. For structural and material changes are acknowledged as having played an important role in the overall changes in class relations that occurred in the years around 1850. Working-class consciousness did have an economic basis in widespread threats to the security and status of a wide range of trades. The vulnerability of labour to the activities of innovating employers also played an important role in the greater subordination of labour to capital after the Chartist period. But it would be unwise to ascribe absolute primacy to structural and economic changes, and attempts to read the course of politics from social bases and changes in work practice have produced ambiguous results, which would appear to be the case in much recent and influential work on the regional experience.

Foster (Oldham), Joyce (Blackburn) and, to a lesser extent, Kirk (Ashton, Stalybridge and Stockport) all relied upon theoretical perspectives based upon a simple dichotomy between the 'formal' and the 'real' subjugation of labour to capital, the emergence of social stability being said to have emerged following the resolution of struggles over the labour process in favour of capital.[93] But the limited value of this line of approach can be highlighted by pointing to its theoretical and empirical weaknesses. One of the main criticisms of Foster concerned his portrayal of the emergence of a class-collaborationist 'labour aristocracy' as the key component in the establishment of mellowed class relations at mid-century. The ambiguities of the labour aristocracy's position in and away from work, the theoretical imprecision of the concept, inaccuracies in Foster's interpretation of evidence and his misapplication of empirical data, all point to the generally unsatisfactory nature of his use of the thesis.[94] Joyce broadened the debate beyond the labour aristocracy thesis, but a weakness in his approach was his reliance on the theoretical and tentative conclusions of Stedman Jones' analysis of the Oldham experience of the second quarter of the nineteenth century. Using this analysis, he made bold claims regarding changes in later periods and over a wider geographical area.[95] Kirk also utilised Stedman Jones' analytical framework, although he did not accord to changes in work practice the primacy that Foster and Joyce gave to their formulations.[96]

In Bolton, as in other Lancashire towns in the 1830s and 1840s, conflict over the nature and execution of work had been particularly intense. But local evidence suggests that structural change proceeded unevenly and ambiguously and was incomplete by mid-century. Stedman Jones identified real subordination with the introduction of self-acting mules in the 1830s. However, Bolton was rapidly becoming the centre of medium-fine spinning and, notwithstanding important advances in mule-spinning technology, there was no real or perceived threat to the spinner-piecer system, and the widespread adoption of the self-acting mule was delayed until the late 1870s. Bolton's hand-loom weaving industry was markedly declining by the 1820s, but this had little to do with the power loom, which could not yet be profitably utilised on Bolton's fine muslin and specialist cloths. Technological change in engineering was clearly a threat, but perhaps equally significant were the changing circumstances produced by the sheer expansion of numbers in specialised, but nevertheless skilled, newer categories of engineering labour. The spread of capitalist relations of production in the building trade was a gradual development, with most of the major conflicts in the industry taking place in the 1860s. In mining, technological change was barely discernible at mid-century, while the transformation of Bolton's bleaching industry dated back to the chemical and technological breakthroughs of the late eighteenth century.[97] Struggles over the labour process were clearly important, but conflicts over wages and conditions were just as frequently and as bitterly fought out. Moreover, from mid-century, the stabilisation and progress of industrial capitalism lay in the triumph and expansion of capitalist market relations which did not require or even seek a complete restructuring of the labour process.

If we accept that structural change proceeded with some ambiguity, then this may go some way in accounting for the emergence of political movements and traditions which operated with a considerable degree of autonomy and which were only partly consistent with shifts in economic developments. Early Chartism was essentially the revival of traditional radicalism, carrying with it political critiques of social relations which, despite the deteriorating relations between labour and capital, continued to hold sway over economic explanations of exploitation. From the radical analysis of society, political and not economic relationships were seen as primary. Chartist ideology certainly had the capacity to address economic relations as such, and was at times severely critical of the existing state of relations between labour and capital. But the attitude towards employers was not one of unqualified hostility and criticisms were couched in moral terms – instances of their tyranny being viewed as unjust and unfair, but unnecessary in economic terms. In the final analysis, workers were deprived of the fruits of their labour mainly through the mechanism of a corrupt Parliament in which misery and oppression were ultimately rooted.

From the viewpoint of working-class radicals, the main crime of the middle class lay not in their economic role as employers of labour or as owners of capital, but in their association with an aristocratic political party, the Whigs, through which they influenced Parliament. Despite the involvement of middle-class reformers in Chartism, working-class radicals retained some suspicion of their motives and felt that they did not wholeheartedly embrace the prospect of genuine political reform. In 1840, for instance, a Bolton spinner told of 'a sullen, deeprooted hatred of the higher classes' among his fellow workers, for whom the main crime of their employers was that they were 'almost to a man arrayed against any change in those political arrangements which are grinding them to the dust'.[98] For Daniel Diggle (operative dyer), the middle class was to be condemned for its apparent reluctance to aid the 'working men' in the fight against unjust laws:

> The middle class now exclusively possess the power of returning the legislators ... They did not return to parliament friends to the working men, but friends of the middle class ... The middle class possessed the only instrument, the tool, by which they might effect the salvation of all, but they pettishly refused to use it for the benefit of the working men, and refused to lend him that instrument or to have a similar one of his own ...[99]

In 1839 John Warden expressed similar themes when he defended Bronterre O'Brien in a letter to the editor of the *Bolton Free Press*, the *Press* having accused O'Brien of deliberately causing a rift between reformers through the use of inflammatory rhetoric:

Mr. O'Brien is charged with fermenting disunion between the middle and working classes, by holding up the former to the hatred of the latter. Mr. O'Brien does not denounce the capitalists, *as capitalists, but as supporters of class legislation*. None can regret more than I do the lamentable hostility which now exists between these classes: none can desire more eagerly for a reconciliation. But I am compelled to say that the middle classes have evinced the most heartless disregard for the sufferings of their less fortunate fellow men, and that they, and they alone, are responsible for all the evils of society. You must admit those evils are the result of *bad legislation*; you must admit that for the last seven years the *middle classes have had the power of choosing our legislators*: therefore, *they are responsible for the continuance of those anomalies* – therefore, they are the parties from which the working classes have to wrest that power which they have shewn themselves unable to wield with interest to *themselves and their fellows*.

Mr. O'Brien says that the 'profitmongers' and capitalists deserve to suffer more than the burglar or the highwayman ... when we reflect that 'profitmongers' have enacted bad laws, that these laws have engendered misery and vice – and that these in turn produce highwaymen and burglars, who, but for them, might have lived to ornament and improve the society in which they were born, we must see that the responsibility comes home to the lawmakers. Perhaps *both* may be the unconscious victims of the circumstances in which they are placed; but there is this difference between them – the ONE *has the power to perpetuate or remove the evils under which* BOTH *labour*, while the other is *perfectly powerless*.[100]

But behind these criticisms lay the desire for a genuine response from the middle-class reformers. The desirability and feasibility of an alliance between reformers was never ruled out of court by either the middle class or working class. At the meeting which launched the memorial for Corn Law repeal and political reform, for instance, all the resolutions were moved jointly by middle- and working-class speakers. A resolution that 'the entire abolition of the corn laws would relieve the present distress, and save the country from ruin', but that 'no permanently good and impartial government' could be achieved without universal male suffrage, as the means of removing 'the other numerous evils' associated with unjust legislation, brought this response from the Chartist Gillespie:

He trusted that the middle and working classes would now go hand in hand, without which they could never obtain their wishes ... It was thought that the people were opposed to the capitalists. They were not so. All they wanted was, that the labour of the working man should be as sacred as the capital of the rich man. – (Cheers) They wanted laws that would prevent extravagance in high places, and which would bring more comfort to the dwellings of the poor. They wanted to break down a system which gave to her Majesty £1,600 per day; a system which gave to the Queen Dowager £300 per day; and to Prince Albert £100 per day ... It has been said that he was hostile to the middle classes ... He had said hard things of them ... He was now ready to bury all in oblivion, – (hear and cheers,) – to go hand in hand with the middle classes, and he hoped, they, on their parts, would be ready to carry out the entire wishes of the people. – (cheers) [101]

Dorothy Thompson would dismiss my interpretation of these sentiments, having argued that 'The Chartist approach to the two major parties, indeed to any conventional politician outside their own movement, was always totally instrumental.' [102] But whilst it is important to recognise the points of conflict within radical ideology, analyses which struggle to identify radicalism or Chartism as exclusively working-class fail to appreciate those points in the radical analysis which gave it much of its inter-class appeal and which made cooperation possible in the first place: the concentration on Old Corruption, taxation, political structures, the conflict between productive and unproductive wealth. These and further affinities between Chartism and Liberalism have been identified by Brian Harrison and Patricia Hollis. [103]

Students of Chartism will be aware that these observations on the ideological content of Chartism do not present novel findings. In a forceful critique of what he sees as the historiographically dominant 'social' approach to Chartism, for example, Gareth Stedman Jones has argued persuasively for a more political interpretation of Chartism, in which central importance is accorded to the role of the state and in which the central radical image is seen as continuing to be one of an excluded 'people', whose oppression was ultimately rooted in that very exclusion from political power. In short, his examination of radical language concludes that ideology was not merely reflective of social bases, but was prefigurative in the construction of social reality, which meant that the trajectory of radicalism can be explained by the fact that it never fully transcended the ideological limits imposed by its eighteenth-century origins. Neither radicalism, nor Owenism, nor trade unionism, maintains Stedman Jones, produced a breakthrough to a genuine proletarian ideology. As such, the essentially inter-class appeal of radicalism continued into the Chartist period. Accordingly, Chartism was not a social, class-based movement, appealing primarily to an economically defined and exploited working class, but essentially a movement of the 'productive classes'. Thus, from the perspective of radical ideology, the main divisions in society were not those between middle class and working class or capital and labour, but those between the politically excluded and economically productive of all social strata on the one side and a parasitic aristocracy and its allies on the other, with the latter maintaining their dominance through their control of a corrupt Parliament which they used to legislate against the interests of the former.[104]

Critics of Stedman Jones' revisionist approach to labour history have primarily attacked his narrowly literal approach, which, in failing to consider other forms of political communication beyond the printed word and in neglecting to account properly for the role of economic production relations as an essential constituent of social reality, places the role of ideology out of historical context.[105] According to Kirk, for instance, Stedman Jones' 'non-referential' approach to the role of language fails to pay sufficient attention to the contribution of economic and social structures and the role of experience in the formulation of ideas, all of which ensured the essentially working-class appeal of Chartism. Thus he contends that '*de-facto* anti-capitalist economic explanations of exploitation and misery did exert considerable influence within Chartism'.[106]

Economic and social structures clearly did play an important role in shaping Chartism in Bolton, but while they certainly have to be taken into account, they also need to be kept firmly in historical context. The bitter industrial conflict of the 1830s and early 1840s deeply influenced and adversely affected class attitudes and relationships. Although the expropriation of capitalist industry was never on the agenda, the intensification of economic conflict along class lines raised questions concerning the basis of existing economic roles and relations. And a political interpretation of exploitation had the effect of raising workplace-orientated struggles beyond that level and linking them with wider questions concerning societal relations and arrangements. In this situation, ideology became an area of struggle between workers and manufacturing bourgeoisie. The resolutions of the Bolton spinners in the Plug Strikes, for instance, demonstrate the developing working-class attack on excessive employer power, increasing economic exploitation and the problems associated with unrestrained capitalist market relations. The correctives could only be a greater equation of industry and the labour market in line with working-class interests and the achievement of political power as a means to permanent improvement. The spinners listed 'with disgust and abhorrence those principles of injustice and tyranny that we, as operatives, have so long laboured under':

... namely, in the reduction of our wages, in unjust and unreasonable abatements, in forcing upon us unreasonable and exorbitant rents, and in meanly and avariciously employing apprentices to supersede the regular journeymen, and in various ways curtailing our wages by not paying up to the list that the masters almost unanimously agreed to, thus proving their unprincipled meanness and trickery.

... That this meeting is of opinion, that a great deal of the distress in the manufacturing districts is owing to the improvements of machinery, which have superseded manual labour, and created a redundant and burthensome population. And this meeting is further of opinion, that the best means to be adopted, would be to establish an efficient Ten Hours' Bill, with restrictions on all moving power, to immediately colonize the Crown Lands, which would employ the redundant population, and at the same time improve and augment the home trade.

... That it is the opinion of this meeting that the above evils arise from class legislation, and we are further of opinion that misery, ignorance, poverty and crime, will continue to exist, until the People's Charter becomes the law of the land.[107]

Kirk is thus correct to insist that Stedman Jones pays insufficient attention to the importance of social and economic structures, but while the experience of deep-seated economic grievances constituted a major obstacle to class reconciliation, ideology served to put certain structures on the understanding of that experience. For it is apparent that, despite the development of '*de-facto*' anti-capitalist ideas within Chartism, the old-style radical social criticism, cast in political and anti-aristocratic terms, continued to be the dominant mode of analysis.

Kirk argues that an 'alternative' reading of 'the very same sources' used by Stedman Jones 'reveals an intensely class-based language which was at the heart of Chartism'. His focus rests upon the factory districts of Lancashire and Cheshire, the area where 'Stedman Jones' political characterisation of Chartism would encounter its most severe test from the attempted determinations of the relatively new mode of production'. However, a primary focus which leans heavily on the views of Peter Murray McDouall and, to a lesser extent, on those other leading south Lancashire Chartists James Leach and Richard Pilling needs to be set in a more specific historical context than that adopted by Kirk.[108]

For, in particular, it was between 1840–2 that radicalism assimilated themes from the trade union and factory movements.[109] In so doing, Chartist language revealed a more searching economic analysis of the position of workers than had ever been evident in the violent rhetoric of 1839. But whereas Chartism now had a greater capacity to address economic roles and relations as such, radicals were seemingly still convinced that their oppression was ultimately rooted in their exclusion from political power. It is still impossible to draw a clear distinction between 'older' analyses denouncing taxation, the priesthood, the political monopolies of Old Corruption and the legislative misdeeds of unrepresentative government, and 'newer' themes condemning profits, employer tyranny, unrestrained market relations and unrestricted economic competition. In short, the verdict of Patricia Hollis on the weight of economic and 'socialist' ideas within the radical 'unstamped press' of 1830–6, that 'The working class debate in the 1830s was a debate not between current alternative theories of society, but between those who invoked the older rhetoric of 1819 and those who innovated on it,'[110] can be extended to the early 1840s. All this is highlighted and confirmed by an examination of Chartist ideology in 1848. This indicates that the themes of factory reform, trade unionism, and exploitation in the productive process were not prominent features of a radical platform now anachronistic as a vehicle for addressing the relations between capital and labour.

The more sustained Chartist interest in the possibilities of mobilising trade union support in the early 1840s owed much to the exertions of McDouall and Leach, perhaps the most important Chartist leaders in south Lancashire at the time (though the executive of the National Charter Association was also aware of the advantages to be gained from such a policy).[111] The usual argument was that, although the tyranny of employers was real enough, the political origins of oppression and misery meant that the economic self-defence associations of the working class could not prevent their increasing immiseration. For McDouall, who lectured in Bolton in August 1840, the sufferings of the working class were caused by 'misgovernment and wrong' and, as such, required a political solution:

He ... saw the distress of the workingmen caused by laws in the making of which they had no influence, and over which they had no control ... When he saw the decline of the hand-loom weavers; when he saw them passing away from the land of their birth – from independence and comfort to wretchedness and destitution – he thought there must be something wrong, and he found the cause of the wrong in the laws of the nation, which were made to benefit the rich, and to crush and oppress the poor ... When he saw this, he then began to look for the remedy. He saw the banner of the Charter unfurled – he saw that that was what the labourer wanted – it was political power and nothing else ... if the English labourers were to receive ten shillings a day ... unless he possessed political power it would not long be advantageous to him. The splendour of the throne would be increased, the church would be extended, the business of the aristocracy would be more costly and refined, and the profits of the capitalist greater; and in a short time the labourer would be in precisely the same condition as he was at that moment ...[112]

Similarly, while Leach condemned the 'grasping avarice' of employers before a Bolton audience in February 1841, he accorded the distress that afflicted the working class to their exclusion from political power:

> They [i.e. trade unions] had been caused by the grasping avarice and tyranny of employers and capitalists. The labourers had seen that some plan was wanting for their mutual protection, and they had conceived that trades' unions would effect that object; but, from what he had seen himself, he contended that they were totally inadequate for that purpose. He had admitted that they had done something to stem the torrent of reduction and check the desire of the grasping capitalist, to reduce wages; but they had only acted as a temporary barrier ... Some trades' unions had certainly been more successful than others, on account of their peculiar nature and the difficulty of applying machinery to the work which the skilled labourer performed. But even these trades were compelled to make great sacrifices in contributions from their wages to maintain those who were out of work, to keep them out of the labour market, and prevent them from offering their services to the employers for less wages, which they would do before they would starve in the streets. The wages of the labourer ought to be secured to him by the laws of the land, and he should not be called on to make such sacrifices to maintain them from his earnings, which ought to be more sacred than any other property in the land. The spinners once possessed the most promising and powerful trades' union in the country, yet that extensive union has always been defeated, and was now almost entirely helpless ... He had made some severe remarks on the factory system, and declared that the power possessed by the masters was of the most demonical nature and ought not to be permitted ... He attributed the evils which afflicted the working classes to class legislation; the higher and middle classes being represented in the present House of Commons ...[113]

The tyranny of employers was thus seen as a symptom rather than a cause of society's ills. In the intellectual and emotional convictions of the Chartists, we catch glimpses of an alternative society – egalitarian, humane and harmonious.[114] But no design for an alternative social order was ever clearly articulated. The above resolutions of the Bolton spinners do not necessarily indicate any desire to transcend capitalist relations of production. The intensified exploitation of the 1830s and 1840s was viewed as an unjust and unfair, but unnecessary, experience. As suggested by Gray, the primary concerns of most workers lay less with major changes in the social order than with the renegotiation of threatened reciprocities with employers.[115]

At the same time, with the aristocracy continuing to appear to dominate English politics, the middle class was able to deflect criticism of the Whig legislation of the 1830s away from itself. A placard issued to 'The Trade Societies of Bolton' from the Workingmen's Association singled out government repression – and not employers – as the main adversaries of trade unions.[116] As regards the New Poor Law, we argued earlier that Liberals were able to appease working-class fears on this issue and, despite the fact that some leading citizens sympathised with the new system, the workhouse test was not applied rigorously in Bolton.[117] There was some sympathy with the broad notion of less eligibility among all guardians, and, combined with a desire to suppress mendicity and encourage self-help, this affected the spirit in which relief was given. In June 1839, for instance, a spinner in the employ of Bolling, in work but on short time, applied for an award to supplement his meagre earnings. But because there were allegedly 'scores, if not hundreds of cases' in the town as bad if not worse, Thomasson was against making the award. It was his opinion that it 'was unfortunate that cotton spinners made no provision for a rainy day'.[118] Earlier in May, amid reports of the existence of near-starvation due to the unwillingness of many to become paupers, a scheme involving the cleansing and white-washing of the houses of applicants was implemented (the pretext was health reasons). In one week alone, 437 houses were whitewashed in Great and Little Bolton.[119] But as regards the treatment of the poor, there was nothing new in such attitudes and it was soon apparent that, despite changes in administration, middle-class hostility to central interference would mean continuity of practice. A further obstacle to the establishment of a rigid anti-pauper system, consistent with the promotion of self-help, came with the formation of the main charity organisations, the Bolton Benevolent Society in 1838 and the Bolton Society for the Protection of the Poor and District Provident Society in 1841. People who were reluctant to apply to the guardians could now apply to these for relief.

From about the mid-1840s, the appeal of the two major parties grew as Chartism, despite a brief revival in 1848, declined in influence and lost much of its earlier strength. With the lifting of the depression of 1837–42, changing circumstances worked to encourage the separation of working-class economic and political agitation that was to become characteristic of the third quarter of the nineteenth century. The demoralisation of defeat in 1839 and 1842 certainly helped to lessen belief in the efficacy of intimidatory political action as a remedy for social and economic problems. At the same time, the Chartist insistence that permanent improvement would only be achieved following the prior extension of political rights to the masses began to lose force as the stabilisation of capitalist market relations gave further encouragement to, and enhanced opportunities for, personal and collective advancement by non-political means. From then on, there was a significant shift towards a definition of the primacy of moral and individual self-improvement as the path to progressive improvement.

One aspect of this process was the fiscal initiatives of central government from the early 1840s. The programme of tariff reform introduced in Peel's budget of 1842 was intended to promote social unity as much as economic reform. The heavy burden of indirect taxation imposed upon the working class was now to be reduced through a drastic reduction of duties on a wide range of articles, coupled with the reimposition of income tax on incomes of over £150 per annum. This limit generally exempted the working class and, in recommending the measure, Peel made a direct plea to the wealthy to shoulder the burden of the nation's financial troubles until the new tariff proposals had brought about a regeneration of manufacturing industry and commerce.[120] Middle-class opinion on this was tempered by a general satisfaction with the new tariff proposals. There is little direct evidence of local working-class reactions to Peel's initiative, but at the national level the Chartists welcomed income tax as a measure of social justice, while the *Bolton Chronicle* claimed that, when news of Peel's programme reached town, 'one universal feeling of joy and admiration pervaded every political circle in the town. One and all ... were ready to bear testimony of their gratitude.'[121] The budget of 1845 and the repeal of the Corn Laws in 1846 were further indications of the state's growing use of fiscal reform to promote economic growth and social unity, while the Ten Hours Act of 1847 further highlighted the removal of grievances which had underpinned radical and Liberal protest movements in the 1830s and 1840s (more will be said on changes in the character of the Victorian state in the next chapter). The effects of all this benefited the Liberals in two ways. Firstly, as prosperity gradually and generally increased from the mid-1840s, the view of the most militant of the Chartists – that such reforms were unthinkable or could not benefit the working class in material terms without a major overhaul of the existing electoral system – was now being effectively undermined. At the same time, those same reforms seemed to confirm the Liberal view of the efficacy of piecemeal and gradual reform. The Liberals actually gained credibility through their championing of causes like financial reform, Corn Law repeal and municipal incorporation, which were seen to be rationalising the range of national taxes and local rates to be levied, and which were in line with what moderate radicals and reformers had argued was needed all along.

The pattern of cultural activity in Chartism indicates that the movement had always contained differing perspectives in strategy and ideology. In 1840, for example, a group of younger Chartists associated with the temperance wing of the movement established a working men's Sunday and evening school. Meeting four nights per week, the range of issues discussed typically displayed particularly strong affinities with Liberalism. These Bolton Chartists located the cause of distress among workers in their lack of determination to obtain an education. It was this that was considered 'the great obstacle in the way of our much desired object – social and political emancipation; and which now renders them the slaves of whatever other class may choose to oppress them. Were this not the fact, we should have more night schools in existence than we have – Mechanics' Institutions, and Mutual Instruction Societies would be better, and such resorts as "Star Inn" and "Finley Fraziers" less attended.' Notwithstanding all this, it has to be stressed again that the view that working-class ignorance and misery was a consequence and not a cause of their lack of political rights was actually dominant in the early 1840s. This was fully illustrated in the contention of the Bolton spinners in the 1842 Plug Strikes, 'that misery, ignorance, poverty and crime, will continue to exist, until the People's Charter becomes the law of the land'.[122]

Symptomatic of the extent to which this position subsequently became inverted, and a notable aspect of Chartist leaders in 1848, was their berating of the working class for excessive drinking and lack of self-discipline, seen as factors undermining the campaign of that year.[123] This development represented a significant ideological shift. Criticism of the middle class, which had been at its peak in 1838–42, now receded. From now on, there was no significant or coherent opposition to the broad values and assumptions of the middle class as regards social policy and the way in which the economy worked in general.[124] Workers now became even more convinced that it was in their interests to join the middle class in the assault upon Old Corruption. The resolutions of the Bolton spinners in 1842 had made no mention of free trade, but in 1844–5 they joined with their employers in agitation to repeal the tax on imported raw cotton, based on the belief that increased remuneration for their labour could only be achieved through a prior increase in employer profit margins.[125] Late in 1845, with food prices rising and famine in Ireland biting hard, the middle class organised public and town council meetings to raise and coordinate demands for an immediate opening of the ports. These were well supported by workers (and by some leading Conservatives on humanitarian grounds), and Chartists failed to pass amendments calling for land reform. The Operative Spinners' Union again agitated independently, with a committee operating from Bolton organising meetings in Bolton and elsewhere in Lancashire.[126] Chartism revived in 1848, but it did not match the scale of earlier peaks of activity. 'Economic' themes from the trade union and factory movements no longer featured prominently in a radical analysis which was now less ambiguously anti-aristocratic and less insistent that working-class self-improvement could only be achieved through the prior acquisition of political power.[127]

Even at its peak, Chartism never completely subsumed movements aiming at more limited or gradual change. Thus, whilst the labour movement had at times been a highly integrated one, with great interconnections of activity and cross-over of personnel, this should not be allowed to obscure the degree to which movements such as factory reform and trade unionism had maintained their own distinct identities and independent organisations. And, as has been seen earlier, many were always prepared to agitate for piecemeal advancement within the existing system or for more limited panaceas than the political and social programme embodied in the Charter. This raises questions as to the extent to which working-class consciousness can be considered revolutionary in the 1840s and reformist after 1850.

By implication, the extent to which the Lancashire working class supposedly only really displayed reformist attitudes to social progress after 1850 depends on a prior evaluation of the revolutionary potential of working-class radicalism in the Chartist period. In *Class Struggle and the Industrial Revolution*, Foster argued that Oldham workers displayed a mass 'revolutionary class consciousness' and were receptive to the calls of radicals leaders for the creation of an 'alternative social system', a 'non-capitalist society'.[128] Revolutionary consciousness then dissipated from the late 1840s, when 'the town moved remarkably quickly towards class collaboration'.[129] Foster subsequently modified his view, denying that his main intention was to portray the content of working-class consciousness in the 1830s and 1840s as 'some early variant of revolutionary class consciousness'.[130] Kirk's examination of Chartism in the south Lancashire cotton district did not endorse Foster's findings, but went further than Briggs' view that Chartism was an umbrella movement embracing a variety of aims, in that, for Kirk, those aims were held together by 'a vision of an alternative social order'.[131] This study supports the view that south Lancashire did experience a mellowing of class tensions and improved social relations in the post-Chartist period. But whilst Chartist leaders forcefully argued that the Charter would give the people the power to determine their own destiny – as the

Bolton Chartist James Parkinson put it: 'The Charter was a means to an end'[132] – only a minority of workers were receptive to their pleas that major political reform was absolutely necessary to bring about a transformation of the existing social order. Many were always prepared to embrace piecemeal reforms and a gradualist approach to social progress.[133]

All this should not deflect us from the fact that 1842 marked something of a watershed in the history of popular radicalism. Loss in the popular belief that social reform had necessarily to be preceded by political reform and the emergence of a more dynamic and stable capitalism – which opened up possibilities for class manoeuvre and compromise – now combined to enhance the appeal of Liberal ideas of social progress. After 1842, not only were single-issue campaigns more successful, further encouraging the separation of working-class political and economic activity, but also the middle class accelerated this trend by giving more active support to the likes of Friendly Societies and the campaign for factory reform. The latter was hitherto a predominantly working-class movement (at least at the local level), while movements which had long received middle-class patronage, such as temperance reform, enjoyed marked increases in success and popularity. The 1830s had actually been the crucial decade for collaboration in the temperance movement. But spectacular gains in 1847 were nevertheless significant, in that they enabled a cause which encouraged growing contacts between middle-class and working-class reformers to compete vigorously for working-class attention when Chartism enjoyed its last major revival in 1848. This brings us to an area which will come under consideration in Chapter Five – namely, the pro-active attempts by the middle class to re-stabilise social relations by a more active promotion of its own values, by the mellowing of its liberalism, and by the building of bridges at the workplace and in the community at large.

Thus, middle-class ideals were taking a stronger hold and were fast crowding out the possibility of the formulation of any working-class alternative programme. This does not alter the fact that the whole process of the consolidation of middle-class hegemony was not an untroubled merger of consenting ideas and values; the mid-Victorian consensus represented a process of social stabilisation rather than class harmonisation. The success of the grass-roots liberalism of the 1850s was the product of a process of negotiation and not working-class capitulation. This will become more apparent after an examination of the relations between labour and capital over the period 1830–50, to which we now turn. For conflict at the point of production remained the major obstacle to full middle-class domination. In the face of the central tenets of orthodox political economy, workers clung stubbornly to surviving artisan notions of customary wage regulation and work organisation, such as the 'just wage' or the 'fair price'. Nevertheless, as expressed by the 1848 annual report of the Bolton Poor Protection Society, the depression of that year actually served to confirm the stability and general acceptance of capitalist relations of production among workers:

> The disorders of Continental Europe have caused much misery amongst ourselves. Still we have had much for which we ought to be thankful. Our manufacturing system, on which the comforts of this district at least so much depend, has been severely tested, and its stability proved. Matters look brighter: and it is hoped that a return of commercial prosperity will soon bring a return of their comforts to our deserving workmen. Their patient endurance of distress and general good conduct, amidst evil unexampled abroad, and incendiary harangues at home, have been eminently conspicuous, and have won for them the admiration of society.[134]

Notes

1. D. Walsh, 'Operative Conservatism in Lancashire, 1833–1846: Some Comments on a Changing Political Culture', University of Salford Occasional Paper in Politics and Contemporary History 11 (1987), p. 7.
2. N. Gash, *Aristocracy and People: Britain 1815–1865* (London, 1979), pp. 160–3. Richards, however, dates this development earlier: 'After the general election of 1837 Russell counted 338 ministry men or Liberals, 318 opponents or Conservatives and only four doubtfuls. Each party had its own recognized leaders, whips and clubs' (P. Richards, 'State Formation and Class Formation, 1832–48', in P. Corrigan (ed.), *Capitalism, State Formation and Marxist Theory* (London, 1980), p. 54).
3. R. A. Sykes, 'Popular Politics and Trade Unionism in South-East Lancashire, 1829–42', University of Manchester Ph.D. thesis (1982), p. 545.
4. The middle class perceived that they could achieve most of their aims with only limited parliamentary reform, and a number of factors worked to inhibit the speed with which they embraced democracy. Benthamite Liberal intellectuals, for instance, influenced by Utilitarian principles and Liberal ideas of progress, had only a limited conception of democracy, firmly based on the ownership of property, which was considered more important than education in making a person fit to exercise the franchise (D. G. Wright, *Democracy and Reform 1815–1885* (Harlow, 1970), pp. 104–5).

    In 1835, before the limits of the Reform Act were evident to the middle-class reformers, Henry Ashworth told a public meeting, held to establish a school in Bolton on the plan of the British and Foreign School

Society, that household suffrage was a 'desirable privilege', to be obtained through the virtues of self-help rather than by lowering the £10 franchise. Education was thus considered a useful tool in the acquisition of property, though clearly subordinate to property as a mark of virtue (*B.C.*, 28 February 1835).

The *Bolton Free Press* vacillated on the question of political reform according to changing political circumstances. At the beginning of the Chartist agitation in September 1838, it declared for universal suffrage. But after the suppression of the national holiday, it then considered household suffrage to be wholly appropriate (*B.F.P.*, 8 September 1838, 14 September 1839).

5. *B.F.P.*, 30 December 1837, 17 December 1838. See also *Northern Star*, 10 February 1838, 15 June 1839 (editorials on 'The Ballot').

6. As we saw in Chapter Three (p. 72), the electors on the committee of the Reform Association initially outnumbered the non-electors, who were predominantly weavers, by 24 to 12. The 1838 annual meeting of the Reform Association indicated that the committee was now belatedly composed of 22 electors and 22 non-electors. No indication as to the occupations of the latter was given, though the speech of a shoemaker was reported (*B.F.P.*, 18 August 1838).

7. J. Belcham, '1848: Feargus O'Connor and the Collapse of the Mass Platform', in J. Epstein and D. Thompson (eds), *The Chartist Experience: Studies in Working-Class Radicalism and Culture 1830–1860* (London, 1982); J. Epstein, *The Lion of Freedom: Feargus O'Connor and the Chartist Movement, 1832–1842* (London, 1982), ch. 3; Gash, *op. cit.*, pp. 140–1, 151–52.

8. *B.F.P.*, 9 February 1839.

9. *B.F.P.*, 18 April 1840.

10. *B.F.P.*, 19 August 1837.

11. For examples, see the exchange between the working-class radicals Lomax and Warden and the middle-class reformer Darbishire (*B.F.P.*, 22 September 1838), recounted below, and comments by P. R. Arrowsmith (*B.F.P.*, 9 February 1839).

12. *B.F.P.*, 12 September 1838.

13. For examples of the urging of unity among reformers, see *B.F.P.*, 20 October, 3 November 1838, 2 February 1839 (editorials on 'Mr. Richard Oastler', 'Union among Reformers', and 'Physical Force'). See *B.F.P.*, 3 November 1838, for the question of torchlight meetings, and 9 February 1839, for the Reform Association dinner in honour of Wood.

14. *B.F.P.*, 20 April 1839.

15. For the 'Sacred Month' in Bolton, see *B.C.* and *B.F.P.*, 17, 24 August 1839; W. Brimelow, *Political and Parliamentary History of Bolton, Vol. 1* (Bolton, 1882), pp. 368–73; J. C. Scholes, *History of Bolton: With Memorials of the Old Parish Church* (Bolton, 1892), pp. 536–7.

16. *H.O. 40/44*, correspondence relating to Chartist activity at Bolton; Heywood Papers, Correspondence 1839, B.A., ZHE/35. On 13 July 1839 it was reported 'that the pike trade has been greatly accelerated ... and

that large numbers have been manufactured … in different parts of the town'. On 10 and 17 August there were reports of seizures of pikes and on 17 August Lord Wilton was reported as saying in the House of Commons that 'Thousands of Persons' were assembling night after night in the immediate vicinity of Bolton, 'with the most violent and seditious speeches' being delivered, and placards in the town referring to recent clashes between Chartists and the authorities at Birmingham (*B.F.P.*, 13 July, 10, 17 August 1839).

17. R. Sykes, 'Physical-Force Chartism: The Cotton District and the Chartist Crisis of 1839', *International Review of Social History* 30 (1985), p. 224.
18. *B.F.P.*, 22 June 1839.
19. Sykes, 'Physical-Force Chartism', p. 225; D. Thompson, *The Chartists: Popular Politics in the Industrial Revolution* (Aldershot, 1986), p. 71.
20. See *Northern Star*, 17 August 1839, 'TO THE WORKING MEN OF BOLTON', for O'Connor's reply to criticism from Bolton Chartists. For example: 'The evidence from nine-tenths of the Kingdom went to show that the people could not, *without organisation*, enter upon the proposed holiday.'
21. *B.C.*, 17 August 1839; *B.F.P.*, 17 August 1839, 11 April 1840.
22. They can be traced in the sources listed above in n. 15.
23. *H.O. 40/44*, Darbishire to Russell, 16 August 1839.
24. Brimelow, *op. cit.*, p. 370; W. E. Brown, *Robert Heywood of Bolton 1786–1868* (Wakefield, 1970), p. 35; *Northern Star*, 17 August 1839.
25. C. Behagg, 'An Alliance with the Middle Class: The Birmingham Political Union and Early Chartism', in Epstein and Thompson, *op. cit.*, p. 61.
26. *B.F.P.*, 29 December 1838.
27. D. S. Gadian, 'A Comparative Study of Popular Movements in North West Industrial Towns 1830–1850', Lancaster University Ph.D thesis, (1976), pp. 102–3.
28. P. Adelman, *Victorian Radicalism: The Middle-Class Experience, 1830–1914* (London, 1984), pp. 22–4.
29. *B.F.P.*, 2 October 1841.
30. Adelman, *op. cit.*, pp. 18–19.
31. E. J. Hobsbawm, *Industry and Empire: From 1750 to the Present Day* (Harmondsworth, 1969), p. 77. Industrial Lancashire also experienced extreme hardship in the cotton famine of 1861–5, but Bolton suffered least of all the major manufacturing towns of the region.
32. *B.F.P.*, 21 March, 15 February 1840.
33. Bolton Society for the Protection of the Poor and District Provident Society – Reports 1841–1858 (B.R.L.). The annual reports and meetings of the Poor Protection Society and the Benevolent Society are also covered in the press.
34. J. Foster, *Class Struggle and the Industrial Revolution: Early Industrial Capitalism in Three English Towns* (London, 1974), p. 21; G. Stedman Jones, 'Class Struggle and the Industrial Revolution', *New Left Review* 9 (1975), p. 38.
35. *B.F.P.*, 7 December 1839.

36. *B.F.P.*, 10 February, 9 June 1838, 7 December 1839 (lecture of Archibald Prentice), 13 June, 7 November 1840 (remarks made by J. B. Smith); *The Anti-Corn Law Circular*, 12 March 1840 (see correspondence from Thomasson).
37. *B.F.P.*, 22 September 1838.
38. *B.F.P.*, 9 February 1839.
39. *B.F.P.*, 16 February 1839.
40. *B.F.P.*, 16 February 1839, 17 June, 12 December 1840, 9 October 1841.
41. L. Brown, 'The Chartists and the Anti-Corn Law League', in A. Briggs (ed.), *Chartist Studies* (London, 1959).
42. See the view of Warden, for example, in *B.F.P.*, 30 November 1839.
43. For examples of this argument, see *B.F.P.*, 22 September 1838, 16 October 1841.
44. *B.F.P.*, 26 February (the same month that Joseph Sturge called the first conference of the C.S.U.), 12 March 1842.
45. Thompson, *op. cit.*, p. 264.
46. *B.F.P.*, 24 December 1842 (and 31 December, for middle-class criticism of this move).
47. The *Northern Star* estimated that 50,000 persons attended this event, the *B.F.P.* 10,000, the *B.C.* 1,000 (*B.C.*, 3 November 1838; *B.F.P.*, 10 November 1838; Brimelow, *op. cit.*, p. 341).
48. *B.F.P.*, 29 February, 7, 21 March 1840. The Bolton Poor Law Union comprised of 26 townships. The 1841 census gives the total population of the union as 97,519, of which 33,609 belonged to Great Bolton and 16,144 to Little Bolton (*B.F.P.*, 31 July 1841). Of the 26,815 signatures attached to the petition, 18,011 came from Great and Little Bolton.
49. *B.F.P.*, 22 May 1841.
50. The *Northern Star* gives 16,600 and 18,500 signatures for the 1839 and 1842 Chartist national petitions (Thompson, *op. cit.*, p. 341).
51. *B.F.P.*, 29 May, 12 June, 3 July 1841; Brimelow, *op. cit.*, pp. 410–17.
52. B.A., ZZ/130/4/9, Miscellaneous Collection of Handbills – Parliamentary Election 1841 Series, 'Operative Cotton Spinners to Bolton Electors, July 1841'.
53. *B.F.P.*, 21 March 1840; B.A., ZZ/130/4/24, Miscellaneous Collection of Handbills – Parliamentary Election 1841 Series, 'Impoverished handloom weavers to the Bolton Electors'.
54. B.A., ZZ/130/4/41, Miscellaneous Collection of Handbills – Parliamentary Election 1841 Series, 'Powerloom Weavers to the Bolton Electors'.
55. *The Anti-Corn Law Circular*, 10 December 1839.
56. *B.F.P.*, 18, 25 September 1841.
57. *B.F.P.*, 25 January 1840.
58. The campaign for factory reform was renewed shortly after the 1841 parliamentary election (*B.F.P.*, 16 October, 31 December 1841).
59. *The Anti-Bread Tax Circular*, 10 February 1842; *B.F.P.*, 5 May 1842. The meeting had been called by a requisition signed by over 700 weavers, though only about 300 persons were reported as being in attendance before the Chartists arrived. If the meeting could be considered small, the

proceedings nevertheless typified the competition between the weavers' committee and the Chartists for the allegiance of the weavers. The Chartists were represented by the cabinet-maker James Lord and the weavers Joseph Lomax, Peter Rigby and John Gillespie, who argued that the best way to achieve the repeal of the Corn Laws was first to secure the Charter. However, they met strong opposition from men who, whilst claiming that they themselves were Chartists (in that they had signed the national petition), clearly felt it expedient to campaign for free trade, which it was felt could be achieved without prior parliamentary reform.

60. 'Impoverished handloom weavers …', *op. cit.*

61. Brimelow, pp. 254–5, 320–1, 416.

62. *B.C.*, 30 March 1833.

63. *B.C.*, 13 April 1833. Bolling's attitude remained implacable until his death in 1848.

64. *B.C.*, 11 February, 15 April, 28 September 1837. At a meeting of the Operative Conservative Association in 1843, Mr Lee, 'an operative', said: '… there were two classes of poor: the industrious and intelligent class – and there was another class who were not industrious, and whose habits were not commendable; consequently, when the last named class were brought into reduced circumstances through their own negligence and evil habits, they were placed upon the same footing as the most worthy, and received the same advantages. He did not mean to say that such characters ought to be badly treated, but under the New Poor Law the vicious and idle man received as much kindness as the most industrious. Let them take, for example, the industrious man, who, often through misfortune, by sickness, want of employment, and so on, was brought under circumstances compelling him to require parish relief, how awful was it that he should submit to a law which said there should be no distinction of characters made' (*B.C.*, 18 March 1843).

65. *B.C.*, 11 February 1837.

66. R. Boyson, *The Ashworth Cotton Enterprise: The Rise and Fall of a Family Firm 1818–1880* (Oxford, 1970), p. 186.

67. *B.F.P.*, 27 March 1840.

68. See *B.F.P.*, 23 March 1839, 27 March 1840, for Fletcher, Hulton and Ridgway.

69. Thus the resolutions passed at the September 1837 meeting merely echoed similar resolutions passed at meetings of ratepayers of the townships of Great and Little Bolton (*B.C.*, 24 May 1834).

70. For the Ashworths, see Boyson, *op. cit.*, ch. 10; B.A., ZZ/130/3/13, Miscellaneous Collection of Handbills – Parliamentary Election July 1837 Series, 'A Fellow Workman to the Working Class of Bolton and Neighbourhood' – attack on Edmund Ashworth for his support of Poor Law reform, importing labourers from the south, etc.; B.A., ZZ/130/4/6, Miscellaneous Collection of Handbills – Parliamentary Election July 1841 Series, 'To the Electors of Bolton' from 'One of the Multitude' – attack on New Poor Law and on John Bowring and Edmund Ashworth for their support of it. See Brimelow, *op. cit.*, p. 415, for Bowring in the

context of the 1841 parliamentary election: 'He was so far inclined towards Chartism as to be in favour of greatly extending the suffrage, reducing taxation, and shortening the duration of Parliaments; but he would continue the Poor-law, moderating its harshness by not separating aged couples.' See *B.C.*, 24 May 1834, for Darbishire's stance on the Act.

71. *Northern Star*, 10 February 1838; *B.F.P.*, 10 February 1838.

72. *B.F.P.*, 27 April 1839.

73. *B.F.P.*, 8, 22 December 1838, 9 March 1839.

74. It can be noted here that the Anti-Corn Law League gathered much evidence on distress in the cotton districts. For Bolton, for instance, Henry Ashworth presented statistical evidence before a meeting in Manchester in December 1841 that claimed that, of 50 mills normally employing 8,124 workpeople, 30 mills employing 6,061 were now either standing idle or working only a four-day week. And a similar level of unemployment was to be found in most other trades. Thus, only 1,325 out of 2,110 engineers, millwrights and machine-makers were now at work; only 49 carpenters out of 150, 16 out of 120 brick-setters, 50 out of 150 stonemasons, 250 out of 500 tailors, and 40 out of 80 shoemakers (*B.F.P.*, 24 December 1841). But a League claim that upwards of 300 families were reduced to extreme distress by the Corn Laws did not go unchallenged. Charles Mott, the assistant Poor Law commissioner, thought that accounts of distress in Bolton were exaggerated. His own investigation produced a report, to which the local Leaguers took exception, saying that the administration of the New Poor Law was contrary to the designs of the Act and that only one of the 300 plus families cited by the Leaguers was actually in serious distress (B.P.P. 1841, II, Correspondence between the Home Office and the Poor Law Commissioners on the Subject of Distress in Bolton; B.P.P. 1842, XXXV, Communications to the Home Office on Distress in Bolton).

75. *B.F.P.*, 29 February 1840; *The Anti-Corn Law Circular*, 12 March 1840, and 4 June 1840 – 'CORN LAWS AND POOR LAWS' – for another statement on the supposed links between the Corn Laws, working-class poverty, and the operation of the Poor Law.

76. *B.C.*, 24 April, 15 May, 19, 26 June 1830.

77. *B.C.*, 5, 26 March, 18 June 1831.

78. *B.C.*, 20 April 1833.

79. *B.C.*, 13 July, 3 August 1833.

80. *B.C.*, 18, 25 January, 1 February, 1 March 1834.

81. *B.C.*, 5, 12, 19 July 1834.

82. *B.C.*, 17 January, 15, 22 August 1835.

83. *B.F.P.*, 24 June 1837; *Manchester Guardian*, 21 June 1837.

84. B.P.P. 1840, XXIV, Report from R. M. Muggeridge on the Condition of the Handloom Weavers of Lancashire, Westmorland, Cumberland and parts of the West Riding of Yorkshire. For a summary of events surrounding the work of the royal commission, see D. Bythell, *The Handloom Weavers: A Study in the English Cotton Industry during the Industrial Revolution* (Cambridge, 1969), pp. 164–8.

85. *B.F.P.*, 30 September, 28 October 1837. Opposition had come from the Tory *B.C.*, which argued that the home market was the best one and was best served by maintaining protective duties, and from Makin, in correspondence to that newspaper, who attacked the weavers' committee as 'self-styled' and unrepresentative of weavers' opinion (*B.C.*, 19 October 1837).

86. *B.F.P.*, 28 April, 5 May 1838.

87. *Northern Star*, 24 October 1840.

88. *B.C.*, 7 November 1835.

89. *B.C.*, 21 November 1835; Sykes, 'Popular Politics', pp. 459–62.

90. *B.C.*, 5 December 1835, 15 July 1836.

91. For example, *B.C.*, 4 June 1836, report of the first O.C.A. 'public dinner', with a claimed 450 members in attendance; *B.C.*, 15 July 1836, report of annual dinner of the O.C.A., republished as *Bolton Operative Conservative Association: Report of the Proceedings at the Meeting of the Bolton Operative Conservative Association Held in the Little Bolton Town Hall, June 1st 1836* (Bolton, 1836).

92. According to the *B.F.P.*, the O.C.A. appears simply to have been the name given to middle-class Conservative dinners. Taking the report of one such occasion, attended by 700–800 persons, from 1 July 1837 edition, for instance. '... the assembly was numerous and highly respectable. We have no doubt of this when we see the names of many of the gentlemen who honoured the company with their presence. But why, in the name of propriety, should such a gathering be called an operative festival? Two-thirds of the Boltonians present were not operatives ... To give the meeting something like the appearance of a collection of operatives, a number of working men were brought from the county ... We have no objection to their calling the concern a Conservative festival, but we consider it nothing less than sheer humbug to speak of it as made up of the working men of Bolton ...'

93. Foster, *op. cit.*; P. Joyce, *Work, Society and Politics: The Culture of the Factory in Later Victorian England* (London, 1980); N. Kirk, *The Growth of Working Class Reformism in Mid-Victorian England* (Beckenham, 1985).

94. Joyce, *op. cit.*, pp. xiv–xv; Kirk, *op. cit.*, pp. 4–12.

95. Joyce, *op. cit.*, p. xix.

96. Kirk, *op. cit.*, p. 24.

97. All of this receives greater attention in Chapter Four.

98. *B.F.P.*, 2 May 1840.

99. *B.F.P.*, 29 February 1840.

100. *B.F.P.*, 6 April 1837.

101. *B.F.P.*, 26 February 1842.

102. Thompson, *op. cit.*, p. 262.

103. *Ibid.*, B. Harrison and P. Hollis, 'Chartism, Liberalism and the life of Robert Lowery', *English Historical Review* LXXXII (1967).

104. G. Stedman Jones, 'The Language of Chartism', in Epstein and Thompson, *op. cit*; G. Stedman Jones, 'Rethinking Chartism', in his *Languages of Class: Studies in English Working Class History 1832–1982* (Cambridge, 1983).

105. J. Foster, 'The Declassing of Language', *New Left Review* 150 (1985); R. Gray, 'The Deconstructing of the English Working Class', *Social History* 11, 3 (October 1986); N. Kirk, 'In Defence of Class: A Critique of Recent Revisionist Writing upon the Nineteenth-Century English Working Class', *International Review of Social History* XXXII (1987); D. Thompson, 'The Languages of Class', *Society for the Study of Labour History Bulletin* 25, 1 (1987).
106. Kirk, 'In Defence of Class', p. 17.
107. *B.F.P.*, 20 August 1842.
108. Kirk, 'In Defence of Class', p. 13.
109. Chartists had, however, always shown some interest in the possibility of mobilising trade union support. Thus a placard addressed to the trade unions of Bolton, from the Workingmen's Association, dated July 1839, called for 'your Declaration of Adhesion in Bodies – as has been done at Birmingham, Newcastle, Manchester, Oldham, Bury, and other places of importance' (*H.O. 40/44*, 'To the Trade Societies of Bolton' from 'The Committee of the Bolton Workingmen's Association', 29 July 1839).
110. P. Hollis, *The Pauper Press: A Study in Working-Class Radicalism of the 1830s* (Oxford, 1970), p. 204, ch. VII *passim*.
111. R. Sykes, 'Early Chartism and Trade Unionism in South-East Lancashire', in Epstein and Thompson, *op. cit.*, pp. 169–71.
112. *B.F.P.*, 29 August 1840.
113. *B.F.P.*, 13 February 1841.
114. D. Jones, *Chartism and the Chartists* (London, 1975).
115. Gray, *op. cit.*, p. 372.
116. See n. 108 for source.
117. W. G. Lumley, an assistant Poor Law commissioner, was of the opinion that the policies adopted by the guardians of Bolton promoted crime and immorality, and were injurious to the propagation of habits of thrift and industry among the labouring population. As such, he thought that they 'furnish examples of the continued prevalence of the demoralizing malpractice which it was the intention of the Poor-law Amendment Act to suppress'. Relief in aid of wages was being made to low-paid hand-loom weavers, thus encouraging weavers to produce less, and to mill-workers temporarily laid off or on short time. And no serious attempt had been made to provide suitable workhouse accommodation and thus to lessen dependency on outdoor relief. (B.P.P. 1846, XXXVI, Copy of Reports received by the Poor Law Commissioners in 1841, on the State of the Macclesfield and Bolton Unions).
118. *B.F.P.*, 22 June 1839.
119. *B.F.P.*, 2, 9, 16 May 1839.
120. P. Adelman, *Peel and the Conservative Party 1830–1850* (London, 1989), p. 36; Gash, *op. cit.*, pp. 220–4.
121. *B.C.*, 19 March 1842; Gash, *op. cit.*, p. 224, for the generally favourable Chartist and working-class reaction at national level to the budget of 1842. In its edition of 19 March 1842 the radical *Manchester and Salford Advertiser*, while calling for a further revision of taxation, generally welcomed Peel's

initiative: 'Did the reader ever hear of a proposal to raise four millions of taxes which should pass over the head of the working man and ... leave him in a better position than it found his ... The poor man is not called upon for a shilling, and, with much of the tax raised from the middle and higher classes, duties upon many articles of consumption are to be reduced so that he will benefit from a reduction of price in many commodities'.

122. *English Chartist Circular* 11, 110; T. Tholfsen, *Working Class Radicalism in Mid-Victorian England* (London, 1976), pp. 107–9.

123. Thus at a meeting in the Temperance Hall in late March, for instance, held for the purpose of appointing a delegate to the National Convention, Ralph Lord 'called upon those present to be steady and sober – to discontinue attending public-houses and beer-houses, observing that the keepers of such places were not their friends, but would, if necessary, be the first to come out bloodily to oppose them'. And James Parkinson similarly noted the close connection between the drink interest and Toryism and urged workers to maintain sobriety: 'The man to be appointed delegate, should be of known opinions, and well tried in the ranks of the radicals of this town; and it would be necessary that they give him the necessary support to enable him to do his duty. They should also keep sober, and refrain from supporting those persons, who, at the last election, resolved on supporting – not the charter – but that member who would endeavour to get *them* certain privileges which would enable them to rob the people to a certain extent of their money. If their pence had been devoted to such purposes as the release of Frost, Williams, and Jones, &c., instead of being carried to public houses, they would not have been there on that evening asking any government for liberty; for it would not have been withheld. Let the government be made acquainted that the Chartists of 1848 were not what the Chartists of bygone days had been, but that they were marching firmly in the direction of progress.' Matthew Stevenson, the elected delegate, gave a report to a meeting in the theatre later in April. His address included criticism of the press for their 'garbled' reports of the proceedings of the Convention, for 'Newspapers were patronised by certain classes, and contained matter to please those parties'. But 'he might say that the working classes were not blameless in this respect; for instead of supporting the press as they should have done, they spent ten times the money which would have been thus required, in stuff that did them no good at all (hear, hear).' Later in May Stevenson complained 'that while the people would neglect their own interests, and support between 3 and 4 hundred beer and public houses in this town, – as seemed to be the case now, the Charter was a century distant' (*B.C.*, 1, 22 April 1848, 20 May 1848).

124. For the social leadership of the middle class in later Victorian Bolton, see the following unpublished theses: G. Evans, 'Social Leadership and Social Control in Bolton, 1870–98', Lancaster University. M.A. thesis (1974); P. A. Harris, 'Class Conflict, the Trade Unions and Working Class Politics in Bolton, 1875–1896', Lancaster University M.A. thesis (1971); also useful is E. Thorpe, 'Industrial Relations and the Social Structure: A Case

Study of the Bolton Cotton Spinners, 1884–1910', University of Salford M.Sc. thesis (1969).

125. In December 1844 the spinners formed a committee which drew up and presented a memorial to Peel calling for the abolition of the duty on raw cotton (*B.F.P.*, 7, 28 December 1844); Webbs' Trade Union Collection, Section A, XXXV, 2, Bolton Cotton Spinners: Extracts from old minute books and reports, 1844–80, note 73.

126. *B.F.P.*, 22 November, 6, 13 December 1845. At a meeting in December the operative cotton-spinners adopted a memorial calling upon Her Majesty's ministers to open the ports to the free admission of foreign corn immediately, and passed a resolution to call a further meeting for the purpose of 'recommending the mechanics and other trades' to do likewise. Shortly thereafter the power-loom weavers produced their own memorial (*B.F.P.*, 13, 20 December 1845, 17 January 1846).

127. There is not the space here for a detailed exposition of Bolton Chartism in 1848, but the main developments can be traced from the following editions of the *B.C.*: 26 February (public meeting), 1 April (selection of delegate to the National Convention), 15 April (editorial), 22 April (correspondence), 22 April (a meeting of over 3,000 selects a delegate to the National Convention), 6 May (National Convention delegate's report), 13 May (meeting of trades), 20 May (report from National Convention delegate), 1 July (female Chartists' petition – signed by 448 females), 15 July (lecture by McDouall), 15 July (editorial – 'The Chartist Trials' – argues that the state has little to lose and much to gain by showing leniency in the trial of the London Chartists), 29 July, 5 August (relations between Chartists and Irish nationalists), 26 August (inquest into death of Joseph Lomax, bed-quilt weaver and prominent Chartist), 9, 16, 30 September (the Chartists and the 1848 parliamentary election, the Chartist candidate Joseph Barker wins the show of hands from a crowd of 6,000–8,000 at the hustings).

128. Foster, *op. cit.*, pp. 1, 107, 148.

129. *Ibid.*, p. 2

130. J. Foster, 'Some Comments on "Class Struggle and the Labour Aristocracy"', *Social History* 3 (Ocotber, 1986).

131. Kirk, *The Growth of Reformism*, pp. 65–6.

132. *B.C.*, 1 April 1848.

133. Report of the Bolton Society for the Protection of the Poor and District Provident Society (year ending 2 December 1848, B.R.L.); *B.C.*, 16 December 1848.

CHAPTER FIVE

The Limits to Middle-Class Hegemony: Technological Change and Industrial Relations

The stability of the middle-class social leadership in the local community depended in the long term on the maintenance of satisfactory economic roles and relations, but for much of the second quarter of the century, as the following comment from the *Bolton Free Press* suggests, the opposite was probably the case:

> At present, looking at the great mass of society, we see the labouring classes and their employers placed in hostile opposition to each other. Here and there ... may be found an individual master who is beloved and respected by those in his employment; but in too many instances the working man looks on the capitalist as one who heaped up wealth chiefly by 'grinding the faces of the poor;' while the capitalist, equally unjust in his opinion, and with less excuse for being so, reciprocates the ill-will, deeming the working classes a parcel of ignorant, discontented beings, whose demands no concessions would satisfy, and who are always least troublesome when their wages are lowest.[1]

In the years around 1850, however, contemporaries began to observe a considerable improvement in this situation, and historians also have noted the changes in industrial relations that took place. They have also described the fragmentation of a working-class movement that, in terms of overlaps in personnel and the interconnections in activity between industrial and political organisations, had been impressive for its generally high degree of solidarity.[2] They have thus shown how the demise of Chartism was accompanied by less frequent and intense industrial conflict and a decline in working-class solidarities, with political and economic agitations tending to separate and trade-union strategies becoming deliberately more sectionalist in character. Such was the pattern in Bolton also, as those organisations aiming to transcend divisions either enjoyed less support or held narrower aims and objectives than earlier broad industrial fronts. The National Association of United Trades (N.A.U.T.), for instance, attracted a far lower level of support than the earlier National Association for the Protection of Labour

(N.A.P.L.). While the N.A.P.L. had taken pride in stimulating organisation in previously unorganised trades and was connected with talk of
uniting 'all Trade, Benefit, and Co-operative Societies, and Political
Unions, in one great cause, and as one Society',[3] the Bolton Trades
Council (formed 1866) restricted its organisational aims to formally
'organised trades' only and its political ambitions to the reform of a few
aspects of trade-union law.[4] In this context, the demise of other unifying
forces, such as the factory movement, was also significant. The later
campaign for shorter hours in bleaching works, which was actually
focused on Bolton, did not attract the level of community support
characteristic of the earlier agitation.[5]

It has to be acknowledged that improving industrial relations, the
increasing separation of working-class political and economic activity,
and the adoption of a narrower outlook and more moderate aims among
the labour movement were all important in helping the middle class
to consolidate its social leadership. Yet whilst such discontinuities in
working-class experience were important, attention to the pattern of
industrial relations in Bolton across the second and third quarters of the
nineteenth century reveals that, in many important respects, social
stability was also based on important areas of continuity, and that one
such key area was that of production relations.

This claim actually goes against some of the more recent investigations into developments in the cotton districts, which, it will be
recalled, saw changes at work as a major area of discontinuity and one
that was fundamental to the overall process of social stabilisation. These
studies have assumed that production relations were restructured in the
1840s, and have placed much emphasis on the demise of craft autonomy
in labour processes and the creation of new forms of labour discipline.[6]
There are, however, some objections to this line of argument.

Some of these objections have been outlined in the previous chapter.
Firstly, it was revealed that the case for the centrality of changes in the
workplace was based on inadequate empirical foundations. Chartism did
receive its strongest support from those trades where technological
change and innovations in work practice were posing a serious threat to
the security and status of workers, but it appears that industrial struggles
did not necessarily provide the motive for working-class involvement in
political reform movements. Within radicalism, political perspectives
and analyses always held primacy over economic considerations. In this
sense, the links between working-class politics and economics were
more conditional and not as closely integrated as has sometimes been
assumed. Changes at work were thus found to have had less of an impact
on political behaviour than some have maintained, and the demise of
militant Chartism can be attributed mainly to political and social causes.

Economic factors were acknowledged as having played a role in the overall process of social stabilisation, especially the expansion and triumph of capitalist market relations, but it is far from certain that those discontinuities in working-class life which did occur were directly connected to changes in work practice. These were important and did have an impact, but they were not the main source of capitalist domination over labour.

Before 1850, as after, the subordination of labour to capital stemmed primarily from labour's reliance upon capitalist market relations for work. This was implicit in labour's recognition of the employer's role in organising the broader market operation, involving the initiation of the production process and marketing the finished product.[7] It is doubtful that the social vision held by the Chartists envisaged any alternative to this dependence beyond the aim of a more regulated capitalism. The Owenites may have wanted more, but it seems that Owenism had only a limited impact on popular attitudes. Bolton workers showed a lukewarm response to Owenism, and the broad industrial fronts with which they were involved in the 1830s were less influenced by Owenite concerns than has sometimes been assumed; they were mainly concerned with everyday trade-union matters and did not envisage the re-creation of community through cooperation.[8]

As will be shown below, however, capitalist control was far from complete, since workers were able to mitigate their dependence upon capitalist market relations for work through an ongoing sphere of independence forged out of the continuing indeterminacy of capitalist managerial authority in the workplace. The extent to which craft control was fractured at mid-century has been exaggerated; even in sectors where major changes occurred, such as engineering, employers still continued to rely upon the autonomy of workers in labour processes throughout the third quarter of the century.[9]

This left scope for considerable expressions of working-class independency and, as will also be shown, work proved to be one of the more fragile areas of the mid-Victorian consensus. Once the pace of technological change slackened and the economy stabilised after the 1840s, there emerged a somewhat finely balanced compromise or stability in production relations. The limits to capitalist control in the workplace were reflected in employers' reliance on essentially paternalistic notions of social hierarchy and the persistence of largely informal systems of labour relations. These remained in place until changing economic circumstances in the 1880s demanded the construction of more formalised and institutionalised collective bargaining procedures. The tone of industrial relations improved nonetheless, allowing the middle class to advance and consolidate its overall position of social leadership.

Workers and labour processes

The picture of industrial development in Bolton between the second and third quarters of the nineteenth century can be broadly portrayed in terms of the demise of a once substantial hand-loom weaving sector, the rise to prominence of the factory system in cotton and engineering, and the spread of capitalist practices to all industries (Tables 5.1 and 5.2 give some indication of Bolton's occupational structure at mid-century).

Table 5.1

Occupational Analysis of Selected South-East Lancashire Towns, 1841

	Ashton		Bolton		Oldham		Rochdale	
	Total	%	Total	%	Total	%	Total	%
Textile manufacturing	6,590	60.1	11,569	51.1	9,563	51.9	15,820	51.8
Textile finishing	44	0.4	365	1.6	20	0.1	1,040	3.4
Engineering and metalwork	396	3.6	1,633	7.2	988	5.4	1,099	3.6
Building	303	2.8	756	3.3	480	2.6	1,046	3.4
Building, allied trades	166	1.5	268	1.2	134	0.7	209	0.7
Clothing	816	7.4	1,260	5.6	1,860	10.1	1,202	3.9
'Upper' craft	59	0.5	193	0.9	76	0.4	219	0.7
Food etc. manufacture	60	0.5	228	1.0	204	1.1	218	0.7
Miscellaneous manufacturing	50	0.5	216	1.0	54	0.3	130	0.4
Domestic service	771	7.0	1,772	7.8	1,066	5.8	1,890	6.2
Transport	149	1.4	391	1.7	410	2.2	804	2.6
General labouring	409	3.7	841	3.7	486	2.6	1,418	4.6
Mining	168	1.5	322	1.4	1,279	6.9	1,710	5.6
Agriculture	123	1.1	221	1.0	305	1.7	1,330	4.4
Others (dealing, industrial service, public service, professionals and property owning)	863	7.9	2,613	11.5	1,496	8.1	2,397	7.9
Occupied population	10,967		22,648		18,431		30,532	

Source: R. Sykes, 'Popular Politics and Trade Unionism in South-East Lancashire, 1829–42', Univ. of Manchester Ph.D thesis (1982), table 1.7.

Table 5.2

Principal Occupations, Bolton Borough, 1851

	Total	Rough % of total occupied population
Cotton manufacture (2,345 males and 3,013 females under 20; 4,969 males and 3,455 females over 20)	13,782	45.0
Labourers (including gardeners and agricultural labourers)	1,058	3.5
Handicrafts (tailors, shoemakers, etc.)	2,183	7.0
Shopkeepers, traders, dealers	1,450	4.75
Building and allied trades	1,534	5.0
Miners and quarry workers	541	1.75
Engineering and metal workers	2,921	9.75
Transport and communications	753	2.5
Domestic service	1,651	5.5
Milliners and seamstresses	784	2.5
Washerwomen, manglers, laundry-keepers, charwomen	558	1.75
Total occupied population	18,963 males	11,593 females

Source: B.P.P. 1854, 1851 Census: Ages, Civil Conditions, Occupations and Birth-Place of the People, 11, pp. 648–53.

Attention to developments in labour processes, however, suggests that, in general, it is difficult to reconcile supposed sudden shifts in working-class attitudes and behaviour with what were really prolonged changes in work practice. It is not necessary to examine every trade in detail to illustrate this point, though the five examined below – cotton-spinning, engineering, building, tailoring and coal-mining – present useful and typical examples in four of the largest adult male occupations.[10]

The crucially important cotton-spinning trade is perhaps the major case in point. Bolton's cotton-spinners were certainly one of the best organised of all trades in the cotton district; they were the key group of workers among the cotton-factory operatives and played a very important role in the popular movements of the period.[11] Changes in mule-spinning technology were at the forefront of technological improvement in cotton during the disturbed second quarter of the century, and this helps to explain the attention given to them by historians and contemporaries. Sykes has shown how technological change in the 1830s posed a serious threat to the spinner, bringing reduced wage levels and substantial unemployment among their ranks.[12] And given the spinners' strategic position in production and the vital importance of cotton in the national economy, it is not surprising that Gareth Stedman Jones saw their battle to defend their industrial and social position as central to the communal basis of class confrontation in the Oldham of the 1830s, and their defeat as having wide social implications.[13] By way of contrast, Michael Huberman recently argued against the portrayal of the spinners' position as generally insecure and deteriorating during these years. He maintains that, in fact, there existed an 'accord between workers and firms in urban areas', the result of a favourable labour market for spinners which enhanced their bargaining power. Far from being vulnerable, spinners were able to manipulate competition for a limited pool of reliable labour to the extent that employers 'had to meet workers' demands' for 'fixed or sticky piece-rates, short-hour working, and lay-offs which were inversely related to seniority'.[14] But Huberman's view of the position of spinners in the 1830s and early 1840s is at odds not only with current received historical wisdom, but also with contemporary observations. With others, I have suggested a different picture, in which urban employers during those years had few problems in obtaining suitable labour and were able to dictate wage rates, hiring and firing practices, and hours of work.[15]

The main threat to the Bolton spinner was technical refinements which allowed the development of the new long mules and the coupling together or 'double-decking' of pairs of mules. This greatly increased the number of spindles worked by a single spinner, resulting in substantial unemployment among spinners.[16] Falling real wages came too, as employers sought to exploit technological changes through reductions or alterations to piece-rate lists, which usually precipitated conflict, often of a bitter and violent nature.

This had been the pattern since 1823, when the principle of discounting was introduced to the Bolton list to take account of increases in mule size, and when a combination of employers had successfully countered a 'rolling strike' for a wage advance with a general lock-out. Hitherto a standard rate had been paid according to the amount and count of yarn produced, but now, for every dozen spindles worked over 324, a discount was made.[17] In 1830 two of the largest firms in the area, Ashworths of Turton and Bollings of Bolton, introduced larger mules and sought to increase the rate of discount. The result was a bitter strike of over six months' duration, involving regular assaults on blacklegs (or 'knobsticks' as they were called). In one incident, during a night attack, sixty persons damaged a school building recently erected by the Ashworths and assaulted knobsticks housed near to their mill. The striking spinners received the backing of their union and spinners working for other employers were certainly involved in intimidatory crowd action, picketing and attacks upon knobsticks.[18] Ashworths and Bollings were two out of only three firms in the area to employ over 1,000 workers in the 1830s and 1840s.

The other was Ormrods, which experienced a violent strike in 1834, when their spinners and power-loom weavers turned out against a reduction. Knobsticks were imported from Scotland. These were put through such an intense campaign of physical and verbal abuse, together with the intimidatory presence of large crowds which gathered outside their place of work, that they were forced to remain within the mill for long periods, not daring to venture out night or day.[19] To give another illustration of the violence that commonly accompanied spinners' strikes in these years, in 1840 the spinners at Taylor and Marsh struck against a reduction in wages. Knobsticks were again procured. These were subsequently subjected to 'abusive and riotous assemblages' that gathered each evening in the vicinity of the mill to deliver 'hootings, execrations, throwing stones and other missiles and in other ways injuring them'. On one occasion, two of them had to be rescued by the police from a crowd of between 300 and 400 people which was threatening to throw them off a railway bridge.[20]

In these and other such disputes the usual result was defeat for the spinners. The importation of knobsticks and the presence of a labour reserve seriously weakened their bargaining power, while the prosecution of offenders for violence usually put a halt to intimidatory tactics. A system of references or discharge notes from previous employers, used to testify to a worker's competence and good behaviour, would have made it difficult for violent offenders or dismissed striking workers to secure future employment in the town.[21] In the twenty-five years leading to 1841, the spinners claimed that they had suffered seven reductions and achieved only one advance.[22] That was in 1836, when the masters agreed to concede the equivalent of 12 per cent after the spinners had threatened strike action.[23] When depression returned in 1837, even this was retrieved by the masters, who compounded their action by making a further alteration in the discounting rate, itself equivalent to a 4 per cent reduction.[24] In June 1840 the employers again altered the list to take account of growing mule sizes, effecting an average reduction of 10 per cent on mules of 324 spindles and 8 per cent on 648-spindle mules.[25]

This failure of employers to comply with negotiated piece-rate lists was among the grievances listed in the resolutions of the spinners in the Plug Strikes. Another was the forcing of spinners into employer-owned housing as a condition of employment (referred to in Chapter One). In 1840, for instance, a spinner who was obliged to move into one of his employer's houses, which he considered to be altogether inferior to his previous residence, referred to this as 'a quiet, silent, but most galling despotism'.[26] The 'apprenticeship' system in spinning was listed as a further cause of bitterness. In the 1830 dispute, anger was further directed at both Ashworths and Bollings for employing 'apprentices' to supersede the regular spinners. At the former firm, piecers graduating to the position of spinner had first to sign contracts binding them to serve two years at 15 per cent and a third year at 10 per cent below the prices paid to the regular spinners. Similarly, apprentices at Bollings had to serve for two years, during which they would receive less payment for their output than spinners being paid the regular prices. The spinners' union reacted to this further attack on their status by instructing its members to refuse to teach their piecers to spin.[27] All this is ample evidence of the poor state of relations between the spinners and their employers in the 1830s and early 1840s.

However, this deterioration in the spinners' material position was not irreversible and cotton-spinning does not provide a significant example of increased capitalist control in the labour process. Far from being cowed or permanently defeated by the 1840s, once the pace of techno-logical change slowed after 1842 and industrial expansion helped to reduced the surplus stock of spinners, the spinners were able to recover some of the ground they had lost, improving their bargaining position considerably from the mid-1840s. In the third quarter of the century they consolidated their trade-union position to remain one of the best organised of all trades, with the ability to mount determined resistance when required, as the town-wide strikes against wage reductions in 1849, 1861, 1867, 1869, 1874 and 1877 demonstrated.[28]

Crucially, there had been no real threat to the division of labour. Stedman Jones originally identified the onset of what he saw as the spinners' 'real' subordination to capital with the introduction of self-acting mules in the 1830s. But in the light of Lazonick's later detailed research, he has since conceded that the continuities in spinning were more marked than he had appreciated, in that the spinners retained a great deal of control over the organisation and pace of their work and that the threat to their position was not as great as he implied.[29] He now supports Lazonick's view that employers preserved the status of the spinners because it made good economic sense for them to continue to delegate responsibility for the recruitment and supervision of assistant labour. Yet it seems that the upshot of technical improvements to the Bolton hand-mule was probably to increase employers' dependence on the technical expertise of the spinner within production. Catling considers that this machine reached a 'remarkable pitch of sensitivity' and became perhaps 'the most complex, and most highly refined, manually controlled tool which has yet been, or will ever be, mass produced', while Eli Spencer in 1880 noted the growing scarcity of spinners able to perform the delicate and highly skilled manual operations on the same mule.[30] In the meantime, technical difficulties in applying the self-acting mechanism to the medium-fine yarns produced in Bolton meant that the self-actor was not widely adopted until the 1860s. When it came, there was apparently little resistance to its introduction; it did not bring wage reductions and technological unemployment among spinners and seemingly did not present a major threat to the spinner's skill, status and security.

The impact of technology in Lancashire had been greatest in engineering, where a capital-intensive phase of development transformed the division of labour between 1830–50. This reduced employers' dependence on labour-intensive methods and the versatile, but time-consuming and expensive, handicraft skills of the millwright. But employers did not have it all their own way, for they still continued to rely on the autonomy of workers in labour processes. Thus, even in one of the most technologically advanced industries, employer control was far from complete by mid-century, and workers continued to make expressions of independence and engage in forms of craft organisation which technological change had been designed to eradicate.

The rapid adoption of the steam engine and an expanding market for textile machinery were crucial to the growth of engineering in Lancashire. But in the early stages of the Industrial Revolution these were characteristically manufactured by labour-intensive methods, and, according to the account of John Hammond, a Bolton 'machine-maker' in 1831, were of necessity often constructed *in situ* and with whatever suitable labour came to hand:

> When a company intended to erect such a mill ... An engineer was
> sent to superintend the works; he generally brought with him such

workmen as he deemed necessary for the undertaking; but, if he could not accomplish that, he was under the necessity of supplying the defect by engaging such as the locality afforded. It is almost needless to state, that those artizans were a medley of trades, various in their operative professions ... Amongst them, the millwright at that time claimed the pre-eminence; the rest were composed of carpenters, joiners, smiths, and clockmakers, who left their original trades for better wages, moulders and turners were then little known, the work being chiefly composed of wood, brass, malleable iron, and steel. Professional turners being then very rare, each artizan was under the necessity of learning to turn his own part. The moulding part being brass, had to be sent to for some distance, and at great expense. The work was all done in places where it had to remain ... Though very operose this work ... soon became finished, and put into active operation, and though many of the workmen were of course dismissed, it was still necessary to retain a part of them on the premises, there being, at that time, no machine shops, and the apparatus must be kept in order.[31]

This heavy reliance on manual skills and dexterity was especially characteristic of the labour of the millwrights, who, as suggested in the above quotation, were at the top of the status hierarchy in early nineteenth-century engineering. For Musson and Robinson they were of particular importance in setting up Lancashire's early mills and factories.[32] Burgess portrays the millwright as 'a pre-industrial craftsman whose skills could be adapted to the needs of the infant industry. Millwrights had little machinery to help them. All depended upon the expertise of the individual workman.'[33] William Fairbairn, himself a former millwright, described the occupation as 'a kind of jack-of-all-trades, who could with equal facility work at the lathe, the anvil, or the carpenter's bench ... He could handle the axe, the hammer, and the plane with equal skill and precision; he could turn, bore, or forge.'[34]

The all-round skill of the millwrights gave them high status, comparatively high wages, regular employment, security, independence (in the form of a relative freedom from supervision) and a high level of social mobility. These favourable working conditions were buttressed by the traditional seven-year apprenticeship which kept their skills at a premium by restricting entry to the trade. This prevented employers from recruiting extra hands to meet an increase in demand, which in turn minimised the number of surplus hands in subsequent depressions.[35]

In the 1830s, however, the wider diffusion of precision machine tools weakened the millwrights' bargaining power. Increasing specialisation in the utilisation of labour brought about a widening of the available labour supply, a lowering of costs, an expanding *per capita* productive capacity, and a reduced employer dependency on the skill of the mill-wright.[36] As outlined by Hammond, this transformation in the utilisation of labour was connected with its increasing deployment in specialist workshops:

> After mills had been a few years established ... Some small shops were established for the construction of such machinery as could be constructed out of the mills, and I believe carding engines were the first things of the kind so undertaken; afterwards other parts of the apparatus began to appear in the shops, such as the jenny and its preparation, and afterwards the mule ... it was then a very portable piece of work, and well adapted to be made [in] a workshop. Machinery began at this time to be improved, workshops spread themselves over the country, and workmen were employed under new masters, viz. Undertakers instead of the proprietors of mills ...[37]

Some indication of the threat that the new technology posed to the millwright's status is revealed in a letter from Naysmith, Gaskell and Co. to a potential buyer for planing machines. It concerned Benjamin Hick and Son's Soho Iron Works, which had been a customer of the firm for machine tools since 1836:

> We are in hand with two such machines for Mr Hick of Bolton who has had a turnout of his millwrights and in consequence came to us for our assistance as he is determined to supply their place entirely with machinery which will be fully attained by a few planing machines.[38]

It is clear that technological change strengthened the hand of the employers, who were now more able to capitalise on booms and in slumps, to shift the burden of adjustment to labour. In the early 1830s employers were able to tap an expanding labour supply and to use 'systematic overtime' and piece-work to exploit prosperity. Then, in the depression of 1837–42, unemployment became a serious problem for engineering workers. This would appear to be confirmed by some statistics on Bolton produced by Henry Ashworth. Ashworth enumerated 2,110 ironfounders, engineers, millwrights and machine-makers in 1836, some of whom were working overtime and earning the equivalent of a nine- to twelve-day week. In 1841 the number employed was reduced to 1,325, who were working on average a four- to five-day week.[39] To cite further evidence of this general pattern, in 1859 the Friendly Society of Iron Moulders, 'one of the best organised and most extensive trade societies in the kingdom', with 1,100 members in forty-eight branches nationwide, celebrated its fiftieth anniversary. During the proceedings it was revealed that the union normally relied on payments of unemployment benefit to maintain wage levels. In the 1840s, however, it had not been able to prevent substantial unemployment in slumps, and the sheer depth of the depression in 1842 had forced it to abandon the payment of benefits altogether, the only occasion during the first fifty years of its existence on which it took this course of action. The engineering trades were hit by a further slump in 1847 and it was also revealed that, by November 1848, the moulders' union had over 1,500 members out of work.[40] It was these circumstances, together with recently imposed wage cuts, which encouraged the engineering workers of Bolton to support the Charter during the Plug Strikes. Two days after the spinners had struck, work placards appeared in the town 'announcing that a meeting of delegates of the irontrade, consisting of engineers, millwrights, smiths, &c ... had resolved that the existing evils arose from misrepresentation and class legislation, and that the remedy was to make the people's charter the law of the land'.[41]

Also significant, however, was the fact that technological change in engineering was not a straightforward linear process of de-skilling, but one which involved some recomposition of skill. Employers were unable to dispose of craft organisation and continued to rely on the autonomy of workers in labour processes. For Hammond, the new 'machine-making mechanics' were as useful as millwrights and 'other mechanical trades' with which they aspired to attain parity of status.[42] To attain this aim attempts were made to exert some degree of control over the labour market through the pursuit of shorter hours and the restriction of entry to the trade.

The strike of over 130 'machine-makers' at Messrs. Dobsons (Bolton's major producers of textile machinery) in June 1831 appears to have been the first by this new type of workers in Bolton. The men claimed that 'they have been degraded by having been shackled with one hour per day more than others' and demanded that the current eleven-hour day be reduced to ten and that the ratio of apprentices be brought down to 'one Lad to four men and the lads to serve five years ... by Legal Indenture'. The strike was attended with violence, for which a number of strikers were successfully prosecuted, after some knobsticks and hands who returned to work were surrounded in a public house and 'driven and beaten in every direction'. The dispute ended in compromise, with the men securing a half-hour off the working day.[43]

There were further sharp conflicts over a range of issues in the 1840s, including attempts to prevent employers imposing new workshop rules aimed at eroding craft autonomy in the workplace.[44] Conflict thus escalated, and the formation of the national Amalgamated Society of

Engineers (A.S.E.) in 1851 brought greater concordance than hitherto between local struggles and national agitation against systematic over-time, piece-work and the employment of 'illegal men'.[45]

Following the decision of the central executive committee of the A.S.E. to ban all overtime piece-work and the employment of 'illegal men', over 2,600 of the town's engineering workers were locked out in the national dispute of 1852 by members of the Central Association of Engineering Employers. Only 390 of these were actually members of the A.S.E., most of whom probably consisted of the more highly skilled fitters and turners who set up and supervised the new machinery operated by semi-skilled machine-minders.[46] But the issues involved covered a wide range of trades and it was significant that the A.S.E.'s demands were nevertheless widely supported by Bolton's other engineering workers. Those non-A.S.E. men at Hick's, for instance, declined their employer's invitation to return to work and ignored his appeal 'to the good will and kind offices which have mutually characterised our long intercourse with each other, and which we believe to have resulted in our mutual benefit'. Those of the town in general resolved at a public meeting that 'we the non-society men ... are determined not to resume work in any conditions less than those required by the Amalgamated Society.'[47] The men eventually returned to work in defeat, but it soon became clear that the employers' victory was largely formal. Between 1850 and 1890 economic circumstances changed as the diffusion of machine technology slowed and investment became as much labour-using as labour-saving. This improved the bargaining power of labour, and the aims of 1851 were progressively achieved as employer prerog-atives on wage payment and overtime regulation were pushed back by militant industrial action involving a wide range of engineering workers in the 1850s and 1860s.[48]

In contrast to cotton-spinning and engineering, the technical nature of work in the building industry might seem to have offered employers little alternative but to leave the labour process in the hands of the workers. But the building industry nevertheless provided another source of intense conflict over work control. Employers had some success in implementing capitalist practices and authority structures from the 1820s, but only after much conflict, and even by the 1880s the area of effective managerial control was still limited and the ability of workers to influence the terms of production remained considerable.

The majority of workers in the principal trades in the north-west were employed in very small units. Over 90 per cent of master carpenters and joiners, and just under 80 per cent of master bricklayers, to give examples, employed less than ten workers in 1851.[49] The small masters thus preponderated in numerical terms. From the mid-1820s, however,

they were increasingly dependent on the general contractors who dominated the industry. These gathered all the crafts together under the
control of a single enterprise to execute the various stages of the construction process.[50] The system was the primary influence determining wages
and conditions from the mid-1820s, but the persistence of restrictive
practices and craft traditions delayed the imposition of the full logic of
general contracting until beyond the 1870s. It was not until 1869, for
instance, that Bolton's employers sought to substitute payment by the
day with the more flexible payment by the hour.[51]

This was despite many employer successes. The formation of the
national Operative Builders' Union (O.B.U.) in 1831 originated from the
systematic attacks of general contractors on craft privileges, wages and
status. This national body comprised seven affiliated societies: bricklayers; carpenters and joiners; painters; plasterers; plumbers and glaziers;
slaters; and stonemasons.[52] In 1833 Bolton workers were involved in the
O.B.U.'s offensive against the general contractors, who initially agreed
to abolish such contracting in principle, but who then countered with a
decisive lock-out after the men had made further demands for increased
union authority in the organisation and execution of production.[53]

The dispute had centred on Manchester, but some masters from
other Lancashire towns were also involved, including Joseph Marsden –
who later became the first chairman of the Bolton Builders' General
Association – and Rowland Hall Heaton, also from Bolton.[54] Heaton, a
timber-merchant, had been involved in an acrimonious dispute with his
sawers from March 1832, when they had struck work 'in consequence of
some misunderstanding about turning a log of timber'. The reasons for
the dispute are not fully clear, but the men complained that Heaton had
made a reduction of two pence in the shilling for providing 'covered
saw-pits and other conveniences' which 'were more immediately to the
advantage of the employer than the employed'. Heaton obtained a fresh
supply of non-union labour, some of whom were intimidated into
quitting by 'great crowds' that 'collected in the vicinity of the timber
yard' each evening. Others suffered from the theft of their saws, physical
assaults and vitriol attacks. There was also an arson attack on Heaton's
timber-yard.[55] By September 1834 the O.B.U. had collapsed, but resistance against capitalist encroachments continued, and the next major
dispute in 1846 and the conflicts of the 1850s and 1860s reveal the
continuing problems of discipline and control facing the employers.

In 1846 a prolonged strike among the building trades of Manchester
and Liverpool spread to Bolton after the town's joiners downed tools for
an increase in their wages from twenty-five to twenty-seven shillings per
week. Following quickly on this action, thirty-eight of the town's leading
builders, complaining of union dictation over the issues of hours, wages,

working practices and hiring and firing, formed the Bolton Builders' General Association. The B.B.G.A. was represented at a meeting of master builders held a few days later at Newton near Manchester and attended by delegates from Leeds, Birmingham and several north-west towns. This declared its intention to form a national master builders' association to combat the growing power of the 'General Trades' Union of all the branches in the building line'.[56] The bargaining power which inter-trade cooperation gave the various trades was illustrated in a circular issued by the B.B.G.A. to its customers and supporters. The circular also revealed the problems of discipline and control facing Bolton's general contractors:

> For some time lately the trades generally, but the joiners in particular, have used strenuous exertions to form in this town what is called a General Trades' Union of all the branches in the building line, and they have succeeded in a majority of the trades – the Sawyers, Flaggers and Slaters, Plumbers and Glaziers, Plasterers and Painters, and Labourers have joined with them; the consequence has been that all who were not enrolled in the aforesaid general union were liable to be struck against, and most of the master builders in this town have had their business distracted in that way – the joiners or the plasterers, as the case might be, have struck against the non-unionists of the other trades ... These have been found to be very annoying and vexatious proceedings, but notwithstanding that, the employers were obliged to submit, or their interests suffer very materially.[57]

The circular also complained that the joiners had recently arbitrarily issued a new code of working rules, which altered previously agreed workshop procedures, including the reduction of the normal working day to eight hours and improved rates for overtime. The main issue was clearly one of workplace authority; the masters offered to concede an advance of one shilling providing that the men withdraw from the General Trades' Union (though, significantly, each trade could retain its own separate union organisation) and abandon the new rules. The general union collapsed after all trades except the joiners subsequently withdrew. However, the masters only achieved a partial victory, for the joiners were able to secure favourable terms when the dispute was eventually settled, the employers reluctantly accepting the new rules and conceding an advance of one shilling (it was reported that they would have preferred to concede two shillings and retain the old rules). This followed eight weeks of violence. The masters obtained fresh hands, who were subjected to regular assaults from pickets stationed at strategic points around the town and, on one occasion, by a large crowd composed predominantly of factory operatives. The masters responded with prosecutions for violence and breach of contract, but the dispute finally turned on their inability to secure fresh hands of a suitable quality.[58]

Capital continued to make encroachments, however, as demonstrated in 1853, when the employers were able to obtain enough suitable non-union fresh labour to defeat a strike against the spread of machine work in the cutting of timber and other aspects of joiners' work. To consol-idate their victory, the masters declared their intention not to employ hands connected with the joiners' club in future.[59] But problems in enforcing discipline and in managerial authority continued, and the joiners recovered their position amid a number of successful actions by building workers in the 1860s. In 1861, for instance, the bricklayers and stonemasons unilaterally imposed new working rules demarcating their work and forbidding the use of pre-prepared or 'worked stone'.[60] And from 1862 to 1864 a range of trades successfully enforced the 'Saturday half-holiday', which prompted the employers to reorganise and form a branch of the national General Builders' Association in 1865 to combat the advances made by labour.[61] The later 1860s then saw a rash of disputes over a range of issues affecting craft control and employer authority, including the use of worked stone and the imposition of hourly payment.[62]

Tailoring was another trade in which workers enjoyed a high degree of autonomy in the labour process (machinery only began to be used in Bolton from the late 1860s).[63] But this could not prevent an increase in the level of capitalist authority as the tailors' ability to exert some degree of control over the labour market declined with the spread of sweated outwork. This brought about a division of the trade into an 'honourable' section, composed largely of organised workers, and a 'dishonourable' section of largely unorganised workers producing cheap inferior goods in poor working conditions. This development steadily undermined the artisan status of the tailors. In London in 1834, after the failure of a strike to equalize conditions across both sections, the dishonourable sector was able to determine conditions.[64] The situation in London was not exceptional, but in Bolton it appears that the main struggle to equalise conditions between the two sections of the trade did not take place until the mid-1840s and was not as conclusive as the 1834 con-frontation in London. After 1850 the trajectory of industrial development actually worked to strengthen the position of the honourable portion of the trade, who were able to regain some of the ground they had lost.

Clearly, conditions for all tailors could only improve if they could manage to exert a greater degree of control over the labour market and so, when the battle to equalise conditions began in earnest early in 1844, the Bolton Tailors' Trade Society made an appeal for all the town's tailors to join the union in an attempt to equalise wages at four pence per hour. This was the rate being paid by 'the respectable masters', who were being undercut by the 'merciless tyrants' whose 'illegitimate establishments' produced inferior goods while paying wages almost two-thirds lower than those paid by the 'fair trader'. At the same time, this system was said to be causing great unemployment among those in the honourable section of the trade, while those in the overstocked dishonourable sector laboured arduously for fourteen to sixteen hours per day, up to 100 hours per week, in poor conditions for low pay.[65]

As revealed at a meeting of the journeymen tailors in March 1845, the honourable part of the trade was synonymous with production in the masters' own workshops. The degradation of the tailors was attributed to the putting-out of work, described as an 'evil system', which promoted the cut-throat competition that had brought about a downward spiral of prices, wages and conditions. The first resolution passed at the meeting expressed the tailors' opinions on the matter:

> That in the opinion of this meeting, the alarming state of the Tailoring Trade, brought about by the unprincipled competition … as certain master tailors have departed from the original mode of employing their workpeople on premises under their immediate direction, which … has proved detrimental to the best interests of the fair trading masters and the employed, and has been the means of extending disease to a frightful extent to all classes of the community, in consequence of clothes being made up in the humble habitations of the workmen, who are compelled, from the low wages paid by such employers, to live in the most densely populated and unhealthy neighbourhoods.[66]

Many of the honourable employers were sympathetic to this position, and at the March 1844 meeting alone at least eleven master tailors found common cause with the journeymen in forming a union to fight the 'evils' and 'injustice of competition' brought by the 'slop' or cheap and ready-made clothes dealers. At this and at a follow-up meeting it was decided to pursue a strategy of agitation for a government inquiry into their grievances and for legislative action – especially the reinstatement of apprenticeship legislation repealed in 1814 – to bring the dishonourable section under control. Significantly, an appeal was made for an end to 'the strikes that had so frequently been made against the masters' even in the honourable part of the trade.[67]

The problem for the journeymen was that, as the dishonourable section was now exerting a major influence in determining conditions in the trade as a whole,[68] many of the so-called honourable masters were finding themselves compelled to resort to 'dishonourable acts'. This forced the journeymen to undertake regular strike action to keep them in line. At a meeting held later in 1845, for instance, it was disclosed that masters from the 'respectable portion of the trade' were 'sending gentlemen's garments to be made in filthy cellars and dirty garrets', and threats were made to petition for a government inquiry into the conditions of the whole trade 'if the masters do not look to the convenience of their men, and provide a comfortable workshop wherein to have their work done'.[69] Thus the distinction between honourable and dishonourable, while important, could not prevent all sections of the trade from being afflicted by strikes.

All of this meant that, in tailoring, the factory was welcome as a preferable alternative to the putting-out system. And when the factory spread in the town from the 1850s, this proved to be instrumental in strengthening the position of the workers. In the 1860s the journeymen tailors' trade union was successful in organising both factory workers and outworkers, in arbitrarily imposing uniform lists of prices, in regulating overtime, in preventing the employers from temporarily distributing work to unorganised outworkers in booms, and in preventing employers from hiring non-union labour.[70]

In coal-mining, the natural conditions of production remained labour-intensive throughout the nineteenth century and provided the colliers with an unequalled freedom from managerial supervision and a control over the labour process unrivalled in capitalist industry.[71] As was the situation in tailoring, therefore, conflict between employers and workers was centred less around the labour process than around efforts to exert some degree of control over the labour market.[72] Local working conditions seem to have been a factor in this, as they may have reduced the ability of employers to replace striking hands with fresh labour. The typical colliery in the Bolton to Worsley coalfield was small-scale, with only a few employing over 100 face-workers. Most of the coal pits were relatively shallow, though the coal workings varied from eighteen inches to seven feet.[73] Many of the thicker of these were apparently worked by Lord Francis Egerton's collieries, the local surgeon, Dr Black, considering that because of this (and because of Egerton's underground canal network which enabled an easier carriage of hewed coal away from the coal-face): 'In this proprietary of mines the labour is not severe.' But labour in the thin seams was arduous and uncomfortable and when miners accustomed to working in these conditions withdrew, they were not easily replaced:

> ... in many other mines, as may be inferred from the thinness of the beds, the work is very constrained and laborious. Indeed, if men were

not brought up to the work from boys, they could not possibly accomplish it, as it requires a very twisted position of the body in many instances, namely, lying upon one hip, and yet directing the action of the hands and arms forwards, and this often in a space of not more than two feet, and sometimes less. For this reason, it was, that in the times of great want of employment among weavers and other operatives, few of them were able or fitted to undertake the most common work of this kind in the mines, even when there were *turn-outs* among the colliers.[74]

This would have given colliers some ability to control the labour supply. But up to 1850 at least, the market structure of the industry was balanced in the employers' favour, as workers could still be made to carry the burden of adjustment in slumps, while in booms higher labour costs could be passed on to the customer. As was the case in tailoring, the attempts of the miners to mitigate this dependence on market conditions and to exert some degree of control in the regulation of wages and conditions focused on attempts to construct an effective organisation. And the Bolton miners were at the centre of some determined efforts to build an efficient trade unionism among the region's miners. In March 1830 the colliers of south Lancashire formed the Friendly Society of Coal Mining, which set up its headquarters at Bolton, where the proximity of local miners to the more diversified economy of the town facilitated cooperation with other trades through the establishment of connections with the N.A.P.L.[75] In April the Bolton colliers went on strike and within a week most had returned to work after the majority of the employers conceded huge advances of between 25 and 40 per cent.[76]

The union consolidated its victory by imposing certain union rules which sought to establish a closed shop, control over job allocation, hiring and firing and customer supply. These were the source of much friction which eventually provoked a counter-offensive from the employers in 1831. In March, for example, William Hulton's colliers downed tools after he had supported two men who had refused to abide by the union rules. Hulton and the other employers responded by demanding that all colliers quit the union.[77] By May matters were coming to a head when Andrew Knowles' colliers walked out, prompting Knowles to complain that the union had repeatedly struck his works for excessive wage advances and for the reinstatement of dismissed workers. Further, they had also taken it upon themselves to dismiss and replace men in arrears with the union without consultation, had also taken it on themselves to allocate work tasks, and had threatened further strike action unless he appointed their choice of checkweighmen and obeyed their orders as to which customers he could serve and at what price. Thus 'these and other regulations of theirs left little for me to do but find money for wages'.[78] In a reply, the men actually corroborated Knowles' claims but defended their action on the grounds of the often unreasonable behaviour of their employer. By this time all the colliers in the Bolton-Farnworth-Westhoughton area were out on strike to preserve the union and, with other Lancashire employers demanding an end to the union, the strike spread over most of the region. This put a considerable strain on the union's resources and it collapsed in August after setbacks at Oldham and Rochdale.[79]

Local miners took part in the next major strike in Lancashire and Cheshire in 1841, which was conducted with only a 'scanty, improvised organization' and soon came to an end.[80] However, after the formation of the Miners' Association of Great Britain and Ireland in 1842, a more substantial organisation was created. In the summer of 1844 the union organised rallies in the Bolton area to build up support. These attracted crowds of between 1,000 and 6,000 persons to hear those prominent miners' leaders W. P. Roberts and William Dixon, whose efforts were boosted by an ongoing strike of the colliers at the firm of Knowles and Stott for more wages.[81]

In 1846, however, the Bolton miners lost a long and bitter strike. This was a major setback and union organisation in the area collapsed. The strike followed the normal pattern in the industry, in that it had turned on the changing balance of conditions in the labour market. The workers had initiated the strike in favourable conditions, but defeat was ensured when an economic downturn brought a fall in the price of coal.[82] The employers' victory was never likely to be permanent, however, for their failure seriously to address the lack of strong managerial control in the labour process meant that trade unionism was always likely to be revived once favourable economic conditions returned. Trade unionism among the miners had thus reappeared by 1851, when local miners were successful in a strike to raise wage rates to the level paid in 1845; operating in the generally more stable economic conditions of the mid-Victorian years, this time they were able to maintain a more durable organisation.[83]

Economic conflict in perspective

As the above examination of industrial relations shows, economic conflict proved to be a regular source of tension between workers and their employers. This was especially the case in the strife-torn second quarter of the nineteenth century. Relations did improve somewhat in the third quarter, but the issues of work control and market regulation over which labour and capital had struggled were not resolved by mid-century and conflict did continue at a fairly high level of intensity. This signalled the limits to middle-class hegemony. However, the social position of the middle class was nevertheless an improved one, in that working-class economic concerns ceased to infuse political radicalism, less effort went into attempts to form broad industrial fronts, and production relations stabilised rather than harmonised. This owed much to the more stable economic conditions of the mid-Victorian period, which allowed a slowing of the pace of technological change and capitalist reorganisation. But it also owed something to the conditions upon which working-class consciousness had been based in the Chartist period. More has to be said on the ideological content of working-class consciousness, the economic basis of the impressive labour solidarity of the 1830s and 1840s, and the relationship between the two.

It has to be understood that there was never a widespread call for the overturning of capitalist relations of production, though many trades shared a concern to control competition in capitalist market relations. A major example of this was the various efforts of Bolton's still numerous cotton hand-loom weavers to secure some form of statutory wage regulation in the 1830s. These came after cut-throat competition had first reduced them to such a pitiful state of dependence that orthodox trade-union methods were largely ineffective, even among the town's more specialist fancy weavers.[84] In turn, the debasement of the hand-loom weavers presented an example to all, on a massive scale, of the ruinous effects of cut-throat competition. As a Bolton manufacturer said to the Select Committee on Weavers in 1834:

> ... when some of our weavers went to certain mills to solicit subscriptions for taking measures for their relief, the spinners said if you get secured we are right, but as long as we have the great example of your oppression we are never safe, we may be brought down to your condition.[85]

Experiences and threatened eventualities were thus important elements of working-class consciousness, and the attack on competition also provided the stimulus for workers to attempt to equalise wages and conditions within their own trades through inter-trade cooperation, firstly through the N.A.P.L. (1829–32), and later the N.A.U.T. (formed 1845).[86]

The technological threats and divisions of labour processes, experienced by a wide range of trades, were also part of the economic basis of working-class consciousness. By the 1830s even workers in relatively privileged trades were finding their position under attack. Thus, for James Pendlebury, hand-loom weaver and Chartist:

That part of the working men which had been in a prosperous condition, such as the mechanics, &c., had not taken so active a part as they ought to have done. But where would be their prospects in a few years? They were fast sinking to the slavish and degraded condition of the spinner. They knew what the condition of the spinner was, and he declared that if he had a choice to make between becoming a spinner and a hand-loom weaver, he should prefer the latter. Humble and miserable as it was, he should weave, until he was grey, before he would endure the sufferings and hardships which were borne by the spinner.

Pendlebury attributed the deteriorating position of the workers to political corruption rather than economic causes. The significance of this was the way in which a political interpretation of exploitation seems to have a hand in mitigating criticism of the economic role of employers. Thus, although it was the 'decided opinion' of Pendlebury that 'the middle class were the enemies of the people', in that they 'laid hold of every fresh scheme to cheapen labour and increase profits', because economic grievances were constantly referred back to the political system, he did not primarily condemn them as employers of labour, but by reason that 'numbers of them said they could like the people's charter; but they were in easy circumstances, and, therefore, would not lift a finger to help the cause along'.[87]

During the years 1838 to 1842 the actual experience of the intensification of economic exploitation came closer than ever before to contradicting radical assumptions about the origins of oppression and misery. But the more economic explanations of exploitation which appeared in radical arguments during those years still continued to be accommodated within a radical analysis of society which ascribed economic evils primarily to a political source. It will be recalled that the resolutions of the Bolton spinners in the Plug Strikes, for example, attributed the 'evils' that they laboured under to 'class legislation'. The Plug Strikes may have been triggered by underlying economic grievances, as the course of the spinners' involvement subsequently revealed,[88] but for one Bolton Chartist at least, they were for the Charter and political:

> If the strike were not for the Charter, what had the mechanics, mill wrights, engineers, tailors, and shoemakers to do with it? They had no interest in the spinners' and weavers' strike. We certainly struck for the Charter ...[89]

This examination of industrial relations supports Robert Gray's view that 'the attitude to employers as such was not generally one of unqualified hostility, but rather of a concern to restore threatened reciprocities'.[90] Even the weavers did not consider the attack on competition to be necessarily anti-capitalist, and in fact many employers supported their campaign for some form of statutory wage regulation in the early 1830s.[91] In all trades, important distinctions were made between the 'fair' and the 'unfair' employers. There was the honourable and dishonourable in tailoring, as described above, and the weavers were also careful to differentiate the 'honourable masters' from the 'avaricious grinders' who were deemed responsible for deteriorating wages and conditions.[92] This perspective can also be seen in the argument of the committee of the Bolton spinners' union, which in 1830 maintained that relations with their employers ought to be characterised by 'mutual duties':

> For though an artizan, not in the service of a master owes no obedience; no sooner does he engage to exchange his labour with a richer fellow – subject for some stipulated renumeration, then his condition is changed: he then owes a reasonable obedience to his employer, and the employer acquires a reasonable authority over his servant.

For their part, the spinners' committee would ensure that 'drunkenness, dishonesty, neglect of work, or insolence to their employers, will be discountenanced by every member of the society; and their individual and collective support given to whatever promotes *peace, harmony*, and *friendship* among them'. On the other hand, because the spinners felt equally as competent as their employers to judge the state of the market for themselves, they were of the opinion that 'our strikes have been neither vexatious nor unjust'. They would remain aloof from attacks on property, political agitation, and violence, 'except against such unjust and oppressive employers, as attempted to make an arbitrary and uncalled for reduction of our wages'.[93]

The working-class analysis of exploitation was thus essentially experiential and conditional in nature and allowed for the possibility of considerable class manoeuvre and compromise. The stabilisation of the economy by 1850 provided the room for this compromise, while the continuing indeterminacy of capitalist authority in labour processes and the ability of trade unions to alleviate the dependency of their members upon market relations encouraged employers to adopt more benign social policies and managerial strategies. This was reflected in their increasing adoption of paternalistic practices which, in turn, were part of those wider community-based middle-class attempts to improve class relations which will come under focus in the next chapter.

Notes

1. *B.F.P.*, 10 February 1838.
2. The social composition of Chartism and its connections with working-class organisations in Lancashire have been covered in considerable detail in the following: D. S. Gadian, 'A Comparative Study of Popular Movements in North-West Industrial Towns 1830–1850', Lancaster University Ph.D thesis (1976); R. A. Sykes, 'Popular Politics and Trade Unionism in South-East Lancashire, 1829–42', Manchester University Ph.D thesis (1982); R. A. Sykes, 'Early Chartism and Trade Unionism in South-East Lancashire', in J. Epstein and D. Thompson (eds), *The Chartist Experience: Studies in Working-Class Radicalism and Culture, 1830–60* (London, 1982).
3. Cited in R. Sykes, 'Trade Unionism and Class Consciousness: The "Revolutionary" Period of General Unionism, 1829–1834', in J. Rule (ed.), *British Trade Unionism 1780–1850: The Formative Years* (London, 1988), p. 185.
4. Webbs' Trade Union Collection, Section A, IV, Bolton Trades Council, short sketch of history.
5. For a useful introduction to the campaign to extend factory legislation to the finishing trade, see B. Narey, 'The 1853–60 Ten Hours Movement in the Bleaching Industry with Particular Reference to the Response of the Master Bleachers of Bolton', Manchester Polytechnic M.A. Dissertation (1988).
6. J. Foster, *Class Struggle and the Industrial Revolution: Early Industrial Capitalism in Three English Towns* (London, 1974); G. S. Jones, 'Class Struggle and the Industrial Revolution', *New Left Review* 90 (1975); P. Joyce, *Work, Society and Politics: The Culture of the Factory in Later Victorian England* (London, 1980); N. Kirk, *The Growth of Working Class Reformism in Mid-Victorian England* (Beckenham, 1985).
7. C. Behagg, 'The Democracy of Work, 1820–1850', in Rule, *op. cit.*, p. 163; R. Price, *Labour in British Society: An Interpretive History* (London, 1986), p. 72.
8. *B.F.P.*, 18 June, 1, 15, 22 October, 12 November 1836, 11 November 1837; Sykes in Rule, *op. cit.*, pp. 186–91.
9. On this point I have arrived at a similar position to that reached by Price, *op. cit.*, ch. 4.
10. A wider range of trades is surveyed in P. F. Taylor, 'Popular Politics and Labour-Capital Relations in Bolton, 1825–1850', University of Lancaster Ph.D thesis (1991), ch. 4.
11. In 1830 Thomas Bruce, secretary of the Bolton spinners' union, claimed that the union was formed on 31 January 1795 (*B.C.*, 26 June 1830). Scattered newspaper references indicate that the union maintained a continued existence throughout the 1830s and 1840s. In 1836, for example, it covered 28 mills (*B.F.P.*, 1 October 1836), and in 1844, 29 mills (*B.C.*, 15 June 1844). Bolton had 69 mills in 1838, 61 in 1845. The 69 mills in 1838 employed 9,918 workers, an average of 143.7 per mill (D. S. Gadian,

'Class Consciousness in Oldham and Other North-West Industrial Towns', *The Historical Journal* 1, 1, 1978, p. 168). In 1841 the borough of Bolton had 55 cotton-spinning and weaving firms, employing 11,965 workers, an average of 217.5 per firm (R. A. Sykes, 'Some Aspects of Working-Class Consciousness in Oldham, 1830–1842', *The Historical Journal* 23, 1 (1980), p. 168). Later in the nineteenth century Bolton had the reputation of being the most completely organised of all spinners' unions (Webbs' Trade Union Collection, Section A, XXXV, 1, Bolton Spinners: Sketch of History).

12. Sykes, 'Popular Politics', ch. 3; Sykes in Thompson and Epstein, *op. cit.*, pp. 181–5.

13. Jones, *op. cit.*, pp. 51–4.

14. M. Huberman, 'The Economic Origins of Paternalism: Lancashire Cotton Spinning in the First Half of the Nineteenth Century', *Social History* 12, 2 (May 1987).

15. M. Rose, P. Taylor and M. J. Winstanley, 'The Economic Origins of Paternalism: Some Objections', *Social History* 14, 1 (January 1989), and the same source for Huberman's response: 'The Economic Origins of Paternalism: Reply to Rose, Taylor and Winstanley'.

16. Sykes in Thompson and Epstein, pp. 181–2; B.P.P. 1842, XXII, Reports by Inspectors of Factories, Report by Leonard Horner for the Quarter ending the 31st of Dec. 1841. For further information on the effects of technological change in mule-spinning, see M. Freifeld, 'Technological Change and the "Self-Acting" Mule: A Study of Skill and the Sexual Division of Labour', *Social History* 11, 3 (October 1986); W. Lazonick, 'Industrial Relations and Technical Change: The Case of the Self-Acting Mule', *Cambridge Journal of Economics* 3, 1979.

17. *The Bad Effects of Combinations of Workmen in the Town and Neighbourhood of Bolton-Le-Moors* (Manchester, 1823); J. Mason, 'Mule Spinner Societies and the Early Federations', in A. Fowler and T. Wyke (eds), *The Barefoot Aristocrats: A History of the Amalgamated Association of Operative Cotton Spinners* (Littleborough, 1987), p. 23. The 'count' of yarn refers to its fineness, being the number of hanks, each 840 yards in length, obtainable from a pound of yarn.

18. *B.C.*, 13, 27 March, 10, 17, 24 April, 8, 15 May, 12, 26 June, 10, 24 July, 7 August 1830; *Manchester Guardian*, 26 June 1830.

19. *B.C.*, 3, 10, 17 31 May, 14 June, 9, 23 August 1834.

20. *B.F.P.*, 4, 11 April 1840.

21. *B.F.P.*, 10 December 1836, 18 April 1840, for the system of references or discharge notes.

22. *B.A.*, ZZ/130/4/9, Parliamentary Election 1841 Series, Operative Cotton Spinners of Bolton to Bolton Electors.

23. *B.C.*, 8 October 1836.

24. *B.F.P.*, 29 April 1837.

25. *B.F.P.*, June 1840.

26. *B.F.P.*, 2 May 1840. For further evidence on the system, see *B.C.*, 13 November 1847, 1 July 1854; A. B. Reach, *Manchester and the Textile*

Districts in 1849, ed. C. Aspin (Helmshore, 1972), p. 49, and the grievances of the Bolton spinners in *B.C.*, 1 July 1854.

27. *B.C.*, 27 March 1830, for the apprenticeship system at the Ashworths; *Manchester Guardian*, 26 June 1830, for the system at the Bollings, where it had been in use since at least 1828. The system seems to have been in widespread use in the town since the early 1820s. In 1840 a Bolton spinner recalled how he commenced spinning in 1823, 'after the long and general turn out of the cotton-spinners in this town and neighbourhood ... at fifteen per cent under the list price, which is the usual way in which young spinners are introduced to the trade' (*B.F.P.*, 2 May 1840).

28. Taylor, 'Popular Politics', pp. 215–6. For strikes in the Bolton cotton industry in the third quarter of the 19th century, see P. F. Taylor, 'The New Paternalism and Labour-Capital Relations, c. 1848–1877', Manchester Polytechnic B.A. Dissertation (1986), ch. 3.

29. G. S. Jones, *Languages of Class: Studies in English Working Class History 1832–1982* (Cambridge, 1983), p. 14.

30. H. Catling, *The Spinning Mule* (Lancashire County Council, 1986), p. 118.

31. Cited in G. W. Daniels, 'A "Turn-Out" of Bolton Machine-Makers in 1831', *Economic History* (a Supplement to the *Economic Journal* 1, 1926–9), pp. 592–3.

32. A. E. Musson and E. Robinson, 'The Origins of Engineering in Lancashire', *Journal of Economic Society* 20, p. 211.

33. K. Burgess, *The Origins of British Industrial Relations: The Nineteenth Century Experience* (London, 1975), p. 5.

34. W. Fairburn is cited in Musson and Robinson, *op. cit.*, p. 211.

35. Burgess, *op. cit.*, pp. 3, 5–7.

36. *Ibid.*, pp. 10–13.

37. Cited in Daniels, *op. cit.*, pp. 594–5.

38. Cited in P. W. Pilling, 'Hick, Hargreaves and Co: The History of an Engineering Firm c. 1833–1939. A Study with Special Reference to Technological Change and Markets', Liverpool University Ph.D. thesis (1985), p. 19.

39. H. Ashworth, 'Statistics of the Present Depression of Trade at Bolton; Showing the Mode in which it Affects the Different Classes of a Manufacturing Population', *Journal of the Statistical Society* V (1842).

40. *B.C.*, 16 July 1859. The depression of 1858 also badly affected the society. In March of that year there were 1,572 out of 6,235 members 'on the funds', 1,333 of whom were out of work.

41. *B.F.P.*, 20 August 1842.

42. Daniels, *op. cit.*, pp. 594–5.

43. *Ibid.*; G. W. Daniels, 'The Organisation of a "Turn-Out" of Bolton Machine-Makers in 1831', *Economic History* (a Supplement to the *Economic Journal* 2, 1930–3); *B.C.*, 11 June, 30 July, 17 September 1831; *Manchester Guardian*, 18 June, 9, 23 July 1831.

44. Taylor, 'Popular Politics', pp. 224–5.

45. See Burgess, *op. cit.*, pp. 9–11, for developments leading to the formation of the A.S.E. and the 1852 lockout.

46. *B.C.*, 13 March 1852.
47. *B.C.*, 10, 17, 24 January 1852.
48. Burgess, *op. cit.*, ch. 1, for the main development phases of the nineteenth-century British engineering industry. For examples of the conflict in engineering in the 1860s, see the material relating to disputes at the firm of Dobson and Barlow between 1865 and 1868 in Bolton Archives, ZDB/2 collection.
49. Sykes, 'Popular Politics', table 2.4. It was still possible for small masters and journeymen to unite in the same organisations in the early 1830s. The Bolton United Society of Plumbers and Glaziers, for instance, 'which was established to secure the interests of both masters and men', celebrated its anniversary in 1831 (*B.C.*, 15 January 1831). Structural changes were making such bodies irrelevant, however, and they seem to have disappeared after the formation of the Operative Builders' Union later in the same year.
50. R. Price, *Masters, Unions and Men: Work Control in Building and the Rise of Labour 1830–1914* (Cambridge, 1980), pp. 22–34.
51. *B.C.*, 3 April 1869.
52. Burgess, *op. cit.*, p. 106.
53. *Ibid.*; Sykes, 'Popular Politics', pp. 315–8; S. and B. Webb, *The History of Trade Unionism* (London, 1911), pp. 112–7.
54. *B.C.*, 13 July 1833, for a report of a conference of master builders at Preston, attended by Heaton and Marsden. The first resolution passed at this conference indicates that the main issue in the dispute was that of authority: 'That it is the decided opinion of this meeting, that it is utterly impossible for any Master Tradesman to maintain his legitimate authority, to fulfil his engagements to his employers, or to enter into any Contract with safety, so long as the General Trades Unions are in existence, it being now clear that the object of these Unions is an improper interference with the private concerns of the employer, and the destruction of that subordination without which society itself cannot exist.'
55. *B.C.*, 7, 28 April, 7 July 1832, 23 August 1834. In 1844 there was an arson attempt on Thomas Graham's timber-yard during a dispute between Graham and the sawyers' union over the employment of non-union labour (*B.C.*, 19, 26 October 1844).
56. *B.C.*, 2, 9, 16 May 1846; *B.F.P.*, 2, 16 May 1846.
57. *B.C.*, 16 May 1846; *B.F.P.*, 16 May 1846.
58. *B.C.*, 2, 9, 16, 23 May, 6 June, 11 July 1846; *B.F.P.*, 16, 23, 30 May, 4, 11 July 1846.
59. *B.C.*, 6, 13 August, 1, 22 October 1853.
60. *B.C.*, 30 March 1861.
61. *B.C.*, 14, 21, 28 June, 12, 19 July, 9 August, 6, 13 September, 4 October 1862, 22 October 1864, 12 August, 2 December 1865.
62. *B.C.*, 2, 16, 23 February, 19 May, 18 August, 27 October, 3 November, 1, 22 December 1866, 2, 9 March, 6, 13 July, 7 September, 30 November 1867, 1 February, 30 May, 13 June, 26 December 1868, 3, 24 April, 1, 8, 15, 22 May, 10 July 1869.

63.   *B.C.*, 28 September 1867.
64.   Price, *Labour in British Society*, p. 26; E. P. Thompson, *The Making of the English Working Class* (Harmondsworth, 1968), pp. 282–5.
65.   *B.F.P.*, 17 February 1844.
66.   *B.F.P.*, 29 March 1845.
67.   *B.F.P.*, 16 March, 6 April 1844.
68.   At a meeting in March 1844 one speaker complained that the slop shops 'monopolised the business of the trade' (*B.F.P.*, 16 March 1844).
69.   *B.F.P.*, 27 September 1845.
70.   *B.C.*, 27 October, 3 November 1860, 1 April 1865, 14, 21 April 1866, 28 September 1867.
71.   Burgess, *op. cit.*, p. 165.
72.   For further explanation of this point, see Price, *Labour in British Society*, p. 76.
73.   Detailed information on the working conditions of local miners can be found in: B.P.P. 1842, XVII, Reports to Commissioners: Children's Employment (Mines); J. Black, *A Medico-Topographical, Geological, and Statistical Sketch of Bolton and its Neighbourhood* (1837, copy available in Bolton Reference Library), pp. 18–29; Taylor, 'Popular Politics', pp. 239–45.
74.   Black, *op. cit.*, p. 27.
75.   R. Challinor, *The Lancashire and Cheshire Miners* (Newcastle, 1972), p. 26; *B.C.*, 3 September 1831 (a public address issued in conjunction by the Coal Miners' Society and the 'Trades' National Association for the Protection of Labour', warning landlords, shopkeepers and small traders that members of the above societies would take their custom elsewhere if they purchased coal from any masters who were trying to force them to quit their unions or enforce reductions).
76.   *B.C.*, 25 September, 2, 9 October 1830.
77.   *B.C.*, 5, 26 March, 2, 9, 16 April 1831.
78.   *B.C.*, 14 May 1831.
79.   *B.C.*, 14, 21 May 1831; Challinor, *op. cit.*, pp. 26–8.
80.   Over 13,000 miners originally came out on strike. By early February the strike was reported as being nearly at an end and that, with the price of coal rising, some masters were conceding advances. Other masters, however, prosecuted workers for breach of contract. By early March only 1,500 miners were still out: *B.C.*, 16, 23 January 1841; *B.F.P.*, 2 January, 2, 6 February, 6 March 1841; Challinor, *op. cit.*, pp. 32–3.
81.   *B.F.P.*, 8, 22 June, 27 July, 28 September, 23 November 1844. Despite this recruitment drive, it seems that union density in the Bolton area was already high. Early in January 1844 a delegate meeting of the union took place in Manchester. The delegate from Great Hulton represented 1,345 colliers, Little Lever 419, Worsley 400 and Bolton 540, a total of 2,714 colliers. The union's performance in north Staffordshire was much less impressive; 3,000 colliers were organised, but this was out of a total of 10,000 in the area. This had a bearing on union strategy, for there were enough coal stocks to supply the mills of Manchester for six weeks, and for

one delegate 'it would be useless for the Lancashire union to strike as long as there was 7,000 pit men in Staffordshire who had not joined the Union. The canals were open and they could supply the Manchester market with any quantity of coal they required' (*H.O. 45/434; H.O. 45/645*).

82. More details of this strike can be found in R. Challinor and B. Ripley, *The Miners' Association: A Trade Union in the Age of the Chartists* (London, 1968); Taylor, 'Popular Politics', pp. 244–5.
83. *B.C.*, 25 October, 29 November, 6 December 1851.
84. For a detailed account of the cotton hand-loom weavers in Bolton see Taylor, 'Popular Politics', pp. 226–32.
85. B.P.P. 1834, X, *op. cit.*, Q5177; D. Bythell, *The Handloom Weavers: A Study in the English Cotton Industry during the Industrial Revolution* (Cambridge, 1969), pp. 178–9, for a different view on the attitudes of the spinners to the decline of the weavers.
86. The N.A.P.L. was formed in Manchester late in 1829, while the propriety of the trades of Bolton joining this 'Union Of All Trades' was first considered at a stormy public meeting in November of the same year. The hand-loom weavers were the first Bolton workers to affiliate, and they were soon followed by another dozen trades. In 1831, however, the Bolton Trades' Union virtually seceded and maintained at best strained relations with the Manchester committee after disagreements over questions of local autonomy and the management of the central strike fund (*B.C.*, 21 November, 5 December 1829, 12 March, 2, 16 April 1831; R. G. Kirby and A. E. Musson, *The Voice of the People: John Doherty, 1798–1854. Trade Unionist, Radical and Factory Reformer* (Manchester, 1975).

    The N.A.U.T. was another attempt to establish a general trades' federation, which enjoyed a far lower level of success in Bolton than the N.A.P.L. The Miners' Association leaders David Swallow – for whom 'Competition was the root of all evil – over-production created misery – it was remorseless, relentless, and yet might be so easily destroyed' – and William Dixon were active in promoting the N.A.U.T. in the town in 1846, lecturing to fairly large meetings of operatives and counterpane weavers (*B.C.*, 2 May 1846; *B.F.P.*, 31 January, 2 May 1846). But they appear to have enjoyed little success and no activity was reported in subsequent years.
87. *B.F.P.*, 22 June 1839.
88. Taylor, 'Popular Politics', pp. 215–6.
89. *B.F.P.*, 27 August 1842.
90. R. Gray, 'The Deconstructing of the English Working Class', *Social History* 11, 3 (October 1986), p. 372.
91. *B.C.*, 13, 20 April 1833.
92. Taylor, 'Popular Politics', pp. 231–2.
93. *B.C.*, 26 June 1830.

CHAPTER SIX

Paternalism and
Class Reconciliation

Historians seeking explanations of the transition to the social stability of the mid-Victorian period have noted important changes in middle-class attitudes. This development is usually interpreted as an attempt to re-establish social order following the years of working-class political insurgency and the conflict-ridden period of trade-union development from 1829 to 1842. Focusing primarily on ideological developments Tholfsen, for instance, has described a 'mellowing of middle-class liberalism, 1834–51', involving a gradual move away from 'the repressive spirit of 1834' to 'a more benign social policy'.[1] Studies which have concentrated largely on developments in the cotton districts have tended to place more emphasis on the relationship between changing economic structures and consciousness. From the viewpoint of these, the success of middle-class initiatives is seen as deriving from their interplay with changes in labour processes or the stabilisation of industrial capitalism.

Joyce thus described the growth of a powerful employer paternalism from mid-century, the success of which he attributed to its role in healing the wounds of working-class dependency left by the consolidation of mechanised production in the factory.[2] Changes in work practice and organisation were accorded similar prominence in a study of Oldham by Foster, who saw the creation of new authority structures at work as comprising the key element in a 'liberalisation' process which he described as a deliberate and conscious bourgeois attempt to defuse the working-class discontent of the 1830s and early 1840s.[3] Kirk attached central importance to the effects of a restabilised capitalism which enhanced scope for class manoeuvre and compromise. His interpretation further differed from Foster's in suggesting that changes and 'concessions "from above" often came about more *as a response* to the newfound "moderation and restraint" of the working class, rather than as the direct consequence of working-class militancy'.[4] But he followed Foster and Joyce in placing the timing of such developments in the late 1840s, noting one important aspect of the mellowing of middle-class attitudes as paternalism, which 'can be interpreted as an

181

attempt to develop worker loyalty to the employer at a time when class conflict and mass commitment to the Charter had already lost much of their earlier force'.[5]

It will be recalled from earlier arguments, however, that developments in the labour process were not necessarily central to the onset of social stability. On the contrary, while changes in work practice were important, capitalist managerial authority at work was far from complete and workers continued to exercise a considerable degree of control over labour processes and labour markets. The growth of employer paternalism from the 1840s was in large part a reflection of these continuing limitations of capitalist managerial authority. Paternalism too had its limits, which allowed expressions of working-class independence and class conflict to continue on a scale sufficient to dispel Joyce's portrayal of class harmony. The Bolton evidence does not support Foster and Joyce's view that a sharp break in social relations was associated with workplace reorientation at mid-century.

Rather, the case has been made that the mid-Victorian compromise in production relations at mid-century owed much to economic stabilisation and the way in which radical ideology helped to shape the working-class political response to industrial capitalism. Employers and workers had always recognised some degree of mutuality and reciprocity in their relations with each other, even at the heights of class tension, and the latter did not view the intensified exploitation of the 1830s and early 1840s as a necessary function of capitalist relations of production. Criticisms of employers for failing to uphold agreements on wages and conditions were couched primarily in moral terms, even when made from the perspective of the radical analysis of society. Thus, while demands for a more controlled system of production featured strongly in Chartist arguments between 1840 and 1842, the 'evils' associated with unregulated economic growth continued ultimately to be attributed to political rather than economic causes. All this meant that, while local Chartists such as John Gillespie often denounced the factory system, the economic practices of groups such as the millowners were never an insurmountable barrier to cooperation between the classes in reform movements.[6] For example, the Liberal candidates in the 1841 election – Ainsworth and Bowring – received the backing of the spinners' union. This was despite the fact that the union's officials – Howarth and Rothwell – doubled as leaders of the factory movement, and regardless of Bowring's well-known opposition to factory reform.

The roots of the mid-Victorian 'consensus', therefore, were already evident in the 1830s. There was never a widespread call for the overturning of capitalist relations of production. Chartism was never an exclusively working-class movement, and the movement of radical workers into Liberalism did not signify political deference or the betrayal of radical working-class politics. Workers, attracted by Liberal objections to political and financial monopolies, were already becoming attached to Liberalism in the 1830s, and from the 1840s few radicals had diffi- culty in coming to terms with an 'advanced' Liberalism that continued to agitate for some measure of parliamentary reform and for the erosion of aristocratic privilege.

This is not to deny that Chartist policy was partly dictated by tactical considerations. In parliamentary elections, for instance, their support for Liberals derived in large part from their inability to mount their own serious challenge. But the Liberals received strong working-class support nevertheless, and the Chartists gave enthusiastic support to the Liberal candidate Dr Bowring in the 1841 and 1847 parliamentary elections – after he had been sufficiently forthcoming on the question of the 'six points'. The pattern of events was a little different during the last major upsurge of Chartism in 1848, but important continuities were again present.

During this campaign Bolton Chartism apparently drew much of its strength from an alliance between English Chartists and Irish repealers, who staged some demonstrations in late July and early August.[7] The middle class did not play a major role in the movement in 1848 and the earlier pattern of formal trade-union support of organisations was not repeated.[8] In the parliamentary by-election of September 1848 the Chartists put forward a candidate for the first time, Joseph Barker, who won the show of hands (he did not contest the poll). However, this development is put into perspective by the fact that the Liberals did not contest the election.[9] The Chartists considered fielding another candi- date in the by-election scheduled for early 1849, but this was only after they had suffered the disappointment of failing to secure a pledge to support the Charter from the Liberal candidate Joshua Walmsley.[10] Some working-class radicals may have continued to aspire to the Charter as the primary aim after 1848, but they were apparently a small minority.[11] From now on, the theme of more limited (though 'progressive') parlia- mentary reform was the popular rallying cry and one which firmly united reformers in the 1850s.[12] The riots of 1839, the strikes of 1842, the success of 1846 and the events of 1848 did not deflect local middle- class Liberals from their commitment to further parliamentary reform. Indeed, Bolton was the only town in Lancashire where the National Parliamentary and Financial Reform Association received significant support.[13]

It would seem, therefore, that what was required from the middle class was not a series of initiatives in the 1840s aimed at transforming social relations, but measures which brought out the essential features of the class collaboration already sketched out, especially the pushing forward of the middle class as leaders of a variety of political and social reform movements on a scale sufficient to improve their image.[14]

This was far from an untroubled process, however, as an examination of middle-class attempts to reform aspects of working-class morals and culture reveals. Local evidence suggests that the concrete results produced by those 'patronage' associations run by the middle class but intended mainly for a working-class membership were not substantial enough to account for an abrupt transformation in working-class consciousness and behaviour. This lends further support to my view of a slow, troubled and, in some respects, incomplete consolidation of middle-class hegemony, rather than a climacteric in social relations at mid-century. There is no sustained evidence of a major shift in employer commitment to social welfare provision in the years around 1850. As the sections on sanitation and local government have shown, and as those on adult education and cultural provision for the working class will further demonstrate, the class struggle did not sufficiently impress upon the middle class an urgency to sink their religious and political differences and make more positive contributions in those areas. It will also be shown below that there is insufficient evidence to suggest that the initiatives undertaken had much direct effect on working-class attitudes and behaviour. Few attended the Mechanics' Institute or cleansed themselves in the public baths. Moreover, it is not clear from the local evidence whether the impact of education can be measured more obviously in terms of the inculcation of moral values than in advances in basic numeracy and literacy. On the industrial front, paternal strategies were more in evidence, but such expressions of employer 'concern' for the welfare of their hands could not prevent the persistence of conflict, albeit at a lower level of frequency and intensity, and class struggle remained an integral part of capitalist relations of production. All this is not to deny that the revitalisation of middle-class paternalism and philanthropy were important elements in attempts at class reconciliation. Rather, it is to put them into historical context by assessing their impact relative to other forces promoting consensus.

For while paternalism did play a role in helping to transform the image of the middle class, the success of certain campaigns which had joint middle- and working-class support had a much greater impact, consolidating their role as the leaders of a variety of reform movements. Some of these, such as the repeal of the duties on raw cotton in 1845 and corn in 1846, have already received attention. In many respects, the 1830s was also an important decade for collaboration. In the discussion on the temperance movement it will be shown that middle-class temperance reformers were able to establish an early convergence with working-class teetotallers in the 1830s, a development usually held to be one delayed until the later 1840s, when the early connections between teetotalism and radicalism are deemed to have weakened. The mellowing state of the relations between labour and capital in the centrally important cotton industry was also important. As will be shown, labour leaders in that industry displayed an increased level of moderation towards their employers from about the mid-1840s, giving some support to Kirk's view that changes in middle-class attitudes were often provoked by the new-found moderation of labour leaders. Also important in this general process of class negotiation were changes in the character of the Victorian state and an accommodation to factory reform on the part of the middle class, a development which is also discussed below. All of this increased hopes of gradual reform, strengthening the position of the moderate reformers at the expense of the militant Chartists, while the image of the middle class was actually enhanced by their involvement in these reform movements, rather than tarnished, as the militant Chartists and some historians have argued.[15]

Paternalism and authority

This section examines the suggestion that the emergence of social stability in the cotton-factory towns of north-west England owed much to the development of a powerful employer paternalism from the 1840s, the provision of the likes of schools, reading-rooms, dinners and excursions being said to have played a significant role in helping to reduce social tensions and cultural divisions between capital and labour.[16] It will be suggested that, while this development was apparently a new trend, in that paternalism was at least much more visible in urban factories from the 1840s, the spread of paternalism can nevertheless be described as the extension and consolidation of more traditional aspects of authority structures and managerial strategies, the paternal and patriarchal model long being a feature of employment relations in the factory. It is further argued that, while paternalism registered some successes both in 'country mills' and urban environments, its overall impact should not be exaggerated, for it did not necessarily make a key contribution to social reconciliation.

David Roberts locates early factory paternalism among the rural 'factory villages' of the Industrial Revolution. It was both experience and necessity which defined this early 'village mill paternalism', for where there were cascading streams, there was often little else. Schools, houses, stores and churches were deemed necessary both to attract labour and to discipline it through evictions and indoctrination.[17] However, in all probability – in the 1830s and early 1840s at least – paternalism and positive attempts by employers to secure the loyalty of their hands were less ubiquitous in the main urban areas.[18]

Most local evidence before the Plug Strikes does indeed come from industry situated in the rural and semi-rural townships surrounding Bolton. In mining, it seems to have been mainly restricted to the largest coal-owners, who appear to have used it as a strategy to compensate for their limited managerial control in underground situations. The aristocratic Francis Egerton built model housing, churches and schools, and established sick-benefit and superannuation societies, clothing clubs, saving banks, and dispensaries which gave medical care to all.[19] Egerton once informed Russell in 1839 that, despite the 'severe distress' induced by economic depression, the attempts of the Chartists to attract support among his miners and others in the Bolton coalfield 'has produced nothing'. It was only in the area around Heywood near Bury, 'where few men of influence and property reside', that the Chartists had met with success.[20] Yet Egerton's paternalism could not prevent the regular occurrence of industrial conflict, and the situation was the same at Hulton's collieries. During a strike in 1831 William Hulton claimed that 'I have never been so happy as in relieving yourselves and your families, under the pressure of sickness and distress; that I have, to the utmost of my power, extended the blessings of education to your children'; therefore, in striking, 'You have wantonly injured me to the full limits of your ability, in my purse; and you have have further wounded my feelings.'[21] Following the termination of the dispute, Hulton vowed never to employ trade unionists again and set up the anti-union Colliers' Association, under his patronage, to provide insurance cover for his workers in the event of sickness, injury or death. There is some evidence that, in the long term, such acts may have improved the standing of the Hulton family in the eyes of their workers.[22] But it is also significant that in the 1830s and 1840s Hulton and Egerton had reputations for being the lowest-paying masters in the area, and their benevolence could not prevent their colliers from involving themselves in the strikes which made mining one of the most conflict-ridden industries in the Bolton area across the second and third quarters of the century.

Paternalistic employers were far more common in the bleaching establishments situated in the northern townships of the Bolton Poor Law Union. Among the leading practitioners were the Ridgways of the village of Wallsuches near Horwich, whose paternalism was overlain with pretensions to squirarchical status. Not only did the family hunt and preside over the Cattle Fair Society, they were also patrons of the local school, building club and sick society. They also built a church, the opening of which in 1830 provided an occasion to regale the workforce, as did the celebrations of Thomas Ridgway's twenty-first birthday in 1838, when 400 workpeople were joined by about 100 'ladies and gentlemen'.[23] Another notable example in bleaching was the Ainsworths of Smithills, who also acted out a squirarchical role and practised an employer paternalism, and who, from about the mid-1830s, extended their influence beyond the workplace to the township of Halliwell through the provision of schools, churches and other 'substantial donations'.[24] Bleachworks were typically large scale,[25] which meant that employers could well afford the paternalistic strategies which appear to have been adopted by most of the large employers by the mid-1840s. In January 1846 alone, Thomas Cross provided what was by then an annual dinner to the 120 bleachers and finishers in his employ, and the firms of Richard and Thomas Barton, Stephen Blair (who was at the time the mayor of Bolton) and R. H. Summer laid on similar treats.[26]

Paternalism in bleaching seems to have registered some successes in what was a relatively conflict-free industry. There was a movement among the operatives for an equalisation of prices over the winter of 1831–2, but this was easily crushed by the powerful employers' organisation (the Bleachers' Association) and strikes were rare thereafter. Bleaching appears to have been the only major local industry where production continued uninterrupted during the Plug Strikes of 1842, and the operatives were unable to maintain a durable organisation until the campaign to extend the Factory Acts to finishing works began in the mid-1850s.[27] Cotton-spinning also furnished a few notable examples. The Ashworth enterprises at Turton were the best known, but Gardner and Bazley's Dean Mills and 'model village' at Barrow Bridge near Halliwell also aroused considerable interest among contemporaries.[28]

Paternalism appears to have been much less common in the main urban area before the 1840s, and I have found only one example of mutual celebrations before then – the Coronation celebrations in 1838, when a number of the larger employers provided feasts for their workers.[29] However, it appears to be the case that, directed by enlightened economic self-interest, public criticism of the factory system, concern over middle-class status and the wider social role of the employer, paternalistic practices were at least much more in evidence in urban Bolton from the mid-1840s, when they became a highly visible feature of industrial relations in those key industries where larger-scale firms and production units predominated – that is, cotton-factory spinning and manufacturing, and engineering.

The apparently greater concern of employers for the welfare of their hands was manifest in its more ephemeral form in the likes of treats for the workforce, celebratory dinners and trips to the seaside or the countryside. There is plentiful evidence of such acts of benevolence, a few examples of which must suffice to illustrate. To take cotton factories first: in May 1845 the Tory-Methodist Robert Knowles celebrated twenty-five years' ownership of the four factories with a soirée which was attended by over 250 of his workers.[30] In 1852 the paternalistic P. R. Arrowsmith served up 'liberal quantities' of beef sandwiches, plum cake, and 'barley bree' for 800 of his workers in celebration of the recent Liberal success in the parliamentary election.[31] In 1853 J. and G. Knowles treated 300 of their employees and some of their relatives to a trip to Fleetwood.[32]

Such occasions, over which the employer and members of his family usually presided, were often held to celebrate the bestowal of more permanent provision, such as libraries or reading-rooms. The occasion of a soirée in 1845 at the Liberal Unitarian P. R. Arrowsmith's Gilnow Mills, situated on the outskirts of the town, was to celebrate the opening of the Lever Street School and Reading-Room provided by the firm. This included a library which held over 400 volumes by April 1846, when Arrowsmith celebrated his son attaining his majority by providing his workers with dinner and entertainments.[33] The Christmas party thrown in 1848 by Robert Knowles for his employees was in celebration of the opening of an 'efficiently warmed and ventilated reading room'.[34] The provision of what became an annual tea-party by the firm of W. Martin and Son was in promotion of the mill school. Established in 1849 for the benefit of the workforce, by 1853 the institution was patronised by over 2,000 persons.[35]

Instances of formal celebrations in the engineering industry also appear to have proliferated after the Plug Strikes. In November 1842, for example, Thomas Dobson, son of the late Benjamin Dobson, regaled his workers on the occasion of his twenty-first birthday.[36] In November 1843 the ironfounder Thomas Jackson entertained about 100 of his workers at the Horse Inn in celebration of his recent marriage, and the workmen employed at Messrs. Musgrave's iron foundry were similarly catered for following the marriage of Ellen Musgrave to the timber-merchant Joseph Marsden.[37]

For their part, workers seem to have appreciated such acts of benevolence, for there were instances of similar initiatives from the operatives – as in December 1845, when about 200 of the workpeople at Henry and Edmund Ashworth's New Eagley Mills organised a tea-party for themselves and their employers, in order to express their gratitude for the provision of books and equipment in the local Sunday school.[38] Cannon and Haslam established a sick society to provide insurance cover for their workers, but when their spinners entertained their employers over dinner in June 1845, it was a response to the firm's immediate implementation of a 5 per cent wage increase granted to the Bolton spinners by the masters – the usual practice was for wage movements to require two weeks' notice either way.[39] Early in 1846 the workers in the employ of the bleacher Harrison Blair 'presented their esteemed master with a beautiful silver cup, on which was engraved a suitable inscription, expressing their gratitude and esteem'.[40] The paternalism of Robert Knowles was continued by his sons, George and John, who in 1852 were each presented with a silver cup from the operatives in their employ 'as a token of gratitude and esteem' for their 'honourable, upright, and disinterested philanthropy'.[41]

There is some evidence of the effectiveness of the facilities provided by the leading paternalists. The Ashworths maintained a rigorous supervision of their workforce, requiring them to be sober, industrious, respectable and regular attenders at church. Their factory school was generally considered to be excellent and 98 per cent of the hands could read and 48 per cent could write.[42] The model industrial village at Barrow Bridge was developed over the 1830s and 1840s by Robert Gardner, already a millowner, and Thomas Bazley, a local merchant. The social policy was more relaxed here and Gardner and Bazley built no church or public house, maintaining that both were socially divisive. No truck was practised and the village shop was managed by a group of workers on their own behalf.[43] Of the 691 hands employed by the firm on 15 April 1844, 688 could read,[44] and this was before the opening of the Barrow Bridge Institute in 1846, built and equipped by Gardner and Bazley at a cost of £3,000 to serve as the educational, recreational and social centre of the village.[45] The paternalism practised by the bleacher J. H. Ainsworth resembled that of the Ashworths in his concern to oversee the moral, cultural and educational condition of his hands. He conducted a survey of his workforce in 1834, which revealed that 227 of his 321 adult male workers could both read and write.[46]

It is easier to measure things like reading and writing, however, than it is to measure the instillation of suitable attitudes and values. Patrick Joyce calculates that the inculcation of thrift, respectability and sobriety touched only a minority of workers and that the ideological penetration into working-class life from above was limited; it was the recreational rather than the purely educative and self-improvement aspect of factory-based leisure facilities which was more apparent and which had the greatest impact. The hegemony of the large factory employers, he suggests, was culturally, rather than ideologically, based. His calculation that less than 10 per cent of adult male workers in later Victorian Lancashire were touched by 'the culture of improvement', across the whole range of factory- and non-factory-based institutions, seems a reasonable estimate.[47]

For it appears that few of Bolton's employers were prepared to provide workplace facilities for the pursuit of intellectual improvement.

At the opening of the Lever Street School and Reading-Room in 1845, the operative spinner Henry Turner intimated that 'education was not duly appreciated, and, consequently, institutions such as that were not so numerous as they otherwise would be'.[48] Turner was hopeful for the future, that 'that day was not far distant when every workshop would have a similar institution', but this ideal was slow to catch on. In 1855 the *Bolton Chronicle* insisted:

> that those who derive their wealth from the labour of the working classes have peculiar duties imposed upon them ... they have peculiar opportunities of doing good beyond all others. In connection with our large establishments how easy it would be to establish schools for adult classes – libraries – cottage dwellings on improved principles, and other matters calculated to improve the minds and to ameliorate the physical condition of the working classes.

Yet, although some employers had set noble examples in this respect, 'very few' manufacturers had as yet fulfilled the duties incumbent upon them.[49]

Even at those establishments where employers did meet their social 'obligations', it is clear that workers did not necessarily internalise the paternalist ethos. The Ashworths had trouble with their spinners, who apparently placed more faith in trade unionism than the milk of benevolence to protect them from the vicissitudes of trade. Trade unions were an implicit challenge to the ethics of the Ashworth's autocratic brand of paternalism and were not tolerated by the firm.[50] Henry Ashworth dismissed seven spinners for membership of the union in 1842 and five in 1844, amid complaints from the union that, while the benefits of paternalism were appreciated, they did not compensate for wages which were lower than those paid by other firms in the area.[51]

Paternalism did record some notable successes. The more relaxed social policy of Gardner and Bazley was apparently successful – there were no recorded strikes at Dean Mills. The Tory bleacher Thomas Ridgway once proudly boasted that 'he had a large number of workmen in his employ, and there was not one of them who was not a Conservative'.[52] While this statement may be received with a fair degree of scepticism, the enthusiasm with which Ridgway's workers celebrated Conservative success in the south Lancashire parliamentary election of 1841 suggests that he was not far wide of the mark.[53] The spinners in the employ of the conspicuous paternalists Robert Knowles, Thomas Taylor and Messrs. Tomlinson did not join the spinners' union and refused to participate in the threatened spinners' strike of 1844, as did those in the employ of Messrs. Ormrod, who maintained stable wages whatever the vicissitudes of trade.[54] The treat may well have been ephemeral, but it may nevertheless have helped to foster feelings of mutuality. On such an occasion at Messrs. Heaton's Egyptian Mills in 1852, when the employers and workers partook of tea with their families, an address from the operatives to their employers stated that 'Social meetings of this nature do much to create and strengthen feelings of friendship and reciprocity between master and men.'[55]

Moreover, where employers provided facilities for rational recreation and aimed to encourage respectability and cultural 'improvement' among their workforce (by offering an alternative attraction to the public-house culture, but without necessarily trying to regulate their leisure time), liberal individualism had a side which was compatible with collective forms and notions of self-help and mutuality. Tholfsen has noted – correctly, the local evidence suggests – that a recurrent theme in mid-Victorian ideology was that of the 'upright and independent working men freely assenting to the views of benevolent employers', the more benign forms of authority characteristically being more effective.[56] Such sentiments were typically expressed at the opening of Arrowsmith's reading-room at Lever Street and at the tea-party to celebrate the furnishing of a mill reading-room by Robert Knowles in 1848.[57]

As far as industrial relations more generally are concerned, however, it seems that paternalism was not the ultimate solution to class struggle. The persistence of economic conflict signified the limits to paternalism in mid-Victorian England. Joyce has portrayed the post-Chartist era rather differently and depicts social relations in Lancashire as being characterised by a remarkable level of class harmony. He concedes that trade unions remained as potential and, at times, actual organs of class struggle, but maintains that rapid developments in collective bargaining after 1850 meant that they actually complemented paternalism by helping to provide the stable economic environment which enabled it to thrive. Nowhere was this state of affairs more apparent than in the Lancashire cotton industry, which by 1893 had the most elaborate institutionalisation of labour relations anywhere in the kingdom.

Joyce argues that the Brooklands agreement of 1893 was in fact 'only the culmination and codification of the practice of industrial peace characteristic from the 1850s'.[58] It appears to be the case, however, that while labour leaders may well have spoken the language of conciliation and compromise, the centralisation and bureaucratisation of trade- union affairs was not sufficiently advanced to permit Joyce's institutionalised calm until beyond the 1870s. Until then at least, economic conflict and trade unionism continued to function as the major obstacles to the full incorporation of the working class. The conditions described by Joyce only really came into being from the 1880s, even in cotton-spinning, where developments were most advanced. In Bolton a well-organised spinners' union and the formation of a permanent masters' association in 1861 facilitated the consolidation of a recognised system of collective bargaining by the 1860s. But at this time procedures were still largely informal and voluntary and both sides relied upon the sanctions of convention rather than on formal, statutory rules and codes. A system of institutionalised collective bargaining was not demanded until the 1880s, when it emerged to meet the changing economic circumstances contingent upon cotton-spinning's adjustment to a less favourable market situation.[59]

The focus of middle-class concern for the working class went beyond the level of the workplace, and the spread of factory paternalism was complemented by the expansion and, to some extent, remodelling of the town's network of voluntary and municipal institutions from the later 1830s. Attention needs to be turned, therefore, to an examination of the wider philanthropic role of the middle class and to an assessment of the impact of the increasing rate of resources allocated to social reform (the focus will be mainly on the adult population), manifest in the growth of charitable, educational, temperance and other social-reforming institutions and by a more active and interventionist strategy into what the middle class identified and constructed as social problem areas in working-class life. Municipal reform assisted 'moral imperialist' strategies in this process by facilitating administrative intervention into working-class living conditions. These changes, together with the growth of civic pride, accentuated the wider social leadership role of the middle classes who were the patrons of the town's high culture as well as the custodians of its peace and the directors of its municipal development.

However, while the impact of middle-class philanthropy in the civil sphere was not without its successes, these should not be exaggerated. The institutional framework through which middle-class values were promoted and social problems alleviated was barely adequate to begin with; though it expanded in the 1840s, it was hard-pushed to cope with rapid population growth. Charity, temperance and educational activists were on the increase, but they found it difficult to make progress. Most workers preferred the conviviality of the public house – a focal point of working-class social activity – indulging in pastimes which middle-class moral reformers saw as unproductive, 'undisciplined' and 'disorderly', rather than partaking of those sober, 'rational' and 'improving' recreations prescribed as a remedy for social problems. Moreover, despite the increased earnestness of the middle class to regulate much of the non-working day of the working class, there was a further factor contributing to the frustration of this ideal. The spread of cultural and educational provision for the working class was further hampered by the same divisions within the middle class that hindered the development of the town's local government.

While the direct impact of middle-class attempts to pacify working-class opinion was limited, they may nevertheless have played a role in social reconciliation, the utilisation of more benign forms of authority helping to transform the popular image of the middle class. In this respect, their significance must be further assessed in the context of changes in the character of the Victorian state. This will be done in the discussion on factory reform that concludes this chapter. Anxieties over social order, public health and moral degeneration provoked a reconsid-eration of economic and social policy by the state. The resultant fiscal and social initiatives of the 1840s were designed to restabilise the economy and reconcile the working class to industrial capitalism. They marked a retreat from the aggressive economic liberalism that the state had promoted in the 1830s. It was this reorientation of state policy that shaped the broad agenda and construction of social reform through which social reconciliation was debated and negotiated at the local level.[60]

Adult education

Contemporaries always attached primary importance to educational provision in their attempts to promote a more secure acceptance of the existing social order, but a greater sense of urgency among religious leaders, social reformers and leading employers was clearly evident from the early 1840s. Most resources and energy were devoted to the education of young persons, but the central educative systems – the Sunday and day school networks – were ill-equipped to make a signif-icant contribution in this area; while there was an absolute increase in school accommodation during the 1840s, this barely kept pace with the rate of population growth. By the early 1850s large numbers of local children were still not part of the daily authority structures of the voluntary denominational and state-aided school system.[61]

The middle class also made greater efforts to provide educational facilities intended mainly for the adult members of the working class. For Bolton's Liberal-Anglican MP and bleacher Peter Ainsworth, speak-ing in December 1843, the initiative lay not with the state but with local persons of means and influence and the place to start was at the workplace:

The rich were called upon to assist those in humble life, to give them an opportunity of raising themselves in society by education ... he held that, where employers drew together large masses of people, it was for the welfare of both that their improvement in intelligence and morality should be carefully attended to. He should say that there was a great responsibility upon an employer, and he was much to blame if he did not do his duty in that respect, and especially to the children of the parents in his service ... Property had its duties, and they ought to be strictly fulfilled. It might be said to him had he always done so? He could say he had, and from the advantages which had resulted to himself and in his brother's works he would advise others to do the same. They would find advantages in the manners of their workpeople, in their confidence and satisfaction, which no time, no circumstances, could change (cheers).[62]

As suggested in the above discussion of employer paternalism, however, it would appear that few employers were to follow Ainsworth's example before 1850, and educational and cultural provision established by the middle class outside of the workplace, intended mainly for the adult members of the working class, also made a limited impact. All of this suggests that education provided by the middle class probably acted as a complementary rather than a directly causal factor of improvements in social relations. The growth of such provision may have been retarded by the limited working-class response to the endeavours of their would-be cultural leaders, but perhaps a greater contributory factor was the same denominational and political differences that had proved so disruptive in Bolton's political life. This gives further support to the suggestion made elsewhere in this book that intra- rather than inter-class relations were of more concern to the middle class. As the 1849 annual report of the Mechanics' Institution complained, social reconciliation and civic pride were often subverted by religious and political rivalry:

> Your committee are convinced that the reason why this Institution does not prosper, is also the reason why another is not erected in its stead – the same reason why the other public Institutions of this town do not prosper, namely, the bitterness of political and religious hate – a feeling ... rendering nugatory all efforts to establish popular institutions that shall not be characterised by any party complexion.[63]

The Mechanics' Institution was founded in 1825 and was at first well supported by Conservatives. Many familiar Tory names appear on the list of benefactors in 1826, including Hulton, Hardcastle, Hick, Ridgway Bridson, Knowles, Rothwell, Scowcroft and Ormrod,[64] but with the emergence of the parliamentary reform movement in the late 1820s, Tory support was largely withdrawn and the institution was boycotted thereafter by all but a few Conservatives. The stated reason for this Tory aloofness was the oft-alleged 'fact of Radicals, Chartists, and Sectarians having hitherto mixed themselves up largely in its affairs'.[65] The institution itself did not provide overtly political or sectarian literature for its members, but many radicals were nevertheless of the opinion that knowledge equalled power and urged workers to obtain a general education as the path to political emancipation through using whatever facilities were suitable or available, especially those of the institution, which in the 1840s had the town's largest public library (and the Bolton Mechanics' Institution concentrated on general rather than technical or scientific education). In 1831, for instance, 'the several societies which have been formed in Bolton and the neighbourhood, for instruction in political knowledge' formed the Society for Instruction in Political Knowledge, and the then radical *Bolton Chronicle* called on the members to join the Mechanics' Institution as a means of obtaining further valuable knowledge and, in turn, political freedom.[66] Such talk was anathema to Conservatives. Moreover, the institution implicated itself in the radical campaign against the newspaper stamp duty, the members signing petitions for its repeal in 1831 and 1836.[67]

The Tory boycott also indirectly affected the institution by promoting an adherence to rule twelve of its constitution. This aimed to conciliate opposition by excluding all literature of a theological or political character (including novels, plays and other fictional works) from the library. This rule amounted to a virtual ban on fiction, which contributed to the general dullness of an institution whose facilities were considered insalubrious; it was not relaxed until 1847, when agitation from the membership forced the middle-class patrons to amend the ban to cover only the more overt and controversial political, deistical, atheistical and theological works.[68] The institution failed to grow at the same rate as the town and membership remained small. About 120 joined in 1825 and there were only 240 in 1844. Moreover, its membership was far from being predominantly working class. In 1844, for instance, speakers at the annual meeting complained about the lack of working-class interest. T. R. Bridson, for example – one of the few Tories active in the management of the institution, whose support probably emanated from his friendship with Robert Heywood – 'regretted that the working classes had not taken that interest in such Institutions which for their own benefit they might have been expected to evince'. Bookkeepers, clerks and tradesmen accounted for 66 members in 1844, with only 80 persons being classed in the categories of mechanics, foundrymen, husbandmen, cotton-factory operatives, building and other handicrafts.[69]

In November 1846 plans were formulated to build a supplementary educational facility to the Mechanics' Institution, an Athenaeum, in an attempt to overcome Tory aloofness while simultaneously satisfying the need for new premises. The scheme was wrecked by a combination of continuing intra-middle-class conflict and popular pressure from below. The Conservative response was initially favourable, much to the satisfaction of its Liberal promoters.[70] Following an appeal for public donations, the estimated £5,000 cost of the project was soon raised. Subscription lists published in the press indicate that many Tories gave donations. For instance, Hick, T. R. Bridson, Slater, Knowles and others gave individual sums of between £100 and £250, and there were also lists of donations from workers under Tory employers. Those in the employ of the engineering firms of Hick, Rothwell, Dobson and Metcalf, and the bleachers Ridgway and Bridson each gave between £101 and £133 collectively.[71]

The parties then quarrelled at a public meeting over the question of the educational content to be promoted at the institution. A resolution that no day school be attached to the Athenaeum, on the grounds that it would raise religious differences, was supported by the Liberal P. R. Arrowsmith and the Tories Hick and Knowles. The resolution was eventually passed, but there was a strong feeling that, as working men had liberally contributed to the scheme, they should have a voice in its management, and Matthew Stevenson, a 'workingman' and Chartist, supported by the Liberal schoolmaster J. H. Raper, upset the apple cart by successfully moving a resolution demanding an amendment to rule fourteen of the institution's governing rules. Rule fourteen was intended to restrict the power to amend rules to the committee and was designed as a safeguard to rule eleven, which prohibited religious and political education from the institution. The amendment to rule fourteen meant that the rules could now be amended by the consent of 80 per cent of a general meeting. This raised the possibility that a future public meeting would sanction the establishment of a day school on a secular basis. Stevenson, a firm advocate of this idea, voiced his opinion that 'children might be educated without being crammed with church or chapel religion'. Arrowsmith himself declared that he had only voted against the establishment of a day school because of the possibility that religious instruction would be attached to it, for 'He would not assent that when a child learned its letters it should be crammed with theology. That was not the case with the middle classes. A parent should himself teach his child theology, or instruct some person to do it for him.' He tried to appease the Tories by further declaring that 'The working classes, however, ought to consider that, while they were dependent on middle class support, they must have middle class restrictions.' But the damage had been done. Tories were obviously not going to support an institution subject to a high degree of popular control. Reverend Slade had declared from the start that he 'could not support any system of education or general instruction, which was not based in religion, and conducted upon religious principle', and the Tories withdrew their subscriptions and diverted their support to his proposal for a Church Institute.[72] When depression hit the cotton districts in 1847, this project was postponed, but it was revived in 1851 and, as if to symbolise the Liberal-noncomformist/Tory-Anglican split, the Church Institute opened in 1855 – the same year that the Mechanics' Institution acquired its long-awaited new premises.[73]

Charity and philanthropy

Merely providing facilities to encourage working-class self-help clearly had its limitations. Where a more direct social intercourse between the classes was advocated, the middle class was able to use charity to effect a more activist and interventionist strategy in perceived problem areas of working-class life. The main local charity organisations, the Poor Protection Society (P.P.S.) and the Benevolent Society (B.S.), operated through a system of home visitors who inquired into the moral and material circumstances of applicants for relief. The visitors of the B.S., for example – the Liberal schoolmaster and temperance campaigner J. H. Raper prominent among them – armed with the 'acknowledged axiom' that 'property has its duties as well as its privileges', visited 682 families in 1845 alone.[74]

The strong sense of moral righteousness held by many middle-class persons meant that this kind of philanthropic activity often took the form of a prying inquisitiveness. Many middle-class philanthropists certainly believed that they possessed a superior set of attitudes and values to the morally deficient masses.[75] While many of them may have resisted the centralising tendencies of the New Poor Law and its harsh remedies, most nevertheless agreed with the analysis of poverty defined in the report of the Poor Law Commission of 1834, which saw poverty arising out of personal moral failings. As the following extract from the annual report of the P.P.S. for 1841 suggests, few middle-class persons saw poverty and its consequences as a function of the economic and social system. The system of home visiting would help to suppress mendicancy by ensuring that charitable relief would be given to the 'deserving poor' *only*, which would serve as a lesson to the morally undeserving and wilfully idle:

One object of this society is to provide a course of inquiry, by which such cases may be properly investigated, and their wants, if no impediment appear, be relieved. By this means the charitable have the satisfaction of knowing that their bounty is conferred upon deserving objects, instead of (as too frequently happens when alms are given indiscriminately at the door) being in most cases bestowed upon unworthy recipients ... In order to impress upon the poor a proper sense of the great importance ... of maintaining a good moral character ... they are given to understand that ... where falsehood, drunkenness, or any other flagrant immorality is detected, the case is dismissed as unworthy of consideration. By this means, it is hoped, that many may be brought to see the value of having a good name, who otherwise might never have been reminded at all of the expediency of virtuous conduct ... The practised beggar, who studies only how to move the feelings and interest his hearer, will tell a more heart-rending tale, than the hesitating, because unaccustomed, petitioner; who, though a greater sufferer, will not deign to resort to the arts of the other. To render justice to both these classes, by exposing the dishonesty of the one, and encouraging the reluctant approach of the deserving poor, is the end proposed by this society.[76]

In this way charity, presented the opportunity to effect a moral reformation and to inculcate in the individual the principles of self-help as a permanent remedy to poverty. And the patrons of the P.P.S. were confident that they could distinguish the genuine case from the fraudulent. Of the 2,564 applicants for relief in 1841, 1,087 were dismissed as unworthy. Among those, 127 characters were dismissed because they were considered 'bad and disorderly'. Another 40 were found to be 'drunkards', and another 60 to be vagrants.[77]

It is difficult to measure the effects that the activities of these organisations had on working-class morals and behaviour, but statistics on applicants were compiled which indicate that their work was not just confined to the poorer or unorganised sections of the working class, especially in years of depressed trade. Their work could even reach the best organised of workers, as was the case in 1841, when a wide range of 'artisanal' trades, including 200 spinners, appeared among the list of applicants for relief to the P.P.S.[78]

At the same time, direct middle-class involvement in working-class self-help institutions appears to have been on the increase, though again it is difficult to measure precise results. Trade unions continued to be impermeable to direct influence from above, though the middle class apparently achieved some success in their relations with friendly societies. During the Plug Strikes of 1842 many local benefit societies obeyed the Chartist call for the people to 'run for gold'. The committee of management of the Loyal Order of Druids issued a circular in the town, deprecating the acts of its members in the affair, but the benefit societies were nevertheless condemned by members of the middle class for withdrawing their funds from local banks and for the fact that some of them were believed to be functioning as 'secret societies'.[79] This may have encouraged the greater middle-class prominence in the activities of Bolton's leading Friendly Societies by the mid-1840s. The largest and most securely established, with a combined membership of over 10,000 by 1845, were the various branches of the Independent Order of Oddfellows, the Ancient Noble Order of United Oddfellows, and the Ancient Noble Order of Oddfellows of the Bolton Union. The town's Liberal MPs, Ainsworth and Bowring were made honorary members of the first organisation in 1843. Many familiar names appear among the benefactors and supporters of an attempt by the various bodies of Oddfellows to establish a Widow and Orphans' Fund in 1845 – the most prominent being John Slater (Tory bleacher and mayor), T. R. Bridson (Tory bleacher) J. Arrowsmith (Liberal cotton master) Bowring, J. H. Ainsworth (Liberal bleacher), P. Ainsworth, John Dean (Liberal Unitarian, first president of the Reform Association), Thomas Cullen (Liberal millowner), R. Walsh (magistrate) and John Taylor (borough coroner and a leading temperance activist).[80]

Progress in the areas of working-class housing and cleanliness was slower to materialise. Municipal reform and the documentation of the appalling conditions of urban areas in the 1840s promoted administrative intervention into working-class living conditions, but little was done before 1850. The Tory-Liberal conflict retarded this development up to the Improvement Act of 1850 and the town council experienced opposition to municipal improvement schemes from vested interests thereafter.[81] Only after that date was there effective municipal regulation of cellar dwellings and lodging-houses. The latter, for example, which had been condemned in the 1840s for their general squalor and communal sleeping arrangements, were blitzed in 1851 after the town council acquired increased regulatory powers. The result was that, within the space of three months, forty-one out of the town's eighty-three lodging-house keepers were successfully prosecuted and their establishments closed, inducing the remainder to raise the standards of their premises.[82] This development was reflective of an increased middle-class concern to safeguard the health as well as the morals of the working class. But while greater personal cleanliness could be encouraged, it could not be enforced or regulated, much to the disappointment of the paternalist J. H. Ainsworth. The Bolton Baths Company opened in 1847 to promote this object, but the working class did not readily avail themselves of the company's facilities. When, over the course of

1849, only 9,431 individual baths were taken by a population of about 60,000, Ainsworth said to the annual meeting of shareholders:

> This was a state of things deeply to be regretted; but he feared that they would not see a change, unless some sanitary regulations were adopted – unless they had a paid and independent commissioner to visit the dwellings of the poor, and enforce upon them the necessity of adopting habits of cleanliness ... So long as the poor were habituated to the sight of filth and indecencies the most disgusting ... no improvement could be expected; the lower classes must first be taught to acquire habits of decency and self-respect.[83]

Temperance

The temperance movement was an area in which an early degree of convergence was achieved between middle- and working-class reformers, strengthening the attachment of the 'respectable' section of the working class to the developing liberal consensus. Some temperance advocates supported Chartism, but, as we saw in Chapter Three, they were situated on the moderate wing of that movement, their willingness to consider individual moral reform distinguishing them from the militant Chartists who insisted that moral improvement could only be achieved through the prior achievement of political reform. As such, the connections between Chartism and temperance were not a serious obstacle to collaboration between reformers. Success was not unqualified, however. The popular culture centred around the public house proved to be largely impervious to the considerable efforts made to reform it. In the 1840s Bolton's temperance reformers broadened their social activities in an attempt to provide a set of counter-attractions to the 'pub', but the limitations of this approach were recognised as early as the middle of the same decade, when the emphasis shifted from moral persuasion to administrative restriction.

The first temperance society in Bolton was formed in 1831 by a group of middle-class Anglicans and was called the Moderation Society – a reflection of the fact that its principles were based upon abstention from spirits and the moderate use of beer and wine.[84] Teetotalism was established in the town in 1833, when, following a promotional visit by teetotal advocates from Preston, the New Temperance Society was formed.[85] Historians have pointed to the strong presence of working-class activists in the teetotal movement, whose fanatical zeal and connections with radicalism usually led to strained relations between moderationists and total abstainers. Brian Harrison has noted that, while there were early attempts at cooperation, 'when an anti-spirits society adopted the teetotal pledge, gentility usually departed in a hurry'.[86] In a more recent evaluation, Shiman has remarked that 'The fundamental spirit of teetotalism was so different from that of the traditional reform of the moderationists that any accommodation of the old principles by the new teetotallers was doomed to failure.'[87] There were affinities between the two stances in the form of a common commitment to education and individual moral reform as the means to self-improvement. For Tholfsen, however, these were submerged in the 1830s and 1840s beneath the radical and moderate perspectives that working-class teetotallers and middle-class moderationists brought to the movement. He argues that class-conscious working-class teetotallers did not seek accommodation with middle-class moderationists, but rather the transformation of the temperance movement's aims and principles, and that their independent stance was not eroded until the original associations with radicalism weakened in the 1850s, when they were assimilated into a movement that became dominated by middle-class cultural patterns.[88]

In Bolton, however, relations do not appear to have been strained and a fair degree of convergence was established in the 1830s. Dr Black noted that differences of opinion did exist between the town's 1,800 moderationists and 4,114 teetotallers in 1836,[89] and the Anglicans appear to have deserted the movement as teetotalism began to make its presence felt. With their departure, the Moderation Society appears to have passed out of existence. However, their places were soon filled by middle-class Wesleyan-Conservatives (including the ironfounder Peter Rothwell, the millowner Robert Knowles and the county – later the borough – coroner John Taylor) and nonconformist-Liberals. The New Temperance Society operated what proved to be an effective compromise – a dual pledge system, whereby members could pledge either for moderationist or teetotal principles – and this appears to have satisfactorily accommodated both teetotallers and moderationists. The founders of the society were from a working-class and petit-bourgeois background, but middle-class patronage was welcomed from the start – Charles Darbishire, Robert Heywood and Edmund Ashworth gave financial support – and middle-class patrons soon established themselves in positions of leadership.[90]

In the mid-1840s the temperance movement became a leading vehicle in the attempts of moral reformers to adapt working-class leisure patterns. Considerable energy and resources were invested in an attempt to build recreational counter-attractions to the popular culture based around the public house. Coffee taverns and temperance hotels were opened, temperance Friendly Societies formed, and temperance tracts and periodicals distributed.[91] The mainstay of temperance organisation was an institutional network comprised of the parent Temperance Society (as the New Temperance Society came to be known), a Youths' Society, and various Methodist and Sunday school branches. These operated through a round of weekly meetings – which represented the hub of social activity – supplemented by regular gatherings of all the various bodies in the Temperance Hall (opened in 1840, it was the largest public assembly facility in Bolton until the town hall was opened in 1873) and, in the summer months, by outdoor meetings and demonstrations. In July 1848, for example, the Temperance Society celebrated its fifteenth anniversary. Four hundred individuals attended a tea-party at the Temperance Hall, after which they were joined by all the branch societies in a procession of 1,500 persons that went along all the main streets, the day's events finally culminating in an outdoor meeting.[92] Much importance was attached to the inculcation of 'the benefits of teetotal principles, and the necessity of their adoption whilst young'. In September and October 1848 the second and third meetings of a series of 'juvenile' gatherings were held in the Temperance Hall, each attended by over 2,000 children and 1,000 youths and adults.[93] The railway excursion was used on an impressive scale in June 1850 when nearly 9,000 adults and children were transported to Duxbury Park near Chorley, in celebration of the first annual gala day of the Bolton Youths' Temperance Society.[94]

Such efforts were not without success. The 1848 annual meeting of the parent society congratulated itself that 1,100 persons had signed the pledge of membership over the last twelve months.[95] By 1859 the various teetotal societies were estimated to have had about 7,000 members, though only about 2,000 of these were above twenty-one years of age.[96] Against this, however, it was calculated in 1848 that Bolton's 116 public houses, 191 beerhouses, and 11 other licensed outlets at which ale and spirits were sold provided one drinking-place for every 25 houses or 200 persons.[97] According to the borough coroner, John Taylor, those persons regularly attending Sunday worship in 1851 were outnumbered nearly three to one by those who preferred to spend their time on the Sabbath in 'folly and sin', drinking and gambling. However, he thought that it was not the sheer scale of drinking that was the problem. Rather, a more formidable obstacle was the strong prejudices that the public-house culture held against temperance and educational reformers. Strategies based on moral and rational persuasion were doomed to failure, 'Because, as he thought, they began at the wrong end'.[98] The broadening of the social activities of the temperance movement was thus not the only strategy adopted by temperance advocates in the 1840s, and Taylor was the spokesperson of a group that sought to contain working-class drinking through restricting the supply. On each annual licensing day from 1846, the group memorialised the magistrates' bench to grant no new licences for public houses. The bench, packed with teetotallers, was usually happy to oblige.[99] Poole notes that, from the mid-1840s to the mid-1870s, the number of licensed victuallers' houses remained almost static at around 118, though the number of beerhouses continued to rise, the magistrates having no power to restrict their licences until the Selwyn-Ibbotson Bill became law in 1869.[100]

Factory reform

Although factory paternalism did not develop on the scale advocated by some contemporaries, and the *direct* impact of middle-class philanthropy upon the moral condition of the working class was limited, social reform and the mellowing of middle-class attitudes and practices nevertheless made a significant contribution to improvements in social relations. This was especially the case in the cotton industry, whose key importance to the local economy meant that it played a pivotal role in determining overall trends. The greater instances of paternalism and philanthropy after 1842 were all the more noticeable to contemporaries because employers had previously achieved notoriety through their acts of malevolence. The prevailing image of the factory masters in the 1830s and early 1840s was in fact that which came from the critique of the factory system. This was composed of various elements and diverse strands of protest – combined most notably and perhaps uniquely in the 'Tory-radical' rhetoric of Richard Oastler – that concertedly criticised factory work as oppressive, exploitative, and injurious to health and morals. Similarly, the portrait of the factory master was characterised by aggression, avariciousness, tyranny and heartlessness.[101] Two studies of cotton Lancashire have suggested that the baneful acts of the cotton masters were central not only to the image but also to the reality of employment relations in the factory in the 1830s and 1840s.[102] In Bolton there were many examples of employer tyranny which lend support to this view. Here at least, however, the image of the employers underwent a transformation from the mid-1840s, and this was in part dependent on changes in their social practices. As suggested by Anthony Howe, the benevolent cotton employer may have been in the minority, but the diversion of sufficient time, energy and talent away from business and into philanthropy ensured that it was his actions that came to characterise the masters as a class.[103]

Of central importance in this process was an accommodation to factory reform. In the 1830s and early 1840s employers and workers had been sharply divided over this question, the aggressive economic liberalism of the manufacturers being countered by demands for a more measured and regulated system of production. By the mid-1840s, however, the debate was being conducted within a language of negotiation and class conciliation, a development that promoted a settlement of the issue.

As Gray argues, much of the ideological framework for this redefining of the question of factory reform took place in the wider context of changes in the Victorian state and the accommodation of interests within it. The 1830s saw the implementation of Benthamite projects of rationalisation, but these provoked widespread resistance at both popular and ruling-class levels, which in turn induced a series of compromises between previously divergent interests. These took place within the legislative and administrative process, where the language of official expertise and social knowledge provided an ideological framework within which evangelical Tories like Ashley could enter into dialogue with Benthamite liberals. The resultant process of negotiation shaped the debate on those social problems subsumed under the general heading of 'the condition of England question' and a revision of the 'harsh' social policies of the 1830s.[104] More needs to be said on how such changes in state policy promoted an accommodation to factory reform on the part of employers at local level.

It seems to be the case that one effect of the growing debate on the condition of England was to heighten middle-class sensitivity to public criticisms of the factory system. One indication of this was an attempt to disassociate wider social problems from those of the factory. In the opinion of the *Bolton Free Press*, for instance, documentation of the sanitary condition of the towns provided evidence that it was quite erroneous to assume a straightforward connection between factory employment and poor health.[105] Similarly, Graham's Factory Bill was seen as a slur on the factory system, in that it was felt to be based on the mistaken assumption that education was more urgently required for the manufacturing population than for the agricultural and other communities.[106] And for contemporaries such as the Unitarian minister Franklin Baker, the well-regulated factory actually offered the solution to social problems, the 'order and regularity enforced upon the operatives' being 'so nearly akin to moral habits'.[107]

It was in this context that working-class advocates of factory reform, in conjunction with a growing number of middle-class social reformers, increasingly deployed the rhetoric of self-improvement and social reform to press the case for factory legislation, couching their arguments in terms of the greater social good that it would bring and the mutuality and respect that it would promote between employers and workers. This development was all the more potent in that it reflected the increasingly common attempts of employers to cultivate an image of employment relations in the factory characterised by natural paternal sympathy and reciprocity.[108]

To illustrate the type of language under discussion here, in September 1845, for example, the factory operatives of Bolton held a public meeting to draw up a memorial soliciting their employers to implement an eleven-hour day in place of the current twelve. They felt 'confident that its adoption will be followed by satisfactory results both to the employer and the employed'. The first resolution suggested that long hours were injurious to the health and morals of the factory population and a deterrent to the pursuit of self-improvement and rational recreation:

> That this meeting of Factory Operatives is conscious from experience that the present system of long hours is injurious to health, and cannot be continued without materially affecting the physical capabilities of the present and future generations; that by excessive toil our mental facilities are cramped, our social and moral improvement unattended to, our religions neglected, and we are thereby debarred the full enjoyment of those blessings which Divine Providence has placed around us.[109]

The operative spinner Henry Turner, speaking in support of the resolution, argued that 'They were so tired as to be incapable of improving their mental faculties to such an extent as the present state of society warranted and demanded.'

To some extent these perspectives were not new and were present before 1842; moreover, earlier phases of the factory movement attracted a similar base of support (clerical and medical persons especially had long supported the operatives' case for factory legislation). As suggested by Gray, however, there was a shift in emphasis and imagery in the mid-1840s as the ten hours' movement increasingly composed its arguments from a repertoire of evangelical moralism and Benthamite enlightened self-interest. The case for factory reform was being promoted within a class-conciliatory language of Ashley's brand rather than the inflammatory rhetoric of Oastler.[110] Oastler could still draw crowds in Bolton, as in the case of his visit in 1844, but by that time the most revered propertied supporters of the movement among local operatives were Ashley and the Bolton MP Peter Ainsworth.[111]

These changing circumstances were also significant in helping to marginalise the associations between factory reform and radicalism that had featured strongly in Chartist arguments between 1840 and 1842. In this situation, employers were apparently more willing to consider the sort of compromises suggested above by the operatives. As early as 1843, when Lord Ashley prepared to move an amendment to Graham's Factory Bill, that ten hours be substituted for twelve, no fewer than eight of the largest employers immediately agreed to support the operatives' proposal that eleven hours be adopted as a suitable and attainable compromise (the ultimate aim of the operatives was still ten hours).[112] Nor were the operatives the only ones to make conciliatory gestures. The 1845 public meeting moved a vote of thanks to the cotton-spinner Robert Knowles for voluntarily implementing an eleven-hour day earlier in April, a gesture which was probably made in imitation of a similar well-publicised experiment at Robert Gardner's firm in Preston.[113] The experiment was deemed successful both in economic and social terms – there was no reduction in wages or profits, and in March 1846 one operative employed by Knowles claimed that, at that firm at least, 'As regarded education, there was no comparison between now and before they worked eleven hours, for he found that nearly double the number were now engaged in night schools, as compared with the twelve hours system.'[114] Other firms soon followed the example set by Knowles.[115]

Also significant was the mounting support that the operatives received from those middle-class social reformers who were unlikely to be directly economically affected by factory legislation. Robert Heywood was in favour of a ten hours Bill because he believed that it would promote temperance and lead to an increase in the membership of the Mechanics' Institution.[116] At a public meeting to launch a petition in support of a ten hours Bill in March 1846, the operatives' short-time committee shared the platform with Ashley, several of the town's leading citizens, and nonconformist clergymen.[117] Another public meeting was convened in 1847 by the mayor, following a requisition notice signed by 121 of the town's leading manufacturers, ministers, professionals, town-centre shopkeepers and traders.[118] Again, it has to be said that a similar base of support was present in earlier campaigns, but in the changing circumstances of the mid-1840s this support appears to have been larger in scale and greater in potency and it played an influential role in the accommodation of much of the manufacturing interest to factory reform.

The greater acceptance of the desirability of factory legislation among Bolton's cotton masters was evident by 1845. The operatives' proposal for the voluntary implementation of an eleven-hour day was turned down, but most employers were nevertheless in favour of shorter hours – they thought it could only be achieved compulsorily through legislation, however, as any voluntary scheme would be wrecked by a few defaulters.[119] There remained a committed minority of opposition right through until May 1847,[120] but once Fielden's Ten Hours Bill passed into law, it was accepted by all but two local manufacturers. The

Ashworths and Mr Hollins were the only local employers to use the infamous relay system to maintain eleven hours for the legally unprotected adult hands.[121] For this, they received the condemnation of all sections of the local community and, no other local manufacturers supported their campaign for an eleven-hour day.[122] The Bolton employers were thus distinguished from those in other towns in south-east Lancashire, notably Ashton and Stalybridge, where the use of relays was more widespread.[123] In February 1850 the Ten Hours Act was dealt a severe blow when the judges of the Court of Exchequer upheld a ruling by the Manchester magistrates that the use of relays was legal. The outcry from Bolton came from all sections of the community, and members of the middle class actually led the protest movement. A public meeting which launched a petitioning movement was chaired by Robert Knowles and Ainsworth and Heywood were among the speakers. Over 50 petitions were forwarded from the Sunday schools. Another received the signatures of 46 clergymen and ministers of all denominations. Yet another was signed by 64 millowners, 21 surgeons and 9 magistrates. A further petition was signed by 151 managers and overlookers of the various mills.[124] The town council also forwarded a petition, deprecating the threat to an Act which it saw as a major contributory factor to the marked improvement in class relations that had clearly taken place since the summer of 1842:

> That your memorialists being residents in an important and populous community have had ample opportunities of forming a correct judgement of the working of the Ten Hours Factory Act. That it is the unbiassed opinion of your memorialists that the said Act has been greatly instrumental in correcting the evils, both physical and social, which have been deemed to be incidental to factory employment; that they believe operatives have embraced the opportunities given by limited hours of labour; and that the measure has led to the formation of evening classes for the instruction of young people of both sexes, and been in various ways productive of beneficial effects; and more than all, your Memorialists believe that the Ten Hours Act, has created a spirit of such general satisfaction amongst the factory workers, that any departure from it, either directly or indirectly, will revive agitation, and spread a distrust in the Government as well as animosity towards employers.[125]

Thus, the accommodation to factory reform was probably more marked in medium-fine-spinning Bolton than in towns such as Ashton and Stalybridge where coarse spinning predominated, and Bolton's cotton employers were apparently more willing to meet their operatives' demands on wages and hours of labour than Dutton and King's 'cotton tyrants of North Lancashire, 1836–54'.[126] Moreover, most of the town's employers recognised the federated United Cotton Spinners Association, which was established in 1842.[127] By the mid-1840s the improving relations between employers and operatives were publicly proclaimed from a variety of sources.[128] Employers were now much less subject to criticism from below. In August 1845 the operative cotton-spinners held a tea-party in the Temperance Hall to celebrate the fact that the employers had acceded to two recent wage advances without the operatives having to resort to the usual threat of strike action. Several employers took up the invitation to attend an event designed, in the words of one operative spinner, 'to cement a feeling which now existed, and he hoped would continue to exist, between the employers and the employed ... A feeling of mutual interest.' Others sent communications, such as those from Messrs. Bolling, which 'in acknowledging the friendly invitation of the "Operative Cotton Spinners," beg to assure them, that they duly appreciate the spirit in which it has been sent, and they trust it will be a means of confirming the good feeling now existing between the employers and employed.'[129] The Bolton spinners had more than an incidental role in the organisation of similar events which were later held in Oldham and Preston.[130] Such proclamations of mutual interests were indicative of the greater cohesion and consensus that now characterised the manufacturing community of Bolton. Those forces promoting conflict within social relations were now being neutralised by those promoting cooperation and compromise. But once again it is important to note that this development represented a process of stabilisation rather than harmonisation. Late in 1847, for instance, depression returned to the town and the cotton employers implemented a 10 per cent wage cut, an action interpreted by some operatives as one to secure recompense for the Ten Hours Act.[131] Cotton strikes became less frequent and less violent in the third quarter of the century, but conflict continued nevertheless, as was also in the case of the town's engineering and coal industries and in building, where conflict actually escalated during the 1860s. As Tholfsen suggests, the mid-Victorian town was 'a community united by common purposes', notable for its general cultural cohesiveness, 'but also an arena in which contending social classes confronted each other in conflict'.[132]

Notes

1.   T. Tholfsen, *Working Class Radicalism in Mid-Victorian England* (London, 1976), p. 124, ch. 4.

2. P. Joyce, *Work, Society and Politics: The Culture of the Factory in Later Victorian England* (London, 1980).

3. J. Foster, *Class Struggle and the Industrial Revolution: Early Industrial Capitalism in Three English Towns* (London, 1974), p. 7.

4. N. Kirk, *The Growth of Working Class Reformism in Mid-Victorian England* (Beckenham, 1985), p. 25. For more on the 'newfound "moderation and restraint"' of the working class in the years around 1850, see S. and B. Webb, *The History of Trade Unionism* (New York, 1920), ch. 1V; R. Harrison, *Before the Socialists: Studies in Labour and Politics 1861–1881* (London, 1965), ch. 1.

5. Kirk, *op. cit.*, p. 292.

6. Of crucial importance here was the failure of the Chartists to move away from a popular theory of market relations that located exploitation in *exchange*, with the capitalist, as *middleman*, cornering the market and depriving the worker of the full fruits of his product, and towards a class-based theory of exploitation within *production* of a social democratic or Marxist kind (see G. S. Jones, 'The Language of Chartism', in J. Epstein and D. Thompson (eds), *The Chartist Experience: Studies in Working–Class Radicalism and Culture, 1830–60* (London, 1982), pp. 20–3. See also N. Kirk, 'In Defence of Class: A Critique of Recent Revisionist Writing upon the Nineteenth-Century Working Class', *International Review of Social History* XXXII (1987), p. 41). For Gillespie, see *B.F.P.*, 31 December 1841. For Bowring's views on the question of factory reform, see *B.F.P.*, 24 September 1842.

7. *B.C.*, 29 July, 5 August 1848.

8. The only reference I have found to any connection between Chartism and trade unionism in 1848 was a meeting of trades held at the Temperance Hall in May, attended by about 700 persons. The event was apparently organised by persons who were both Chartists and leaders of the Miners' Association of Great Britain. Among the speakers were the miners' leaders W. P. Roberts and David Swallow, who attacked the anti-trade union 'Gagging Bill'. Primacy was still attached to political relations, and Roberts considered that economic relations were not necessarily an obstacle to political alliances between the two major classes: 'He then dwelt at considerable length on the necessity of the Chartists supporting the middle class movement. Though the middle classes had been enemies to the Chartists he believed they were now honest in the course they were taking, inasmuch as they saw no probability of a reduction of taxation being effected under the present system' (*B.C.*, 13 May 1848).

9. *B.C.*, 9, 16, 30 September 1848. The Liberals later claimed that they did not field a candidate as a mark of respect for the seat becoming vacant upon the death of the Tory MP William Bolling. The appointment of the Liberal MP Dr Bowring to the consulship of Canton did not bring forth a similar gesture (subsequent remarks by the Liberal cotton master Joseph Crook, *B.C.*, 10 July 1852).

10. *B.C.*, 23 December 1848.

11. Public meetings of Chartists were small and very infrequent after 1848,

though the last recorded meetings did not occur until 1853. An attempt at revival was made in the summer and Chartist meetings were staged all over Lancashire. The one in Bolton only attracted 150 people (*H.O. 45/6731, 6794*, mayor to Home Office, 28 and 31 July 1853); *B.C.*, 6 August 1853). In November Ernest Jones, still advocating the Charter as a 'grand cure' for the problems afflicting trade unions, lectured to a small audience at the Temperance Hall (*B.C.*, 5 November 1853).

12.   For example, see the sizeable and enthusiastic support of the 'non-electors' – whose leaders included ex-Chartists – for the Liberal candidates in the 1852 parliamentary election (*B.C.*, 3, 31 July).

13.   A. Howe, *The Cotton Masters 1830–1860* (Oxford, 1984), p. 233; *B.C.*, 16 February, 30 March 1850.

14.   I generally support Howe (*op. cit.*, pp. 307–9) here, but do not necessarily follow his view that economic calculation was subordinate to the wider social ideals and cultural ambitions of the cotton masters. Henry Ashworth, for example, once estimated that the 'order and content' of his 1,200 workers was worth fifty pounds per week (D. Roberts, *Paternalism in Early Victorian England* (London, 1979), p. 174).

15.   For example, Kirk, *The Growth of Reformism*, pp. 54, 56, 63–4.

16.   The argument comes mainly from P. Joyce, *op. cit.*, but also see Kirk's views mentioned at the start of this chapter.

17.   Roberts, *op. cit.*, ch. 7.

18.   *Ibid.*, pp. 180–3. M. Huberman, in his 'The Economic Origins of Paternalism: Lancashire Cotton Spinning in the First Half of the Nineteenth Century', *Social History* 12, 2, argues that paternalism originated in urban and not rural areas, but see the criticisms in M. Rose, P. F. Taylor and M. J. Winstanley, 'The Economic Origins of Paternalism: Some Objections', *Social History* 14, 1.

19.   Roberts, *op. cit.*, pp. 219–20; *B.F.P.*, 21 August 1841.

20.   *H.O. 40/44*, Egerton to Russell, 6 August 1839.

21.   *B.C.*, 26 March 1831.

22.   See, for example, the celebrations of the 'coming of age' of W. B. Hulton in 1866 and his marriage in 1867: *B.C.*, 11 August 1866, 27 April 1867.

23.   Howe, *op. cit.*, p. 272; *B.C.*, 1 September 1838; *B.F.P.*, 18 August 1838. In 1843 the late Joseph Ridgway left £26,000 in various charitable bequests, to take effect after the decease of his widow. The largest were £2,000 for the erection of a school at Bolton, £1,000 to the Bolton Dispensary and a further £1,000 to the Chester Church Building Society (*B.F.P.*, 1 July 1843).

24.   P. A. Whittle, *Bolton-le-Moors* (Bolton, 1857), pp. 334–7, 409; *B.F.P.*, 7 December 1844. Peter Ainsworth also owned a quarry and in 1846 he provided a dining- and reading-room for his quarrymen (*B.F.P.*, 17 January 1846).

25.   37 bleachworks in the neighbourhood of Bolton, Bury and Manchester, listed by the 1854 Bleachworks' Commission, employed an average of 170 workers. Ainsworths of Bolton was the largest firm, with a total of 508 hands, Hardcastle's of Bolton the second largest, with 440. No other firm employed above 400. At the bottom end of the scale, 9 firms employed

between 50 and 90 workers (B.P.P. 1854–5, Commission for Inquiring into the Expediency of Extending the Acts Relative to Factories to Bleach-works, &c., p. 19).

26. *B.C.*, 3 January 1846.

27. P. F. Taylor, 'Popular Politics and Labour-Capital Relations in Bolton, 1825–1850', Lancaster University Ph.D thesis (1991), pp. 218–9.

28. R. Boyson, *The Ashworth Cotton Enterprise: The Rise and Fall of a Family Firm 1818–1880* (Oxford, 1970); D. O'Connor, 'Barrow Bridge, Bolton. Dean Mills Estate: A Victorian Model Achievement' (typescript in B.R.L., 1972).

29. *B.F.P.*, 23, 30 June, 7 July 1838.

30. *B.F.P.*, 31 May 1845.

31. *B.C.*, 7 August 1852.

32. *B.C.*, 27 August 1853.

33. *B.F.P.*, 20 September 1845, 11 April 1846. Arrowsmith also provided two ranges of model cottages, Cobden Place and Bright Terrace, in which his spinners presided.

34. *B.C.*, 30 December 1848.

35. *B.C.*, 5 March 1853.

36. *B.F.P.*, 26 November 1842.

37. *B.F.P.*, 18 November 1843. The Musgraves and Marsdens were both Wesleyans. The Joseph Marsden referred to was the same Joseph Marsden – timber-merchant and general builder – who played a prominent role in action against the Operative Builders' Union in 1833 and who became the first chairman of the Bolton Builders' General Association in 1846 (see Chapter Five). He later became a master cotton-spinner. This was confirmed in *B.C.*, 5 November 1859, which reported on the celebrations of Marsden's son's 'coming of age' in the Baths Assembly Rooms, at which his workers were present. Marsden was in the chair on the occasion, and his speech included an account of his business career.

38. *B.F.P.*, 3 January 1846.

39. *B.F.P.*, 21 June 1845.

40. *B.C.*, 3 January 1846.

41. *B.C.*, 20 November 1852.

42. Roberts, *op. cit.*, p. 172.

43. Biographical information on Bazley can be found in W. D. Billington, *Barrow Bridge: The History, Natural History and Tales of the Village* (Halliwell Local History Society, Bolton, 1988).

44. B.A., ZHB/1/5, Return of employees working at Dean Mills.

45. *B.F.P.*, 5 September 1846.

46. B.A., ZZ/109/3, John Horrocks Ainsworth Papers, Times and Wages Book. This source gave details relating to general literacy rates, religious attendance, family, and other details on the adult male members of the workforce.

47. Joyce, *op. cit.*, ch. 5 (especially pp. 171–2).

48. *B.F.P.*, 20 September 1845.

49. *B.C.*, 27 October 1855.

50. Boyson, *op. cit.*, ch. 8.
51. *B.F.P.*, 28 December 1844.
52. *B.C.*, 7 November 1835.
53. *B.C.*, 10 July 1841.
54. *B.F.P.*, 6 July 1844.
55. *B.C.*, 17 January 1852.
56. Tholfsen, *op. cit.*, p. 210.
57. *B.C.*, 30 December 1848.
58. Joyce, *op. cit.*, pp. 64–82.
59. T. B. Boothman, *Bolton Master Cotton Spinners' Association 1861–1961 Centenary Commemoration* (Bolton, 1961); P. F. Taylor, 'The New Paternalism and Labour-Capital Relations in the Bolton Cotton Industry, c. 1848–1877', Manchester Polytechnic B.A. Dissertation (1986), pp. 43–6; E. Thorpe, 'Industrial Relations and the Social Structure: A Case Study of Bolton Cotton-Mule Spinners', Salford University M.Sc. thesis (1969); Webbs' Trade Union Collection, Section A, XXXV, Bolton Cotton Spinners: sketch of history and extracts from old minute books and reports, 1844–80 (British Library of Political and Economic Science).
60. P. Richards, 'State Formation and Class Struggle, 1832–48', in P. Corrigan (ed.), *Capitalism, State Formation and Marxist Theory* (London, 1980).
61. I have based this brief summary on the following sources: J. Black, 'A Medico-Topographical, Geological, and Statistical Sketch of Bolton and its Neighbourhood', *Transactions of the Provincial Medical and Surgical Association* V (1837), pp. 40, 69, 70–3 (a copy of this work is available in B.R.L.); W. Brimelow, *Political and Parliamentary History of Bolton, Vol. 1* (Bolton, 1882), pp. 379–82; H. Ashworth, 'On the State of Education in the Borough of Bolton in 1837' (copy available in B.R.L.); Whittle, *op. cit.*, pp. 151–2; *B.C.*, 30 December 1848; *B.F.P.*, 17 June 1843
62. *B.F.P.*, 23 December 1843.
63. *B.C.*, 10 November 1849.
64. Annual Reports for the Bolton Mechanics' Institution, 1825–1877 (B.R.L.).
65. This example, *B.C.*, 25 April 1846.
66. *B.C.*, 7 May 1831.
67. W. E. Brown, *Robert Heywood of Bolton 1786–1868* (Wakefield, 1970), p. 19.
68. *B.C.*, 30 October, 6 November 1847.
69. *B.F.P.*, 12 October 1844.
70. *B.C.*, 28 November 1846; *B.F.P.*, 5 December 1846.
71. *B.C.*, 14, 21 November 1846.
72. *B.C.*, 20, 27 March, 3 April 1847; *B.F.P.*, 30 October 1847. Slade is quoted in T. Dunne, *Bolton Public Libraries 1853–1978: One Hundred and Twenty-five Years in Retrospect* (Bolton Metropolitan Borough Arts Department, 1978), p. 9, who attributes the collapse of the Athenaeum project to Slade's personal influence.
73. *B.C.*, 18, 25 January, 17 May, 5 July 1851, 2 June, 3 November, 29 December 1855.

74. *B.F.P.*, 13 December 1845; Bolton Society for the Protection of the Poor and District Provident – Reports, 1841–58 (B.R.L.). The Benevolent Society and Poor Protection Society were supported by all sections of the middle class and were not marked by the internal strife that had been so disruptive in other areas of the town's institutional network.
75. D. Fraser, *The Evolution of the British Welfare State* (Basingstoke, 1984), ch. 6.
76. Bolton Society for the Protection of the Poor and District Provident Society – Reports, 1841–58.
77. *Ibid.*
78. *Ibid.*
79. *B.F.P.*, 20, 27 August 1842.
80. *B.F.P.*, 14 January 1843, 29 March, 19 April, 13 December 1845.
81. The 1854 Bolton Improvement Bill, for example, lost many of its provisions after such opposition. After first being divested of its cemetery and gasworks clauses, due to opposition from groups of ratepayers, it then lost its main object, which was the extension of the existing waterworks. This came after plans to make alterations to the Belmont Reservoir aroused opposition from the proprietors of mills and bleachworks who were supplied from a stream flowing from that body of water and who felt that their interests would be adversely affected (*B.C.*, 1 April, 20 May, 1 July, 18 November 1854).
82. *B.C.*, 15 February, 22 March, 7 June 1851.
83. *B.C.*, 15 December 1849.
84. *B.C.*, 23 July 1831.
85. *B.C.*, 27 July 1833, 15 March 1862.
86. B. Harrison, *Drink and the Victorians: The Temperance Question in England 1815–1872* (Pittsburgh, 1971), p. 137.
87. L. L. Shiman, *Crusade against Drink in Victorian England* (Basingstoke, 1988), p. 18.
88. Tholfsen, *op. cit.*, pp. 68–72, 229–40.
89. Black, *op. cit.*, pp. 52–3.
90. *B.C.*, 15 March 1862.
91. *B.C.*, 13 June 1846, 14 October 1848, 29 September 1849, 11 August 1855, 15 March 1862.
92. *B.C.*, 29 July 1848.
93. *B.C.*, 9 September, 14 October 1848.
94. *B.C.*, 24 June 1850.
95. *B.C.*, 5 February 1848.
96. *B.C.*, 19 March 1859.
97. *B.C.*, 26 August 1848.
98. *B.C.*, 6 September 1851.
99. *B.C.*, 25 August 1855, remarks by J. H. Raper, recalling how the strategy was first adopted in 1846.
100. R. Poole, *Popular Leisure and the Music Hall in 19th-Century Bolton* (Centre for North-West Regional Studies, University of Lancaster, Occasional Paper 12), p. 41.

101. R. Gray, 'The Languages of Factory Reform in Britain, c.1830–1860', in P. Joyce (ed.), *The Historical Meanings of Work* (Cambridge, 1987), p. 146. In *McDouall's Chartist Journal and Trades' Advocate*, 25 September 1841, 'The Factory Master's Portrait' detailed the employer as a scheming tyrant, obsessed with the pursuit of profit maximisation and grossly ignorant on all other subjects.

102. H. I. Dutton and J. E. King, 'The Limits of Paternalism: The Cotton Tyrants of North Lancashire 1836–1854', *Social History* 7, 1 (January, 1982); Kirk, 'In Defence Of Class'.

103. Howe, *op. cit.*, p. 273.

104. Gray, *op. cit.*, especially pp. 167, 170; Richards, *op. cit.*

105. *B.F.P.*, 19 November 1842.

106. *B.F.P.*, 8 April 1843.

107. F. Baker, *The Moral Tone of the Factory System Defended* (London, 1850), p. 15.

108. To give an example of the language of paternal mutuality: in 1850 the Tory-Wesleyan cotton-spinner Thomas Taylor addressed his workforce during a dinner party which he had laid on for them. His speech included the following remarks: 'When he looked around at the decorations, the thought struck him that they might be viewed in an emblematical light. For instance, let the flowers be taken to represent the beauty and loveliness of the union, as he trusted it existed – and he thought there was good evidence that it did exist – between employers and employed ... Let them still go on unitedly without hostile opposition to one another; for he always regarded the interests of the servants as the interests of the master, and the master's interests as those of the servants' (*B.C.*, 2 November 1850).

109. *B.F.P.*, 6 September 1845.

110. Gray, *op. cit.*, p. 172.

111. *B.F.P.*, 20 April 1844 for Oastler, 19 October 1844 and 6 September 1845 for Ashley and Ainsworth; *B.C.*, 24 April 1847 (Ashley acknowledges a gift bought for him and his wife by the operatives in the employ of the millowners Cannon and Haslam).

112. *B.F.P.*, 8, 15 April 1843.

113. *B.F.P.*, 15 March, 26 April, 6 September 1845.

114. *B.F.P.*, 7 March 1846. It seems probable that advances in mule-spinning technology implemented at the firm in the early 1840s had made shorter hours economically viable. For these had reduced the cost of spinning 60's twist from 5d. down to 2d. per lb, without reducing the earnings of the spinner (W. P. Crankshaw and A. Blackburn, *A Century and a Half of Cotton Spinning 1797–1947: The History of Knowles, Limited of Bolton* (Bolton, 1948), p. 21.

115. *B.F.P.*, 14 March 1846.

116. *B.F.P.*, 4 October 1845; *B.C.*, 9 March 1850.

117. *B.F.P.*, 7 March 1846. J. T. Ward has noted 'close connections between prominent nonconformist divines and leading capitalist opponents of (factory) reform' (J. T. Ward, 'The Factory Movement', in J. T. Ward (ed.), *Popular Movements c.1830–1850* (London, 1970), p. 59). In Bolton,

however, there was no marked correlation between political and religious allegiance and attitudes to factory reform. If anything, Anglican clergy were not prominent in the campaigns of the 1840s.

118. *B.C.*, 23 January 1847; *B.F.P.*, 23 January 1847.

119. *B.F.P.*, 18 October 1845, 20 June 1846.

120. B.P.P. 1847, XLVI, Memorials of the Master Manufacturers in the County of Lancaster, with respect to the Ten Hours Bill of 1847.

121. *B.C.*, 20 January, 31 March 1849.

122. *B.C.*, 31 March, 23, 30 June 1849.

123. *B.C.*, 30 June, 21 July 1849.

124. *B.C.*, 16 February, 9, 16 March, 13, 20 April 1850. As suggested above, this pattern of events probably does not lend itself to any universal application. The situation in Ashton and Stalybridge was apparently very different: see Kirk, *The Growth of Reformism*, pp. 246–7.

125. *B.C.*, 11 May 1850.

126. Dutton and King, *op. cit.*

127. S. and B. Webb, 'Bolton Spinners: Sketch of History (1892)', Trade Union Collection, Section A, XXXV, 1.

128. *B.F.P.*, 23 December 1843 (editorial), 13 December 1845 (remarks by the operative spinner Henry Turner at a meeting at Lancaster calling for the immediate opening of the ports to supplies of foreign corn), 25 September 1847 (notes some comments made by the *Economist* on the national picture).

129. *B.F.P.*, 9 August 1845.

130. *B.F.P.*, 27 September, 29 November 1845.

131. *B.C.*, 24 December 1847.

132. Tholfsen, *op. cit.*, p. 156.

Conclusion

It will be recalled from the introduction to this study that those historians concerned with the origins of the celebrated mid-Victorian 'consensus' and who focused attention on the cotton districts of Lancashire and Cheshire have generally portrayed a sudden and major shift in social relations in the years around 1850. This examination of popular politics and labour-capital relations has demonstrated that, for the community of Bolton at least, the overall process of change was more protracted in nature. Moreover, although the conclusions of any study with such a limited geographical focus do not necessarily lend themselves to general application, the presentation and analysis of evidence throughout this book have suggested a revision of, and further research into, many key areas of the region's pattern of social relations. It is unlikely that all aspects of Bolton's political and social development would have been atypical, especially since national factors seem to have influenced its course.

Thus I have argued that the onset of mid-Victorian stability was not necessarily dependent on changes in the organisation and execution of work.[1] It has further been proposed that, although those explanations of change which attached central importance to the relationship between structures (especially economic) and consciousness furthered our knowledge and understanding of the period under consideration,[2] they nevertheless paid insufficient attention to the precise content and role of ideology and the actions of the state in conciliating popular opinion. Economic developments did have a role to play in the overall process of social stabilisation, and those changes in attitudes and behaviour which have been documented in this work were undoubtedly facilitated by an easing of the pressures on capital accumulation from about the mid-1840s. While acknowledging the importance of these developments, however, I have suggested that, considered within a framework of explanation which pays attention to the role of the state in setting the agenda for 'the condition of England question' and which incorporates an account of ideology that acknowledges the relative autonomy of political traditions, it is evident that the national political framework, and not the local economic sphere, was the major influence shaping the working-class political response to industrial capitalism.[3] Thus, while class tensions and considerations were seldom, if ever, absent from political protest and social reform movements, ideology, in the case of Bolton at least, often served to unite middle-class Liberals and working-class radicals, even in the strife-torn early Chartist period.

The view that social change was linked to advances in the labour process, involving a progression from the formal to the real subsumption of labour to capital, is theoretically simplistic and difficult to demonstrate empirically. It is also hard to reconcile with evidence relating to Bolton's pattern of industrial development which shows that such changes were incomplete by mid-century. Not only did economic conflict continue after 1850, but the nature of industrial disputes in the 1850s and 1860s reveals little change in the fundamental nature of those issues of wages, conditions and, significantly, work control which divided labour and capital both before and after 1850. On this count alone, the explanatory power of linking what were really prolonged changes in work practice with sudden shifts in working-class attitudes and behaviour is unconvincing when applied to the local context.

The most significant economic advancement was the expansion and stabilisation of capitalist market relations from mid-century, but the movement of working-class reformers into Liberalism did not wait for this development. Attention to the progress and social composition of reform movements reveals that this was a gradual, if somewhat conflict-ridden development, and that ideology played a crucial role in cementing links between reformers as early as the late 1820s and throughout the 1830s and 1840s. Both working-class radicals and middle-class Liberals sought political solutions to problems of poverty and distress which were commonly believed to emanate from the political monopolies associated with a corrupt Parliament. The major theme of this political critique, essentially inter-class in appeal, was that the exploitation of the people was linked to the ability of a parasitic aristocracy and its allies to make unjust exactions through their control of Parliament.

It was of crucial significance that the central themes of this radical analysis of society, which had begun to crystallise in the 1760s, were not fundamentally altered by the later development of Owenite cooperative, quasi-socialist, or so-called '*de-facto* anti-capitalist' economic themes and perspectives. In the early 1840s these did give Chartism a more distinctly working-class appeal, but they did not displace the anti-aristocratic attack on political and financial monopolies from the centre of radical arguments. Owenism gave the assault on unrestrained market relations its most coherent analysis, but it is significant that Owenites and radicals considered the tenets of their respective programmes to be mutually exclusive when they debated the merits of their agendas at a public meeting in Bolton in November 1837.[4] The Owenite emphasis on the evils associated with capitalist competition and of uniting all social classes through the implementation of a cooperative economy had little influence on a radical analysis which continued to accord central importance to the political origins of misery and oppression. The emphasis was always primarily on class legislation and taxation and not production relations and profits. This situation may have been partly due to the fact that, although Bolton was one of the stronger centres of Owenism in the region, it was nevertheless relatively weak, both in influence and in numbers of adherents, in comparison with radicalism.[5] Most local working-class efforts at bringing capitalist competition under greater restraint apparently did not envisage 'a different structure of labour and product markets from those of industrial capitalism', or 'the reconstruction of community through co-operation'.[6] The most impressive example of attempts to control excessive economic competition in the cotton districts was made by the inter-trade N.A.P.L., which Sykes convincingly argues was not inspired by 'Owenite communitarian ideals of a co-operative re-organisation of society'. Rather, its aims were limited to the more bread-and-butter issues associated with the everyday economic experience of the workplace.[7] Further illustration of this general point is the fact that the same analysis of excessive domestic competition which motivated the N.A.P.L. also underpinned the attempts of the hand-loom weavers in 1834 to establish boards of trade to equalise and regulate piece-rates. This campaign was orchestrated by manufacturing and working-class Tories who certainly did not share the 'utopian' visions of mainstream Owenism.

The failure of Owenite economic themes to impart a more economic flavour to Bolton radicalism, however, was less an indication of Owenism's local strength than a reflection of the ideological limits imposed by radicalism's predominant emphasis on national political structures. Contemporary political reformers from all social classes held a comprehensive view of society in which local abuses were ultimately linked to national political structures. It has been shown in Chapters One and Two that the radical petite bourgeoisie and the Liberal middle class considered the oligarchical domination of the unrepresentative and out-moded court leets of Bolton to have derived from Old Corruption at Westminster, while Chapter Three has demonstrated that Chartism was a national political movement in aim and ideology, in that the link between distress and political exclusion was never displaced as the central radical image.

These same ideological limits also served to restrict the potential for themes from the trade union and factory movements to produce a breakthrough to a more proletarian political ideology. Even in the Chartist period, Bolton's trade unionists remained, for the most part, preoccupied with the everyday practical issues of wages and conditions. Although there was some cross-over of personnel between the various strands of working-class protest, the links between radicalism and the trade union and factory movements were more limited than has some-times been suggested. The leaders of the various hand-loom weavers' organisations, the key Bolton Spinners' Union, and the local short-time committees never seem to have become radicals or Chartists, despite the attempts to persuade them that their causes had necessarily to be subverted to the pursuit of political reform. Aside from the early 1840s, therefore, when Chartism assimilated themes from the factory and trade union movements, industrial issues and organisations aiming at wider social change were not necessarily as closely interwoven as some historians have maintained. And even in this particular instance, irre-spective of the fact that Bolton was located in the region where the capitalist mode of production was most advanced, these 'economic' perspectives remained subordinate to older themes denouncing political monopolies.

There was thus no complete synthesis between political relations and industrial issues in the radical critique. The significance of this was manifold. Firstly, it left the way open for cooperation between reformers. The emphasis on the political monopolies of Old Corruption, the conflict between productive and unproductive wealth, and the moral distinction between earned and unearned income all represented important affini-ties between radicalism and Liberalism.[8] These were strengthened by a growing acceptance of the merits of personal advancement through self- and collective means which gained ground from the mid-1840s, when the militant Chartist insistence on the necessity of prior political reform to achieve permanent improvement began to be undermined by the resolution of economic crisis. This gave enhanced scope for class manoeu-vre and compromise at the local level, and, by changes in the character of the Victorian state, sought to remedy the deficiencies of the Whigs' economic liberalism and political failings of the 1830s with a concilia-tory programme of fiscal and social reform. It must also be emphasised that attention to the sometimes strained relations between the Chartists and the Liberals should not be allowed to obscure the Liberals' success in attracting support for their policies among the majority of the working class, who were not Chartist activists. All this did not mean an untroubled merger of consenting value systems – far from it – but, in Bolton at least, the movement into Liberalism did not signify the sharp break in working-class consciousness that Foster and Kirk portrayed in the other important regional centres of Ashton, Oldham, Stalybridge and Stockport. The success of middle-class movements like the Anti-Corn Law League in attracting working-class support has been unduly discounted by those historians who have narrowly focused on its relations with the militant Chartists, while radicalism in at least one of the major south-east Lancashire towns had more in common with areas like Crossick's Kentish London – which was 'of a traditional kind that could inform mid-Victorian Liberalism as easily as Chartism' – than Kirk's analysis has allowed.[9]

The emphasis on political roles within radicalism was further significant in masking the realities of capitalist exploitation and thereby inhibiting the working class from developing a more rigorous economic understanding of its own situation. Low wages and poor conditions were not seen as necessary products of capitalist relations of production, but were ultimately attributed to the apparent hegemony of a parasitic aristocracy which extracted the wealth of the economically productive of all strata through its monopoly of Parliament. Political reform was seen as the key to a more equitable system of exchange relations between labour and capital, but mainstream working-class demands for a more regulated economy did not envisage a more fundamental alternative to capitalist market relations (the employers' role in initiating and directing the broad market operation went unchallenged). Even when 'economic' themes infused Chartist arguments in the early 1840s, criticisms of employers remained couched in moral terms which expressed desires for the restoration of threatened reciprocities. Thus employers were often severely criticised for introducing labour-saving technology and de-skilling capitalist practices and innovations. But the focus of working-class radical criticisms of the middle class was primarily directed to the moderation of their attempts to secure the reform of those political structures that sustained the aristocratic depredations on industry (for instance, they were unwilling to sanction the more intimidatory and violent 'physical force' or 'mass platform' tactics). The working-class political response to industrial capitalism was thus largely channelled within the constraining parameters of the political language of the radical-Liberal critique. Ideology imposed a structure on the understanding of the intensified economic exploitation of the 1830s and 1840s and thereby played an important role in the consolidation of middle-class hegemony over the working class.

The overall process of social stabilisation was a many-sided one, however, and the establishment of a satisfactorily smooth middle-class leadership of the local community further depended, in large part, on the significant alleviation of those internal tensions which had accompanied middle-class formation. Attention to the internal affairs of the middle class has revealed the complexity of 'middle-class consciousness' and has enabled the portrayal of a more coherent account of the nature of Bolton politics than a simple concentration on social relations between the two major classes would have revealed. Hopefully, moreover, it has produced a more informative and scrupulous historical synthesis.[10]

The increasing ability of the national Liberal and reforming middle class to procure parliamentary measures to forward its interests, despite the obvious limitations of the 1832 Reform Act, was indicative of the peculiar configuration of its hegemony.[11] Local government reform and the freeing of trade were especially important in this respect. However, as much of the foregoing pages have revealed, before 1850 these issues did not automatically translate into Liberal dominance at the local level. They actually provided a further source of disruptive internal conflicts for a middle class deeply divided along denominational, cultural, political and kinship lines. The predominant endemic rivalry in the town was that between the rival sections of the middle class, and not one between middle class and working class or rich and poor.[12] From the viewpoint of the middle class, their own struggle was usually more important than conflict between labour and capital or between themselves and the working class.[13] Moreover, intra-class relations were often more important in determining the parameters of class action than relations with either Parliament or the working class. This was especially the case in local government, into which the working class made only limited forays on its own behalf, but local government was an important area of struggle between petit-bourgeois and middle-class groupings throughout the second quarter of the century. Between 1838 and 1850 the exercise of power was often frustrated by conflict and the multiplicity and complexity of the local institutional network. By 1850, however, against the background of the remodelling of the town's local government – a process completed by 1850 – there was at least general agreement on how the town should be governed. Also important in effecting a compromise among rival sections of the middle class was a growing Tory accommodation to financial reform.

In terms of the internal power relations of the middle class, the ascendancy achieved by the Liberals in the early 1840s proved to be a fragile one. The net result of this in the long term, however, was a broadening of the base of the hegemony that the middle class exercised over the working class. By the 1860s popular support for both sections of the middle class had deepened and the working class was firmly assimilated into the two-party system. Space prohibits a detailed account of this development, but it is worth mentioning that, from mid-century, the Liberals were able to capitalise on such issues as the aristocratic mismanagement of the Crimean War and the boost that the American

Civil War gave to demands for parliamentary reform, to strengthen and consolidate the position which they had achieved by 1850 as the leaders of a variety of reform movements.[14] At the same time, as shown in Chapter Two, the Tory revival in local politics followed soon after they were forced to accept the legitimacy of the new town council in 1842, and from the late 1840s there were signs of a Tory resurgence in national politics too.[15] As demonstrated in Chapter Three, Conservatism achieved only a low level of support among the working class in the 1830s and 1840s. The massive Irish Roman Catholic immigration into the cotton districts following the famine, however, and the continuing Tory endorsement of traditional forms of leisure and amusement in the face of Bolton's increasingly visible temperance movement, worked to enhance its appeal in the 1850s, and by the 1860s it had grown in popularity to enjoy a mass following.[16]

The stabilisation of social relations was thus many-sided and gradual. It did not signal an end to class conflict or the emergence of an untroubled middle-class rule. Nor was there an end to the internal tensions and divisions within the middle class. The shared economic experiences of workers across a wide range of trades, subjected to threats to their status and security, ensured the presence in the second quarter of the century of a working-class consciousness based on common struggles against excessive competition and the inequality of capitalist market relations. The extent and depth of class antagonisms, however, were not universalised to the point that this class consciousness became revolutionary in content. Few workers sought to transcend capitalist relations of production through Owenite schemes of cooperation and, notwithstanding the wide appeal of Chartism, many had always sought less radical ways to permanent improvement than the Chartist insistence on the necessity of a prior major overhaul of the electoral system. The working class did not suddenly become liberalised or reformist. Reformist Liberalism achieved mass popularity as early as the 1840s, when class hostilities were at their height, not beyond 1850 as has so often been assumed. At the same time, the working class did not become deferential. 'Physical force' and 'mass platform' radicalism declined, but there were continuing demands by reformist workers for a more democratic franchise and for a more open local Liberal organisation. These ensured that the popular Liberalism of the 1850s would continue to be subject to the sort of class tensions that had so marked the Liberalism of the 1830s and 1840s. Workers may have aired their grievances more peacefully, but these continued to be informed by a strong sense of class pride and independence. The mid-Victorian consensus represented a process of social stabilisation rather than class harmonisation.

224   *Conclusion*

Notes

1. J. Foster in *Class Struggle and the Industrial Revolution* (London, 1974), and P. Joyce in *Work, Society and Politics* (London, 1980), have suggested otherwise.

2. Foster, *op. cit.*; G. S. Jones, 'Class Struggle and the Industrial Revolution', *New Left Review* 90 (1975); Joyce, *op. cit.*; N. Kirk, *The Growth of Working Class Reformism in Mid-Victorian England* (Beckenham, 1985).

3. This is contrary to the view expounded by N. Kirk in his 'In Defence of Class: A Critique of Recent Revisionist Writing upon the Nineteenth-Century English Working Class', *International Review of Social History*, XXXII (1987).

4. *B.F.P.*, 11 November 1837.

5. *B.F.P.*, 18 June, 1, 15, 22 October, 12 November 1836, 11 November 1837; D. S. Gadian, 'A Comparative Study of Popular Movements in North-West Industrial Towns', Lancaster University Ph.D. thesis (1976), pp. 220–3.

6. R. Price, *Labour in British Society: An Interpretive History* (London, 1986), pp. 54–55. It also appears that Foster (*op. cit.*, pp. 110–4) has exaggerated the influence of Owenism upon workers in nearby Oldham. See the criticisms by R. Sykes, 'Trade Unionism and Class Consciousness: The "Revolutionary" Period of General Unionism, 1829–1834', in J. Rule (ed.), *British Trade Unionism 1750–1850: The Formative Years* (London, 1988), pp. 188–91.

7. R. Sykes, *op. cit.*, pp. 180–6.

8. These distinctions between types of wealth and income were held to represent the moral superiority and greater social usefulness of industrial over aristocratic wealth (the former being generated by a process which benefited the whole and not just a small minority of society). The relations between wages and profits began to receive attention from the 1820s, but the focus was limited to the inequalities of exchange relations, and the radical critique continued to be primarily directed at the idleness and parasitism of the aristocracy. The employer's role as exploitative middleman within exchange relations was condemned by theorists of 'unequal exchange', but, as Stedman Jones says, the political origins of oppression remained clear: 'The employer, like the shopkeeper, was subsumed under the category of the middleman. He literally occupied a middle or intermediate position between the labouring producer and the idle consumer and was subject to the pressures of both. As a middleman, whose interest was to buy cheap and sell dear, he certainly took up a position alongside other oppressors, but more as lackey than controller of the system' (G. S. Jones, in Epstein and Thompson, *op. cit.*, pp. 20–1). For more on the affinities between Chartism and Liberalism see B. Harrison and P. Hollis, 'Chartism, Liberalism and the life of Robert Lowery', *English Historical Review* LXXXII (1967).

9. G. Crossick, *An Artisan Elite in Victorian Society: Kentish London 1840–1880* (London, 1978), p. 204; N. Kirk, *The Growth of Reformism*, p. 8.

10. In the attempt to provide a more coherent historical synthesis, I was influenced in the first place by some remarks made by Simon Gunn in his 'The "Failure" of the Victorian Middle Class: A Critique', in J. Wolff and J. Seed (eds), *The Culture of Capital: Art, Power and the Nineteenth-Century Middle Class* (Manchester, 1988), pp. 17–18.

11. D. Nicholls, *op. cit.*, pp. 48–9; J. Saville, 'Some Notes on Perry Anderson's "Figures of Descent"', in Barker and Nicholls, *op. cit.*, pp. 36–8.

12. This was probably the case in most urban areas: see D. Fraser, *Urban Politics in Victorian England: The Structure of Politics in Victorian Cities* (Leicester, 1976), pp. 14, 115.

13. Again, Bolton was far from unique in this respect: see, for instance, V.A.C. Gatrell, 'Incorporation and the Pursuit of Liberal Hegemony in Manchester 1790–1839', in D. Fraser (ed.), *Municipal Reform and the Industrial City* (Leicester, 1982).

14. *B.C.*, 3 March 1855, 14, 21, 28 February, 20, 27 June 1863, 11 February, 16, 23 December 1865.

15. *B.C.*, 19 June, 31 July 1847 (for the unprecedented popularity of William Bolling in the 1847 parliamentary election campaign).

16. J. R. Egan, 'The Irish in Bolton: 1841–1871', University of Sheffield M.A. thesis (1985); R. Poole, *Popular Leisure and the Music Hall in 19th-Century Bolton* (Centre for North-West Regional Studies, Occasional Paper 12, 1982).

Bibliography

This bibliography is organised in the following manner:

1. Primary Sources

1a. Newspapers and journals
1b. Manuscript collections
1c. Miscellaneous reports and transactions
1d. Parliamentary papers
1e. Books, articles and pamphlets by contemporaries

2. Secondary Sources

2a. Miscellaneous publications and unpublished typescripts on Bolton
2b. Unpublished dissertations
2c. Books and articles

For abbreviations, see the list at the beginning of the book.

PRIMARY SOURCES

1a. Newspapers and journals

Bolton Evening News, 18 September 1867 (supplement on Dobson and Barlow Limited).
Bolton Chronicle, 1825–70.
Bolton Free Press, 1835–47.
Bolton Journal, 10 December 1881 (Bolton religious census).
Bolton Journal and Guardian, 23 March 1895 ('Rise and Progress of Roman Catholicism in Bolton').
Bolton Protestant Association Monthly, 1851.

English Chartist Circular 11, 110 (temperance Chartism in Bolton).
Manchester and Salford Advertiser, 1842.
Manchester Guardian, 1830–45.
McDouall's Chartist and Republican Journal, 1841.
McDouall's Chartist Journal and Trades' Advocate, 1841.
Northern Star, 1838–50.
The Anti-Bread Tax Circular, 1841–3.
The Anti-Corn Law Circular, 1839–41.

1b. Manuscript collections

Ainsworth (J. H.) Papers: ZAH series, business correspondence and
    diaries, B.A.
Bolton Biographical Notes (consisting of seven bound volumes of
    mainly newspaper pen-portraits and obituaries), B.R.L.
Bolton Operative Bleachers', Dyers' and Finishers' Association, FT/1,
    Box 2 (1). Quarterly reports, balance sheets, and miscellaneous
    material, spring 1853–1890, B.A.
Correspondence relating to Chartist activity and local politics in
    Bolton, *H.O. 40/44* and *H.O. 45* series, Public Record Office, Kew.
Dobson and Barlow machine-makers, ZDB/2 series, correspondence
    and miscellaneous material relating to workshop disputes, 1865–8,
    B.A.
Heywood Papers, ZHE series, correspondence 1829–67, diaries 1818–68,
    B.A.
Material relating to Bank Street Chapel deposited at John Ryland's
    Library, Manchester.
Material relating to Dean Mills, ZHB series, Barrow Bridge, B.A.
Minute book of the local committee for promoting the success of
    the proposed factory workers' exhibition and bazaar, 1850–2,
    B.R.L.
Minutes of the Bolton hand-mule spinners' trade union, 1873–7,
    Manchester University Library.
Miscellaneous collection of handbills and other material, ZZ 130 series:
    ZZ/130/1, Bolton parliamentary election 1832; ZZ/130/2, Bolton
    parliamentary election 1835; ZZ/130/3, Bolton parliamentary
    election 1837; ZZ/130/4, Bolton parliamentary election 1841;
    ZZ/130/5, Bolton parliamentary elections after 1841; ZZ/130/6,
    Bolton parliamentary elections, miscellaneous; ZZ/130/8, Church
    and ecclesiastical matters, 1793–1856; ZZ/130/9, clubs and societies,
    1823–31; ZZ/130/10, education, literature and libraries, 1815–46;
    local government and politics, 1797–1876. B.A.

Miscellaneous material relating to the bleaching industry, located in ZZ series (this useful collection includes material relating to the activities of the employers' Bleachers' Association and the monthly pay lists of J. H. Ainsworth, 1829–34, and the same firm's time book 1840–3), B.A.

Transcript of the proceeding of the court leet of Little Bolton, MLB/2, 1797–1841, B.A.

Webbs' Trade Union Collection, Section A, IV, Bolton Trades Council, short sketch of history, British Library of Political and Economic Science.

Webbs' Trade Union Collection, Section A, XXXV, Bolton Cotton Spinners, sketch of history and extracts from old minute books and reports, 1844–80, British Library of Political and Economic Science.

1c. Miscellaneous reports and transactions

Annual reports for the Bolton Mechanics' Institution, 1825–77 (incomplete).

Bolton Society for the Protection of the Poor and District Provident Society, Reports 1841–58.

General reports of the overseers of the poor of Great Bolton, for the years 1820, 1823, 1831, 1832, 1833.

Reports of the superintendent of Police, 1847–9.

The Twentieth Annual Report of the Bolton Temperance Society (Bolton, 1854).

1d. British Parliamentary Papers

Reports of Inspectors of Factories, 1838–50.

1833, VI, Select Committee on the Present State of Manufactures, Commerce, and Shipping in the United Kingdom.

1834, X, Select Committee on Hand-Loom Weavers.

1835, V, Select Committee on Accidents in Mines.

1835, XIII, Select Committee on Hand-loom Weavers' Petitions.

1837–8, VII, Select Committee on the Education of the Poorer Classes.

1837–8, VIII, First and Second Reports from the Select Committee on Combinations of Workmen Together with Minutes of Evidence.

1840, X, Select Committee on Mills and Factories.

1840, XXIV, Report from R. M. Muggeridge on the Condition of the Handloom Weavers of Lancashire, Westmorland, Cumberland and parts of the West Riding of Yorkshire.

1840, XXXIX, Bolton Police: Account of Monies Received and Expended for Police Purposes in the Borough of Bolton ... and Return of all Persons Appointed as Members of the Police Force etc.

1841, II, Correspondence between the Home Office and the Poor Law Commissioners on the subject of Distress in Bolton.

1841, XX, Municipal Corporations: Report of Captain Jebb on the Bolton Corporation.

1842, XV, First Report of the Commissioners on the Employment of Children (Mines).

1842, XVII, Reports to Commissioners: Children's Employment (Mines).

1842, XXXV, Communications to the Home Office on Distress in Bolton.

1844, XVIIL, First Report of the Commissioners for Inquiring into the State of Large Towns and Populous Districts.

1845, XVIIIL, Second Report of the Commissioners for Inquiring into the State of Large Towns and Populous Districts.

1846, XXXVI, Copy of Reports Received by the Poor Law Commissioners in 1841 on the State of the Macclesfield and Bolton Unions.

1847, XXI, Bolton Improvement: Report of the Commissioners Appointed to make Preliminary Inquiries Respecting the Bolton Improvement Bill, with Minutes of Evidence.

1847, XLVI, Memorials of the Master Manufacturers and Millowners in the County of Lancaster, with Respect to the Ten Hours Bill of 1847.

1849, VII, Select Committee on the Prevention of Accidents in Coal Mines.

1849, VII, Select Committee on Accidents in Mines.

1852–3, XXXVII, Select Committee on Public Houses and Places of Public Entertainment.

1854, XIV, Select Committee on Public Houses and Places of Public Entertainment.

1854, 1851 Census: Ages, Civil Conditions, Occupations and Birth-Place of the People, 11.

1854–5, XVIII, Commission for Inquiring into the Expediency of Extending the Acts Relative to Factories to Bleaching Works, &c.

1857–8, XI, Select Committee on Bleaching and Dyeing Works.

1868–9, XXXI, Trade Union Commission: Manchester Outrages Inquiry.

1e. Books, articles and pamphlets by contemporaries

A Letter Addressed to the Members of Both Houses of Parliament on the Distresses of the Hand Loom Weavers, as a Remedy for which the Expediency and Practicability of a Board of Trade for the Equalization of Wages is Proposed and Considered by the Committee of Manufacturers and Weavers of the Borough of Bolton (Bolton, 1834).

Arrowsmith, J. H., *Essay on Mechanics' Institutes, with a Particular Relation to the Institute Recently Established in Bolton* (Bolton, 1825).

Ashworth, H., *On the State of Education in the Borough of Bolton in 1837* (copy available in B.R.L.).

Ashworth, H., *An Inquiry into the Origin, Progress, and Results of the Strike of the Operative Cotton Spinners of Preston, from October 1836 to February 1837* (Manchester, 1837).

Ashworth, H., 'Statistics of the Present Depression of Trade at Bolton; Showing the Mode in which it Affects the Different Classes of a Manufacturing Population', *Journal of the Statistical Society* V (1842).

Ashworth, H., *The Preston Strike: An Enquiry into its Causes and Consequences* (Manchester, 1854).

Ashworth, H., *Historical Data Chiefly Relating to South Lancashire and the Cotton Manufacture* (Manchester, 1866).

Ashworth, H., *Recollections of Richard Cobden, MP, and the Anti-Corn Law League* (London, 1876).

Atkin, F., *The Philosophy of the Temperance Reformation* (Bolton, 1874).

Authentic Report of the Great Protestant Meeting Held in St George's Schoolroom, Little Bolton, 9 November 1840, for the Purpose of Forming a Branch Association, to be Called the Bolton and Halliwell Association (Bolton, 1840).

Baker, F., *A Letter to the Rev. John Lyons, M.A., Occasioned by a Sermon Preached in St George's Church, Little Bolton, on Sunday, June 27, 1841, by that Gentleman, being Previous to the Election of Members for the Borough of Bolton* (Bolton, n. d.).

Baker, F., *The Moral Tone of the Factory System Defended* (London, 1850).

Baker, F., *The Rise and Progress of Nonconformity in Bolton* (London, 1854).

Bank Street Chapel Bolton, Bi-Centenary Commemoration 1696–1896 (Manchester, 1896).

Barton, B. H., *Historical Gleanings of Bolton and District* (Bolton, 1881).

Black, J., 'A Medico-Topographical, Geological, and Statistical Sketch of Bolton and its Neighbourhood', *Transactions of the Provincial Medical and Surgical Association* V (1837).

Bolton Operative Conservative Association: Report of the Proceedings at the Meeting of the Bolton Operative Conservative Association Held in the Little Bolton Town Hall, June 1st 1836 (Bolton, 1836).

Brimelow, W., *The Ainsworths of Smithills* (Bolton, 1881).

Brimelow, W., *Political and Parliamentary History of Bolton, Vol. 1* (Bolton, 1882).

Clegg, J., *A Chronological History of Bolton* (Bolton, 1878).

Clegg, J., *Annals of Bolton* (Bolton, 1888).

Engels, F., *The Condition of the Working Class in England*, translated and edited by W. O. Henderson and W. H. Chaloner (Oxford, 1958).

Entwistle, J., *A Report of the Sanitary Condition of the Borough of Bolton* (Bolton, 1848).

French, G. J., *A Short History of the Volunteer Movement in Bolton* (Bolton, 1886).

Hilton, R. S., *Sunday Closing: Being a Reply to 'Observer's' Letter which Appeared in the Bolton Chronicle of June 18th 1853; and Containing a Refutation of Calumnies and Misrepresentations of that Letter, a Word in Defence of the 'Mob' and a Brief Examination of 'Observer's Church* (Bolton, 1853).

Horwich Operative Conservative Association First Anniversary Dinner, 1836 (Bolton, 1836).

Marx, K. and Engels, F., *Articles on Britain* (Moscow, 1971).

Musgrave, J., *Origins of Methodism in Bolton* (Bolton, 1865).

Paul, W., *History of the Origin and Progress of Operative Conservative Societies* (Leeds, 1838).

Peaples, F. W., *History of the Great and Little Bolton Co-Operative Society Limited, Showing Fifty Years' Progress, 1859–1909* (Manchester, 1909).

Pickvance, W. W. (Prize) *Essay on the Advantages Working Men Will Receive by Visiting the Exhibition of 1851* (Bolton, 1851).

Reach, A. B., *Manchester and the Textile Districts in 1849*, edited by C. Aspin (Helmshore, 1972).

Rowley, J. (ed.), *H.M. Richardson, Reminiscences of Forty Years in Bolton* (Bolton, 1885).

Scholes, J. C., *History of Bolton: With Memorials of the Old Parish Church* (Bolton, 1892).

The Bad Effects of Combinations of Workmen in the Town and Neighbourhood of Bolton-lLe-Moors (comprising republished correspondence to the *Manchester Guardian*, Manchester, 1823).

Whittle, P. A., *Bolton-le-Moors* (Bolton, 1857).

Winder, T. H., *A Life's Adventure* (autobiography, Bolton, 1921).

SECONDARY SOURCES

2a. Miscellaneous publications and unpublished typescripts on Bolton

Billington, W. D. (ed.), 'Recollections of Nineteenth Century Bolton' (typescript in B.R.L., n. d.).

Billington, W. D., *Barrow Bridge: The History, Natural History and Tales of the Village* (Halliwell Local History Society, Bolton, 1988).

Boothman, T. B., *Bolton Master Cotton Spinners' Association 1861–1961 Centenary Commemoration* (Bolton, 1961).

Brown, W. E., *Robert Heywood of Bolton 1786–1868* (Wakefield, 1970).

Crankshaw, W. P. and Blackburn, A., *A Century and a Half of Cotton Spinning 1797–1947: The History of Knowles, Limited of Bolton* (Bolton, 1948).

Daniels, W. G., 'A "Turn-Out" of Bolton Machine-Makers in 1831', *Economic History* (a Supplement to the *Economic Journal* 1, 1926–9).

Daniels, W. G., 'The Organisation of a "Turn-Out" of Bolton Machine-Makers in 1831', *Economic History* (a Supplement to the *Economic Journal* 2, 1930–3).

Deakins Ltd. 100 Years of Bleaching and Dyeing: The Story of a Family Enterprise at Belmont (1950).

Dunne, T., *Bolton Public Libraries 1853–1978: One Hundred and Twenty-Five Years in Retrospect* (Bolton Metropolitan Borough Arts Department, 1978).

Greathead, G., 'A Study of Handloom Weaving Decline in the Mid-Nineteenth Century' (typescript in B.R.L., n. d.).

Hamer, H., *Bolton 1838–1938: A Centenary Record of Municipal Progress* (Bolton, 1938).

Hartley, S., 'A History of the Bleaching Industry: With Special Reference to the Turton Area of Lancashire' (typescript in B.R.L., n. d.).

Haslam, W. H. and Morris, F. E., *John Haslam and Co. Ltd, 1816–1920* (B.R.L., n. d.).

Longworth, J. H., *The Cotton Mills of Bolton 1780–1985* (Bolton, 1986).

Muschamp, R., 'The Society of Friends in the Bolton District', *Transactions of the Lancashire and Cheshire Antiquarian Society* XLV (1928).

O'Connor, D., 'Barrow Bridge, Bolton. Dean Mills Estate. A Victorian Model Achievement' (typescript in B.R.L., 1972).

O'Connor, D., 'The Temperance Movement in Bolton' (typescript in B.R.L., 1974).

Poole, R., *Popular Leisure and the Music Hall in 19th-Century Bolton* (Centre for North-West Regional Studies, University of Lancaster Occasional Paper 12, 1982).

Poole, R., 'Leisure in Bolton, 1750–1900' (typescript in B.R.L., a study undertaken for the Bolton Research Award in 1980–1).

Ramsden, M., *A Responsible Society: The Life and Times of the Congregation of Bank Street Chapel, Bolton, Lancashire* (Horsham, 1985).

'Short Histories of Famous Firms, Hick Hargreaves and Co.', *The Engineer*, 25 June and 30 July 1990.

'Short Histories of Famous Firms, V., Messrs. Rothwell and Co., Bolton', *The Engineer*, January to June 1920.

2b. Unpublished dissertations

Dale, P. N., 'A Study of the Growth of Churches in Bolton during the Industrial Revolution', University College of North Wales Ph.D. thesis (1984).

Egan, J. R., 'The Irish in Bolton: 1841–1871', University of Sheffield M.A. thesis (1985).

Evans, G., 'Social Leadership and Social Control in Bolton, 1870–98', University of Lancaster M.A. thesis (1974).

Gadian, D. S., 'A Comparative Study of Popular Movements in North West Industrial Towns 1830–1850', University of Lancaster Ph.D. thesis (1976).

Harris, P. A., 'Class Conflict, the Trade Unions and Working Class Politics in Bolton, 1875–1896', University of Lancaster M.A. thesis (1971).

Narey, B., 'The 1853–60 Ten Hours Movement in the Bleaching Industry with Particular Reference to the Response of the Master Bleachers of Bolton', Manchester Polytechnic M.A. dissertation (1988).

Pilling, P. W., 'Hick Hargreaves and Co., the History of an Engineering Firm c.1833–1939: A Study with Special Reference to Technological Change and Markets', University of Liverpool Ph.D. thesis (1985).

Sykes, R. A., 'Popular Politics and Trade Unionism in South-East Lancashire, 1829–42', University of Manchester Ph.D. thesis (1982).

Taylor, P. F., 'The New Paternalism and Labour-Capital Relations in the Bolton Cotton Industry, c. 1848–1877', Manchester Polytechnic B.A. dissertation (1986).

Taylor, P. F., 'Popular Politics and Labour-Capital Relations in Bolton, 1825–1850', University of Lancaster Ph.D. thesis (1991).

Thorpe, E., 'Industrial Relations and the Social Structure: A Case Study of Bolton Cotton Mule-Spinners, 1884–1910', University of Salford M.Sc. thesis (1969).

Trodd, G., 'Political Change and the Working Class in Blackburn and Burnley, 1880–1914', University of Lancaster Ph.D. thesis (1978).

2c. Books and articles

Adelman, P., *Victorian Radicalism: The Middle-Class Experience, 1830–1914* (New York, 1984).

Adelman, P., *Peel and the Conservative Party 1830–1850* (London, 1989).

Anderson, P., 'Origins of the Present Crisis', *New Left Review* 23 (1964).

Anderson, P., 'The Figures of Descent', *New Left Review* 161 (1987).

Bailey, P., *Leisure and Class in Victorian England: Rational Recreation and the Contest for Control, 1830–1885* (London, 1987).

Barker, C. and Nicholls, D. (eds), *The Development of British Capitalist Society: A Marxist Debate* (Manchester, 1988).

Behagg, C., 'An Alliance with the Middle Class: The Birmingham Political Union', in J. Epstein and D. Thompson (eds), *The Chartist Experience: Studies in Working-Class Radicalism and Culture, 1830–60* (London, 1982).

Behagg, C., *Politics and Production in the Early Nineteenth Century* (London, 1990).

Belcham, J., 'English Working-Class Radicalism and the Irish 1815–1850', *North West Labour History Society Bulletin* 8 (1982–3).

Belcham, J., '1848: Feargus O'Connor and the Collapse of the Mass Platform', in J. Epstein and D. Thompson (eds), *The Chartist Experience: Studies in Working-Class Radicalism and Culture, 1830–60* (London, 1982).

Benson, J., *British Coalminers in the Nineteenth Century: A Social History* (Dublin, 1980).

Best, G., *Mid-Victorian Britain 1851–75* (London, 1971).

Best, G. F. A., 'Popular Protestantism in Victorian England', in R. Robson (ed.), *Ideas and Institutions of Victorian Britain* (London, 1967).

Biagini, E. F. and Reid, A. J., *Currents of Radicalism: Popular Radicalism, Organised Labour and Party Politics in Britain, 1850–1914* (Cambridge, 1991).

Blake, R., *The Conservative Party from Peel to Thatcher* (London, 1985).

Boyson, R., 'The New Poor Law in North-East Lancashire, 1834–71', *Transactions of the Lancashire and Cheshire Antiquarian Society* LXX (1960).

Boyson, R., *The Ashworth Cotton Enterprise: The Rise and Fall of a Family Firm 1818–1880* (Oxford, 1970).

Briggs, A., 'Middle-Class Consciousness in English Politics, 1780–1846', *Past and Present* 9 (1956).

Briggs, A. (ed.), *Chartist Studies* (London, 1959).

Briggs, A., 'The Language of "Class" in Early Nineteenth-Century England', in A. Briggs and J. Saville (eds), *Essays in Labour History* (New York, 1960).

Brown, L., 'The Chartists and the Anti-Corn-Law League', in A. Briggs (ed.), *Chartist Studies* (London, 1959).

Burgess, K., *The Origins of British Industrial Relations* (London, 1975).

Burgess, K., *The Challenge of Labour: Shaping British Society* (London, 1980).

Bythell, D., *The Handloom Weavers: A Study in the English Cotton Industry during the Industrial Revolution* (Cambridge, 1969).

Bythell, D., *The Sweated Trades: Outwork in Nineteenth-Century Britain* (London, 1978).

Catling, H., *The Spinning Mule* (Lancashire County Council, 1986).

Challinor, R., *The Lancashire and Cheshire Miners* (Newcastle, 1972).

Challinor, R. and Ripley, B., *The Miners' Association: A Trade Union in the Age of the Chartists* (London, 1968).

Chaloner, W. H., 'The Agitation against the Corn Laws', in J. T. Ward (ed.), *Popular Movements c.1830–1850* (London, 1970).

Chapman, S. D., *The Cotton Industry in the Industrial Revolution* (London, 1972).

Chapman, S. J., 'The Regulation of Wages by Lists in the Spinning Industry', *Economic Journal* IX (1899).

Chapman, S. J., 'Some Policies of the Cotton Spinners' Trade Unions', *The Economic Journal* X (1900).

Chapman, S. J., 'An Historical Sketch of Masters' Associations in the Cotton Industry', *Transactions of the Manchester Statistical Society* (1901).

Clements, R. V., 'British Trade Unions and Popular Political Economy 1850–1875', *Economic History Review*, 2nd series, XIX, 16 (1961).

Cole, G. D. H., *A Short History of the British Working-Class Movement 1789–1947* (London, 1948).

Coleman, B., *Conservatism and the Conservative Party in Nineteenth-Century Britain* (London, 1988).

Cronin, J. E. and Schneer, J. (eds), *Social Conflict and the Political Order in Modern Britain* (London, 1982).

Crossick, G., *An Artisan Elite in Victorian Society: Kentish London 1840–1880* (London, 1978).

Crossick, G. and Haupt, H.-G. (eds), *Shopkeepers and Master Artisans in Nineteenth-Century Europe* (London, 1984).

Crouzet, F., *The Victorian Economy* (London, 1982).

Cunningham, H., 'The Language of Patriotism, 1750–1914', *History Workshop, a Journal of Socialist Historians* 12 (Autumn, 1981).

Dennis, R., *English Industrial Cities of the Nineteenth Century* (Cambridge, 1984).

Dutton, H. I. and King, J. E., 'The Limits of Paternalism: The Cotton Tyrants of North Lancashire 1836–1854', *Social History* 7, 1 (January, 1982).

Edsall, N. C., *The Anti-Poor Law Movement 1834–1844* (Manchester, 1971).

Edsall, N. C., 'A Failed National Movement: The Parliamentary and Financial Reform Association, 1848–54', *Bulletin of the Institute for Historical Research* (1976).

Epstein, J., *The Lion of Freedom: Feargus O'Connor and the Chartist Movement, 1832–1842* (London, 1982).

Epstein, J., 'Understanding the Cap of Liberty: Symbolic Practice and Social Conflict in Early Nineteenth-Century England', *Past and Present* 122 (February, 1989).

Epstein, J. and Thompson, D. (eds), *The Chartist Experience: Studies in Working-Class Radicalism and Culture, 1830–60* (London, 1982).

Evans, E. J., *Social Policy 1830–1914: Individualism, Collectivism and the Origins of the Welfare State* (London, 1978).

Evans, E. J., *The Forging of the Modern State: Early Industrial Britain 1783–1870* (London, 1983).

Farnie, D. A., *The English Cotton Industry and the World Market 1815–1896* (Oxford, 1979).

Foster, J., *Class Struggle and the Industrial Revolution: Early Industrial Capitalism in Three English Towns* (London, 1974).

Foster, J., 'The Declassing of Language', *New Left Review* 150 (1985).

Foster, J., 'Some Comments on "Class Struggle and the Labour Aristocracy"', *Social History* 3 (October, 1986).

Fowler, A. and Wyke, T. (eds), *The Barefoot Aristocrats: A History of the Amalgamated Association of Operative Cotton Spinners* (Littleborough, 1987).

Fraser, D., 'The Agitation for Parliamentary Reform', in J. T. Ward (ed.), *Popular Movements c.1830–1850* (London, 1970).

Fraser, D., *Urban Politics in Victorian England: The Structure of Politics in Victorian Cities* (Leicester, 1976).

Fraser, D., *Power and Authority in the Victorian City* (Oxford, 1979).

Fraser, D. (ed.), *Municipal Reform and the Industrial City* (Leicester, 1982).

Fraser, D., *The Evolution of the British Welfare State* (Basingstoke, 1984).

Fraser, W. H., 'Trade Unionism', in J. T. Ward (ed.), *Popular Movements c.1830–1850* (London, 1970).

Freifeld, M., 'Technological Change and the "Self-Acting" Mule: A Study of Skill and the Sexual Division of Labour', *Social History* 11, 3 (October, 1986).

Gadian, D. S., 'Class Consciousness in Oldham and Other North-West Industrial Towns 1830–1850', *The Historical Journal* 21, 1 (1978).

Garrard, J. (et al.), *The Middle Class in Politics* (Farnborough, 1978).

Garrard, J., *Leadership and Power in Victorian Industrial Towns 1830–80* (Manchester, 1983).

Gatrell, V. A. C., 'Incorporation and the Pursuit of Liberal Hegemony in Manchester 1790–1839', in D. Fraser (ed.), *Municipal Reform and the Industrial City* (Leicester, 1982).

Gash, N., *Aristocracy and People: Britain 1815–1865* (London, 1979).

Gilbert, A. D., *Religion and Society in Industrial England: Church, Chapel and Social Change 1740–1914* (London, 1976).

Gillespie, F. E., *Labor and Politics in England 1850–1867* (1927, republished in London, 1966).

Gosden, P. H. J. H., *Self-Help: Voluntary Associations in Nineteenth-Century Britain* (London, 1973).

Gray, R. Q., *The Labour Aristocracy in Victorian Edinburgh* (Oxford, 1976).

Gray, R. Q., 'The Deconstructing of the English Working Class', *Social History* 11, 3 (October, 1986).

Gray, R. Q., 'The Languages of Factory Reform in Britain', in P. Joyce (ed.), *The Historical Meanings of Work* (Cambridge, 1987).

Greenwood, J., 'The Conservative Party and the Working Classes: The Organisational Response' (University of Warwick, Department of Politics, Working Paper 12, June, 1974).

Gunn, S., 'The "Failure" of the Victorian Middle Class: A Critique', in J. Wolff and J. Seed (eds), *The Culture of Capital: Art, Power and the Nineteenth-Century Middle Class* (Manchester, 1988).

Hammond, J. L. and B., *The Age of the Chartists 1832–1854: A Study of Discontent* (New York, 1967).

Hanham, H. J., 'Liberal Organisations for Working Men, 1860–1914', *Society for the Study of Labour History Bulletin* 7 (1963).

Harrison, B., *Drink and the Victorians: The Temperance Question in England 1815–1872* (Pittsburgh, 1971).

Harrison, B., 'Teetotal Chartism', *History* 58 (1973).

Harrison, B. and Hollis, P., 'Chartism, Liberalism and the life of Robert Lowery', *English Historical Review* LXXXII (1967).

Harrison, R., *Before the Socialists: Studies in Labour and Politics 1861–1881* (London, 1965).

Hennock, E. P., *Fit and Proper Persons: Ideal and Reality in Nineteenth Century Urban Government* (London, 1973).

Hinton, J., *Labour and Socialism: A History of the British Labour Movement 1867–1974* (Brighton, 1983).

Hobsbawm, E. J., *Labouring Men: Studies in the History of Labour* (London, 1964).

Hobsbawm, E. J., *Industry and Empire: From 1750 to the Present Day* (Harmondsworth, 1969).

Hobsbawm, E. J., *Worlds of Labour: Further Studies in the History of Labour* (London, 1984).

Hollis, P., *The Pauper Press: A Study in Working-Class Radicalism of the 1830s* (Oxford, 1970).

Hollis, P., *Class and Conflict in Nineteenth-Century England, 1815–1850* (London, 1973).

Hollis, P. (ed.), *Pressure from Without in Early Victorian England* (London, 1974).

Honeyman, K., *Origins of Enterprise: Business Leadership in the Industrial Revolution* (Manchester, 1982).

Hopwood, E., *A History of the Lancashire Cotton Industry and the Amalgamated Weavers' Association* (Manchester, 1969).

Howe, A., *The Cotton Masters 1830–1860* (Oxford, 1984).

Huberman, M., 'Invisible Handshakes in Lancashire: Cotton Spinning in the First Half of the Nineteenth Century', *Journal of Economic History* XLV, 4 (December, 1986).

Huberman, M., 'The Economic Origins of Paternalism: Lancashire Cotton Spinning in the First Half of the Nineteenth Century', *Social History* 12, 2 (May, 1987).

Huberman, M., 'The Economic Origins of Paternalism: Reply to Rose, Taylor and Winstanley', *Social History* 14, 1 (January, 1989).

Hume, C. H., 'The Public Health Movement', in J. T. Ward (ed.), *Popular Movements c.1830–1850* (London, 1970).

Hutchins, B. L. and Harrison, A., *A History of Factory Legislation* (London, 1966).

Jenkin, A., 'Chartism and the Trade Unions', in L. M. Munby (ed.), *The Luddites and Other Essays* (London, 1972).

Jenkins, M., *The General Strike of 1842* (London, 1980).

Johnson, R., 'Educational Policy and Social Control in Early Victorian England', *Past and Present* 48 (November, 1970).

Jones, D., *Chartism and the Chartists* (London, 1975).

Jones, G. S., 'Class Struggle and the Industrial Revolution', *New Left Review* 90 (1975).

Jones, G. S., 'The Language of Chartism', in J. Epstein and D. Thompson (eds), *The Chartist Experience: Studies in Working-Class Radicalism and Culture, 1830–60* (London, 1982).

Jones, G. S., *Languages of Class: Studies in English Working Class History 1832–1982* (Cambridge, 1983).

Joyce, P., 'The Factory Politics of Lancashire in the Later Nineteenth Century', *The Historical Journal* XVIII, 3 (1975).

Joyce, P., *Work, Society and Politics: The Culture of the Factory in Later Victorian England* (London, 1980).

Joyce, P., 'Labour, Capital and Compromise: A Response to Richard Price', *Social History* 9, 1 (January, 1984).

Joyce, P., 'Languages of Reciprocity and Conflict: A Further Response to Richard Price', *Social History* 9, 2 (May, 1984).

Joyce, P. (ed.), *The Historical Meanings of Work* (Cambridge, 1987).

Kirk, N., 'The Myth of Class? Workers and the Industrial Revolution in Stockport', *Society for the Study of Labour History Bulletin* 51, 1 (April 1986).

Kirk, N., *The Growth of Working Class Reformism in Mid-Victorian England* (Beckenham, 1985).

Kirk, N., 'In Defence of Class: A Critique of Recent Revisionist Writing upon the Nineteenth-Century English Working Class', *International Review of Social History* XXXII (1987).

Kirby, R. G. and Musson, A. E., *The Voice of the People: John Doherty, 1798–1854. Trade Unionist, Radical and Factory Reformer* (Manchester, 1975).

Koditschek, T., *Class Formation and Urban Industrial Society: Bradford, 1750–1850* (Cambridge, 1990).

Lacquer, T. W., *Religion and Respectability: Sunday Schools and Working-Class Culture 1780–1850* (London, 1976).

Lazonick, W., 'Industrial Relations and Technical Change: The Case of the Self-Acting Mule', *Cambridge Journal of Economics* 3 (1979).

McCleod, H., *Religion and the Working Class in Nineteenth-Century Britain* (London, 1984).

McCord, N., 'Cobden and Bright in Politics, 1846–1857', in R. Robson (ed.), *Ideas and Institutions of Victorian Britain* (London, 1967).

McCord, N., *The Anti-Corn Law League 1838–1846* (London, 1968).

Mather, F. C., *Public Order in the Age of the Chartists* (Manchester, 1959).

Mather, F. C., *After the Canal Duke: A Study of the Industrial Estates Administered by the Trustees of the Third Duke of Bridgewater in the Age of Railway Building, 1825–1872* (Oxford, 1972).

Mather, F. C., *Chartism and Society: An Anthology of Documents* (London, 1980).

Matthew, H. C. G., 'Disraeli, Gladstone, and the Politics of Mid-Victorian Budgets', *The Historical Journal*, 22, 3 (1979).

Midwinter, E. C., *Victorian Social Reform* (Harlow, 1968).

Moorhouse, H. F., 'The Marxist Theory of the Labour Aristocracy', *Social History* 3, 1 (1978).

Morris, R. J., *Class and Class Consciousness in the Industrial Revolution 1780–1850* (London, 1979).

Morris, R. J. (ed.), *Class, Power and Social Structure in British Nineteenth-Century Towns* (Leicester, 1986).

Musson, A. E., 'The Ideology of Early Co-operation in Lancashire and Cheshire', *Transactions of the Lancashire and Cheshire Antiquarian Society* LXVIII (1958).

Musson, A. E., *British Trade Unions 1800–1875* (London, 1972).

Musson, A. E., 'Class Struggle and the Labour Aristocracy, 1830–60', *Social History* 3 (October, 1976).

Musson, A. E. and Robinson, E., 'The Origins of Engineering in Lancashire', *Journal of Economic Society* 20 (1960).

Musson, A. E. and Robinson, E., *Science and Technology in the Industrial Revolution* (Manchester, 1969).

Neale, R. S., *Class and Ideology in the Nineteenth Century* (London, 1972).

Neale, R. S., *Class in English History 1680–1850* (Oxford, 1981).

Newby, H., 'The Deferential Dialectic', *Comparative Studies in Society and History* 17 (1975).

Newby, H., 'Paternalism and Capitalism', in R. Scase (ed.), *Industrial Society: Class, Cleavage and Control* (London, 1977).

Nicholls, D., 'The English Middle Class and the Ideological Significance of Radicalism, 1760–1886', *Journal of British Studies* 24 (1985).

Nicholls, D., 'Fractions of Capital: The Aristocracy, the City and Industry in the Development of Modern British Capitalism', *Social History* 13, 1 (January, 1988).

Nicholls, D., 'The Personnel, Methods, and Policies of English Middle-Class Radicalism, 1760–1924', *The International Journal of Social Education* 3, 1 (Spring, 1988).

Payne, P. L., *British Entrepreneurship in the Nineteenth Century* (London, 1988).

Perkin, H., *Origins of Modern English Society* (London, 1985).

Pickering, P. A., 'Class without Words: Symbolic Communication in the Chartist Movement', *Past and Present* 112 (August, 1986).

Pollard, S., 'Nineteenth-Century Co-Operation: From Community Building to Shopkeeping', in A. Briggs and J. Saville (eds), *Essays in Labour History* 1 (1960).

Pollard, S., 'The Factory Village in the Industrial Revolution', *English Historical Review* 79 (1964).

Price, R., 'The Other Face of Respectability: Violence in the Manchester Brickmaking Trade 1859–1870', *Past and Present* 66 (February, 1975).

Price, R., *Masters, Unions and Men: Work Control in Building and the Rise of Labour 1830–1914* (Cambridge, 1980).

Price, R., 'The Labour Process and Labour History', *Social History* 8, 1 (January, 1983).

Price, R., 'Conflict and Co-operation: A Reply to Patrick Joyce', *Social History* 9, 2 (May, 1984).

Price, R., *Labour in British Society: An Interpretive History* (London, 1986).

Prothero, I., *Artisans and Politics in Early Nineteenth Century London: John Gast and his Times* (Folkestone, 1979).

Richards, P., 'The State and Early Industrial Capitalism: The Case of the Handloom Weavers', *Past and Present* 83 (May, 1979).

Richards, P., 'State Formation and Class Struggle, 1832–48', in

P. Corrigan (ed.), *Capitalism, State Formation and Marxist Theory* (London, 1980).

Roberts, D., *Paternalism in Early Victorian England* (London, 1979).

Rose, A. G., 'The Plug Riots of 1842 in Lancashire and Cheshire', *Transactions of the Lancashire and Cheshire Antiquarian Society* LXVII (1957).

Rose, M. E., 'The Anti-Poor Law Agitation', in J. T. Ward (ed.), *Popular Movements c.1830–1850* (London, 1970).

Rose, M., Taylor, P. and Winstanley, M. J., 'The Economic Origins of Paternalism: Some Objections', *Social History* 14, 1 (January, 1989).

Royle, E., *Chartism* (Harlow, 1980).

Royle, E. and Walvin, J., *English Radicals and Reformers 1760–1848* (Brighton, 1982).

Rubinstein, W. D., 'Wealth, Elites and the Class Structure of Modern Britain', *Past and Present* 76 (1977).

Rubinstein, W. D., 'The End of "Old Corruption" in Britain 1780–1860', *Past and Present* 101 (1983).

Rule, J. (ed.), *British Trade Unionism 1750–1850: The Formative Years* (London, 1988).

Samuel, R., 'The Workshop of the World: Steam Power and Hand Technology in Mid-Victorian Britain', *History Workshop: A Journal of Socialist Historians* 3 (Spring, 1977).

Sanderson, M., *Education, Economic Change and Society in England 1780–1870* (London, 1983).

Saville, J., *1848: The British State and the Chartist Movement* (Cambridge, 1987).

Seed, J., 'Unitarianism, Political Economy and the Antinomies of Liberal Culture in Manchester, 1830–50', *Social History* 7, 1 (January, 1982).

Seed, J., 'Theologies of Power: Unitarianism and the Social Relations of Religious Discourse, 1800–50', in R. J. Morris (ed.), *Class, Power and Social Structure in British Nineteenth-Century Towns* (Leicester, 1986).

Shiman, L. L., *Crusade against Drink in Victorian England* (Basingstoke, 1988).

Smethurst, D. J., *Lancashire and the Miners' Association of Great Britain and Ireland 1842–1848* (Eccles and District Local History Society, 1978).

Stevenson, J., *Popular Disturbances in England* (London, 1979).

Storch, R. D., 'The Problem of Working-Class Leisure', in A. P. Donajgrodzki (ed.), *Social Control in Nineteenth Century Britain* (London, 1977).

Sykes, A. J., *Concerning the Bleaching Industry* (Manchester, 1925).

Sykes, R. A., 'Some Aspects of Working-Class Consciousness in Oldham, 1830–1842', *The Historical Journal* 23, 1 (1980).

Sykes, R. A., 'Early Chartism and Trade Unionism in South-East Lancashire', in J. Epstein and D. Thompson (eds), *The Chartist Experience: Studies in Working-Class Radicalism and Culture, 1830–60* (London, 1982).

Sykes, R. A., 'Physical-Force Chartism: The Cotton District and the Chartist Crisis of 1839', *International Review of Social History* 30 (1985).

Tholfsen, T., *Working Class Radicalism in Mid-Victorian England* (London, 1976).

Thomis, M. I., *The Town Labourer and the Industrial Revolution* (London, 1974).

Thompson, David, *Nonconformity in the Nineteenth Century* (London, 1979).

Thompson, Dorothy, *The Early Chartists* (London, 1971).

Thompson, Dorothy, *The Chartists: Popular Politics in the Industrial Revolution* (Aldershot, 1986).

Thompson, Dorothy, 'The Languages of Class', *Society for the Study of Labour History Bulletin* 25, 1 (1987).

Thompson, E. P., *The Making of the English Working Class* (Harmondsworth, 1968).

Thompson, E. P., 'The Moral Economy of the English Crowd in the Eighteenth Century', *Past and Present* 50 (1971).

Thompson, E. P., 'Eighteenth-Century English Society: Class Struggle Without Class?', *Social History* 3, 2 (May, 1978).

Turner, H. A., *Trade Union Growth, Structure and Policy: A Comparative Study of the Cotton Unions in England* (Toronto, 1962).

Vincent, J., *The Formation of the Liberal Party 1857–1868* (London, 1966).

Walsh, D., 'Operative Conservatism in Lancashire, 1833–1846: Some Comments on a Changing Political Culture' (Salford University Occasional Paper in Politics and Contemporary History 11, 1987).

Walton, J. K., *Lancashire: A Social History, 1558–1939* (Manchester, 1987).

Ward, J. T., 'The Factory Movement in Lancashire 1830–1855', *Transactions of the Lancashire and Cheshire Antiquarian Society* 75–6 (1965–6).

Ward, J. T. (ed.), *Popular Movements* c.1830–1850 (London, 1970).

Webb, S. and B., *The History of Trade Unionism* (New York, 1920).

Wiener, M., *English Culture and the Decline of the Industrial Spirit* (Cambridge, 1981).

Winstanley, M. J., *The Shopkeeper's World 1830–1914* (Manchester, 1983).

Wolff, J. and Seed, J. (eds), *The Culture of Capital: Art, Power and the Nineteenth-Century Middle Class* (Manchester, 1988).

Wright, D. G., *Democracy and Reform 1815–1885* (Harlow, 1970).

Wright, D. G., *Popular Radicalism: The Working-Class Experience 1780–1880* (Harlow, 1988).

Index

adult education 16, 17, 188–91,
193–7
agitation to repeal the tax on
imported raw cotton 137
Ainsworth family (Anglican) 67, 187
Ainsworth, John Horrocks 189,
199–200
Ainsworth, Peter 54 n. 80, 71,
95–6, 118, 120, 182, 193–4,
199, 205, 207
Amalgamated Society of Engineers
162–3
Ancient Noble Order of United
Oddfellows of the Bolton
Union 199
Anderson, Perry 57
Andrews family (Presbyterians and
Unitarians) 63–4
Anglicans 25, 28, 29, 31, 35, 37,
40, 58, 64, 67–9, 95–6, 200
anti-Corn Law agitation 92, 109,
113, 114–20, 123, 124–5, 128,
136, 137–8
Anti-Corn Law League 113, 116,
119, 145 n. 74
Arrowsmith, James 82, 199
Arrowsmith, Peter Rothwell 109,
110, 115, 122, 188, 191, 196
Ashley, Lord 204 ff.
Ashton-under-Lyne 12, 126, 207,
220
Ashworth family of Turton (Quaker)
60, 63, 64, 122, 157, 158, 187,
188, 190, 207

Ashworth, Edmund 74, 107, 201
Ashworth, Henry 71, 74 ff., 83,
118, 140–1, 145 n. 74, 161,
190, 210 n. 14
Associated Master Cotton-Spinners
of Bolton 91
Astley Bridge 68
Aston, John (hand-loom weaver) 47
Athenaeum project 72, 98 n. 69,
195–7

Baker family (Unitarian) 64
Baker, Franklin 55 n. 80, 61,
73, 204
Bancroft, Thomas 95 n. 42
Bank Street Unitarian Chapel 60,
62, 63, 65, 66, 73–4
Barker, Joseph 183
Barlow, Edward 68
Barnes family (Unitarian) 64
Barrow family (Unitarian) 60, 64
Barrow, Isaac 49, 74
Barrow Bridge 187, 189
Barton, Richard and Thomas
(textile bleachers) 187
Bayley family (Unitarian) 64
Bazley, Thomas 187, 189, 190
Behagg, Clive 27, 113
Benbow, William 111, 112
Birmingham 26–7, 82, 113, 117, 165
Birmingham Political Union 41
Black, Dr 168, 201
Black, Thomas (boot- and shoe-
maker) 47

Blackburn 12, 126
Blackrod 67
Blair, George 67
Blair, Harrison 189
Blair, Stephen 67, 92, 187
Bleachers' Association 187
bleaching operatives 66–7, 114
Bolling family (Anglican) 68, 157,
   158, 208
  Bolling, Edward 68
  Bolling, William 41, 70, 78,
   120, 121, 135
Bolton Anti-Corn Law Association
   113, 117
Bolton Benevolent Society 91, 114,
   135, 197
Bolton Builders' General Association
   164, 165
Bolton Cattle Fair Society 71, 186
Bolton Chronicle 38–9, 42, 46, 50
   n. 12, 52 n. 32, 59, 86–7, 91,
   121, 136, 190, 195
Bolton District Association of
   Protestant Unitarian
   Dissenters 72
Bolton Free Press 70, 82, 89–90, 91,
   109, 110, 128, 141 n. 4, 151, 204
Bolton Gas Company 67, 83, 85
Bolton Improvement Act (1847) 86
   (1850) 59, 88–9, 199
   (1854) 213 n. 81
Bolton Market Hall 88
Bolton Operative Anti-Corn Law
   Association 119
Bolton Operative Conservative
   Association 125, 146 n. 92
Bolton Political Union 20, 42,
   44–8, 73, 74
Bolton Poor Protection Society 91,
   114, 135, 138, 140, 197, 198
Bolton Reform Association
   73–4, 99 n. 79, 105 ff., 119, 141
   n. 6, 199

Bolton Tailors' Trade Society 166–7
Bolton town council 71, 77, 82–4,
   86, 88, 89, 91, 92, 101–2, 207
Bolton Trades Council 152
Bolton workhouse 32
Bolton Working Men's Association
   41, 74, 109–10, 135
Bolton Youths' Temperance
   Society 202
bookkeepers 195
Bowring, John 118, 120, 122, 182,
   183, 199
Bridgeman family (Earls of
   Bradford) 65, 89
Bridgewater Estate trustees 89
Bridson, Henrietta 68
Bridson, Thomas Ridgway 67, 72,
   194 ff., 199
Briggs, Asa 11, 60, 138
Brimelow, W. 61
Brown, James (clogger) 47, 74
Brown, James (boot- and shoe-
   maker) 74
Buck, John 63
building industry 127, 163–4
building workers 114, 145 n. 74,
   156, 163–6, 194
Burke, Edmund 61–2
Burnley 13

calico-printers 14
Callender, W. R. 74
Cannon and Haslam (cotton
   spinners) 188–9
Cannon family (Wesleyan) 69
   Cannon, William 65
Cargon, John (hand-loom weaver)
   47, 125
Catholic Association (of Ireland) 46
Catling, Harold 159
Central Association of Engineering
   Employers 163
Chadwick, Edwin 84–5

charity and philanthropy 91, 192–3, 197–200, 203

Chartism 7, 8, 12, 14–15, 18, 19, 20–1, 28, 40, 41, 43, 49, 55–6, 58–9, 74, 82, 91, 115, 125, 151 ff., 182–3, 185, 186, 200, 205, 209–10, 223
  and Irish repealers 183
  and relations between reformers 106–7, 109–13, 116–20, 218, 220–1
  ideological content 106, 108–9, 128–38, 209 n. 6, 220–1
  'National Holiday' riots 112, 141–2
  national petitions 117
  Plug Strikes 117, 119, 131, 158, 162, 172, 187, 198
  tactics and organisation 108–9, 110–12, 209 n. 8

Church and King Club 61–2, 71, 72, 96 n. 46
Church Institute 197
Church of England 35–7, 44, 59, 60, 61, 64, 72, 91, 98 n. 71
church rates 31, 36–7, 52 n. 41, 52–3, 59, 72–3
churchwardens 30, 31, 33–7, 52 n. 39, 70, 78
Clegg, Ashworth 64
clerks 195
coal industry 65, 66, 68, 127, 168–9
coalminers 156, 168–70
Cobden, Richard 75, 117–18
Commission Street Unitarian Chapel 63
Conservatism 13, 66, 69–70, 223
Conservatives 25, 28 ff., 34, 35, 38 ff., 41–2, 47, 53 n. 51, 59, 61, 64–8, 105, 140 n. 2, 219
  and attitudes to Corn Laws and economic protection 70, 90, 91–2, 123, 137–8, 222

  and attitudes to New Poor Law and factory reform 70, 120–2
  and relations with working class 109, 120–5, 190, 223
  conflict with Liberals over municipal reform 72–93, 222–3
  leisure culture and social attitudes 71–2, 98 n. 69, 194–6
Cooper, Thomas 61
Co-operative movement 14, 16–17
cotton industry 17, 18, 22, 50 n. 3, 64, 67 ff., 96 n. 52
  and commercial depressions 114
  and industrial relations 156–9, 185, 208
  and significance in general patterns of social relations 7, 12–13, 17, 21, 22, 203, 217
  and technological change 114, 127
cotton mule-spinners 41, 45, 47, 109, 114, 118, 119, 128, 131–2, 137, 156–9, 171, 208
  trade union 118, 137–8, 157–8, 172, 173, 174–5, 190, 208, 220
cotton operatives 114, 118, 145 n. 74, 195
  and factory reform 205, 206–7
Cottrill family (Anglican) 68
court leets 29, 32–3, 44, 45, 65, 66, 71, 77, 83
Crompton family (Unitarian) 64, 66
Crook family (Unitarian) 64
  Crook, Joseph 73, 74
Cropp, Thomas (proprietor of *Bolton Chronicle*) 42
Cross family (Anglican, cotton spinners) 68
Cross Street Unitarian Chapel (Manchester) 60, 64
Cross, Thomas (textile bleacher) 187

Crossick, Geoffrey 13, 16–17, 50
    n. 10, 221
Cullen, Thomas 199

Daly, Richard (Great Bolton
    trustee) 34
Darbishire family (Unitarian) 60, 64
    Darbishire, Charles 55 nn. 80 &
    87, 73, 74, 76, 82, 110, 112,
    122, 201
    Darbishire, Samuel 64
Dean, John 74ff., 199
Dean Mills 187, 190
Diggle, Daniel (operative dyer) 128
Dixon, William 170, 179 n. 86
Dobson family (Anglican) 68
    Dobson, Benjamin 188, 196
    Dobson, Isaac 68
    Dobson, Thomas 188
Dobson and Barlow's (textile
    machinery makers) 68, 162
Dorning family (Unitarian) 64
    Dorning, Francis 64
'drink' 137, 148 n. 123, 202
Dutton, H. I., and King, J. E. 208
Dyer, J. C. 74

Edinburgh 13, 17
Egerton, Francis (Duke of Bridge-
    water) 65, 124, 168, 186
engineering industry 18, 22,
    68–9, 127
engineering workers 68, 113–14,
    145 n. 74, 156, 159–63
    and Chartism 162, 172, 195
Exchange Newsroom 71
exclusive dealing 26–7, 41, 49

factory reform movement 20, 42,
    119, 132, 133, 136, 138, 139,
    152, 182, 185, 187, 203–8,
    219–20
Fairbairn, William 160

Farnworth 79ff., 170
Fletcher family 66
    Fletcher, John 121
    Fletcher, Ralph 66, 95 n. 42,
    99 n. 72
Foster, John 12, 15, 16–18, 21,
    26–7, 29ff., 41, 126, 127, 138,
    181, 182, 220, 224 n. 8
Foster, John (editor of *Bolton
    Chronicle*) 121
Fraser, Derek 29, 59, 75
Free Trade and Anti-Bread Tax
    Society 119
friendly societies 139, 198–9, 201
Friendly Society of Coal
    Mining 169
Friendly Society of Iron Moulders
    161–2

Gadian, David 15, 22, 26–7, 113
Gardner, Robert 187, 189, 190, 206
Garrard, John 22
Gash, Norman 72
Gattrell, V. A. C. 61, 63
General Builders' Association 166
Gillespie, John (hand-loom weaver
    and Chartist) 112, 129–30, 182
Glasgow 124
Goodwin family (Unitarian) 64
Graham's Factory Bill (1843)
    204, 206
Gray, Robert 13, 16–17, 135,
    172–3, 204, 205
Gray, William 64
Great and Little Bolton Water
    Company 83, 85–6, 101 n. 107
Greenhalgh, W. (jobbing
    carpenter) 47
Gunn, Simon 22, 225 n. 10

Halliwell, Philip (hand-loom
    weaver) 123ff.
Halliwell Road Free Church 63

Halliwell township 79–81
Hammond, John ('machine maker')
 159, 161, 162
hand-loom weavers 14, 30, 42, 45,
 47, 70, 109, 110, 114, 118,
 119–20, 143–4, 171–3
 and politics 123–5
Hardcastle family (Anglican) 68
 Hardcastle, Elisa 67, 68
 Hardcastle, James 67, 68
 Hardcastle, Thomas 54 n. 80,
 67, 71, 78, 194
Hargreaves, Edith 68
Harrison, Brian 130, 200–1
Harrison, Royden 11
Harwood family (Unitarians and
 Anglicans) 60, 64, 66
 Harwood, George 64
 Harwood, John 65
Haselden family (Unitarian) 64
Haslam family (Unitarian) 60, 64ff.
 Haslam, John Percival 65
 Haslam, Ralph Marsden 65
Haulgh 79–81, 89, 102 n. 121
Hayhurst, W. (publican) 47
Heaton, Messrs. (cotton
 spinners) 191
Heaton, Rowland Hall 164
Hesketh family (Anglican) 68
Heywood (near Bury) 186
Heywood family (Unitarian) 60,
 64, 66
 Heywood, Robert 41, 65, 66,
 70, 71, 73ff., 82–3, 98 n. 69,
 102 n. 120, 112, 195, 201,
 206, 207
Hick family (Anglican) 68
 Hick, Benjamin 68, 69, 71, 78,
 161, 163, 194, 196
highway surveyors 30, 37–8, 40,
 52 n. 53
Hobsbawm, Eric 15–16
Holland family (Unitarian) 64

Holland, John 61
Hollis, Patricia 130, 133
Honeyman, Katrina 93 n. 1
Horwich 52, 67, 79–81
Howarth, Samuel (spinners' union
 official) 41, 118, 119, 182
Howe, Anthony 22, 203
Huberman, Michael 156
Hulton family (Anglican) 66
 Hulton, William 66, 121, 122,
 169, 186, 194
Huntite radicalism 28

improvement trusts and trustees
 39–40, 52 n. 51, 67 ff., 82, 83,
 85–6, 87 ff., 101 n. 107, 102
 n. 120
income tax 91, 102–3, 136
Independent Order of Odd-
 fellows 199
industrial relations 12–13, 106,
 128, 151–3
 in building 163–6
 in coalmining 168–70
 in cotton spinning 156–9, 190,
 191–2, 207–8
 in engineering 159–63
 in tailoring 168
 in textile bleaching 187
Irish 14, 15, 86, 96 n. 46, 183, 223
 and ethnicity 13, 19

Jackson, Thomas 188
Jebb, Captain 76, 77
Jones, Gareth Stedman 17–19,
 127, 130–2, 156, 224 n. 8
Jones, Noah 63
Joyce, Patrick 12–13, 15, 16, 18,
 21, 126, 127, 181, 182, 189,
 191

Kay family (Unitarian) 64
Kentish London 13, 17, 221

Kirk, Neville 12, 13, 15 ff., 18–19, 21, 126, 127, 131, 132, 138, 181, 185, 220
Knowles, Andrew 120, 169–70
Knowles family (Wesleyan) 69
  Knowles, George 188, 189
  Knowles, John 188, 189
  Knowles, Robert 188 ff., 194, 196, 201, 206, 207

labour aristocracy 14, 16–17, 126–7
labour process 14, 16 ff., 20, 181–2
  and work control 12–13, 15, 18–19, 27, 126–7, 152–3, 156–70, 177 n. 54, 218
Lancashire and Yorkshire Railway Company 89
Lancashire Reformers' Union 66
Lazonick, William 159
Leach, James 20, 132 ff.
Leypayers' Committee 30, 32, 42
Liberalism 13, 21, 25, 28, 47, 60, 62, 64, 73, 105–6, 136, 137, 139, 182–3, 220–3
Liberals 9, 25–6, 34, 39, 40, 43, 48, 53 n. 51, 59, 64–5, 66, 67, 69, 70, 73, 105, 140 n. 2, 222
  and attitudes to New Poor Law 122–3, 135
  and conflict with Tories over municipal reform 72–93
  and the hand-loom weavers 123, 124–5
  and relations with working-class reformers 7–8, 69, 106–20, 135–40, 182–3, 218–23
Little Hulton 66, 78–81
Liverpool 164
Lloyd, George (joiner and Chartist) 112
lodging houses 88, 199
Lomax family (Unitarian) 66

Lomax, Joseph (hand-loom weaver) 110
London 166
Loyal Order of Druids 199
Lum, Joseph 118

McConnell, James 125
McDouall, Peter Murray 20, 132, 133
'machine makers' 162–3
magistrates 30, 33–6, 38, 44, 51 n. 29, 65, 66, 70 ff., 77, 78, 91, 95 n. 42, 100 n. 91, 203
Makin, John 123
Manchester 26, 42, 47, 60, 61, 63, 64, 66, 75, 82, 113, 164
Manchester Political Union 42–3
Mangnall family (Unitarian) 64
Marsden family (Wesleyan) 69
Marsden, Joseph 164, 188, 211 n. 37
Martin, William 188
Marx, Karl 18
Mason family (Unitarian) 64
  Mason, Mary 64
Mechanics' Institution 71–2, 184, 194–5, 197, 206
middle-class politics 7–9, 20, 21–2, 140–1, 222–3
  and attitudes to Parliament 57–8, 60
  and mid-Victorian stability 8–9, 13–14, 139
millwrights 159–61, 162
Miners' Association of Great Britain 170, 179 n. 86
Moderation Society 200, 201
Moor Lane Unitarian Chapel 63
Morley, Mr (hatter) 32
Mort family (Unitarian) 66
Mosley Street Unitarian Chapel (Manchester) 60, 64
Municipal Corporations Act 57, 74–5, 113

municipal reform 8, 59, 222
Musgrave family (Wesleyan)
    69, 188
  Musgrave, Ellen 188
  Musgrave, John 68, 69
Musson, A. E. 12, 160

Naisby, William 30 ff., 35–6, 37, 42,
    44, 47, 49, 50 n. 12, 51 nn. 21,
    23 & 29, 52, 54 n. 79, 74, 110
National Association for the
    Protection of Labour 151–2,
    169, 171, 179 n. 86, 219
National Association of United
    Trades 151, 171, 179 n. 86
National Charter Association 133
National Parliamentary and
    Financial Reform Association
    92, 183
National Reform Union 66
National Union of the Working
    Classes 47
Naysmith, Gaskell and Co. 161
Needham, Richard (hand-loom
    weaver) 123 ff.
New Temperance Society 200 ff.
Nonconformists 35, 36, 59–60,
    62–5, 69, 188
  and attitudes to recreation 71
  and conflict with Conservatives
    71–2, 197
  and factory reform 206, 207
  and temperance 201
Nuttall, Charles (pawnbroker) 36

Oastler, Richard 120, 203, 205
O'Brien, Bronterre 55 n. 89, 128–9
O'Connor, Feargus 112, 117
occupational profile of Bolton
    22–3, 154, 155
Oldham 12, 15, 16–18, 26–7, 29,
    50 n. 5, 126, 127, 156, 170,
    181, 208, 220, 224 n. 8

Operative Builders' Union 164
Orangeism 72, 96 n. 46, 99 n. 72
Ormrod family (Anglican) 68, 157,
    190–1
  Ormrod, Emily 68
  Ormrod, James 67
  Ormrod, Peter 37, 67, 71,
    78, 194
  Ormrod, James (currier) 42,
    52 n. 35
overseers 30–1, 33–7, 51 n. 21, 76,
    78, 91
Owenism 19, 130, 153, 218–19,
    223, 224 n. 8

Paine, Thomas 61
Parish Constables' Act 83
Parish Vestries Act 31
Parkes, Joseph 74–5
Parkinson, James (brass-moulder)
    55 n. 90, 139, 148 n. 123
paternalism 13, 14, 153, 181, 182,
    184, 187–92, 203, 214 n. 108
  in coalmining 186
  in cotton spinning 188–90
  in engineering 188
  in 'factory villages' 185–7
  in textile bleaching 186–7, 189
Paulton, A. W. 118
Peel, Robert 91, 116, 136
Peelites 92, 93
Pendlebury, James (hand-loom
    weaver and Chartist) 171–2
Pennington, Sarah 64
Peterloo 66, 108
petite bourgeoisie, politics 9, 25–8,
    58, 219, 222
  and local political system 28–40
  and national politics 40–8, 219
  relations with middle-class
    reformers 28, 48, 69, 74, 92–3
  relations with working-class
    reformers 26–8, 40–8

Pillin, William (hand-loom weaver) 124, 125
Pilling, Richard 132
Pitt Club 69, 71
police and policing 29–30, 31–3, 34, 36, 38–9, 44, 49, 64, 65–6, 70, 76, 77, 82, 83, 100–1
Poole, Robert 71, 203
Poor Law Amendment Act 20, 28, 31, 34, 58, 87, 120–1, 197
    and anti-Poor Law movement 122
    and Bolton Poor Law Union and Guardians 78, 79–81, 90–1, 117, 118, 121–3, 135–6, 147 n. 117
Potter family (Unitarian) 60
Potter, Thomas 74
power-loom weavers 114, 118
Preston 124, 200, 206, 208
public baths 71, 184, 199–200
public health 83, 84–5, 86–8, 101–2
Public Health Act (1848) 58, 87, 88

Radcliffe, William 123
radicalism, ideological content of 42–9, 218–19
Ramsden, G. M. 63
Raper, J. H. 196, 197
Rasbotham family (Unitarian) 64
Reform Act (1832) 57, 112, 222
Reform Bill agitation 9, 20, 27, 41–3, 53 n. 54, 74, 108–9, 112
Reform Ratepayers' Association 101 n. 109
religious attendance 63
religious opinion and political allegiance 69, 97–8
Ricardian Socialism 19
Ridgway family (Anglican) 67, 186–7
    Ridgway, Joseph 67, 71, 121, 196
    Ridgway, Thomas 187

Roberts, David 185
Roberts, W. P. 170
Robinson, Duncan (hand-loom weaver) 110
Robinson, E. 160
Robinson, J. (provision dealer) 47
Rochdale 170
Rothwell, Charles 125
Rothwell, Henry (spinners' union official) 118, 119, 182
Rothwell, Peter 68, 78, 194, 196, 201
Rubinstein, W. D. 57
Rushton, Thomas 68

Scott family (Unitarian) 60
Scowcroft, James 32, 51 n. 26, 54 n. 80, 194
Seed, John 62, 94 n. 33
Select Vestries Act 30
Selwyn-Ibbotson Bill 203
Shawcross family (Manchester) 64
Shiman, L. L. 201
shoemakers 145 n. 74, 172
shopkeepers 9, 25–6, 30, 41–3, 45, 47, 49, 55 n. 89, 207
Simpson family (Unitarian) 64
Skelton, Joseph 36, 53 n. 47, 74
Slade family (Anglican) 68
    Slade, James 35, 37, 52 nn. 39 & 44, 68, 72, 98 n. 69, 196–7
Slater, John 196, 199
small masters 9, 25, 26, 30, 47, 49
Smith, James (Unitarian) 64
Smith, Thomas (hand-loom weaver) 47
Spencer, Eli 159
Stalybridge 12, 126, 207, 220
Stanley family (Earls of Derby) 65
Staton, P. (barber) 47
Stevenson, Matthew 148 n. 123, 196
Stockdale, Richard 88
Stockport 12, 126, 221

Sumner, R. H. 187
Sunday schools 188, 193, 207
Swallow, David 179 n. 86
Sykes, Robert 26–7, 156, 219

tailors 145 n. 74, 156, 166–8, 172
Taylor family (Unitarian) 61, 64
   Taylor, Elizabeth (née Mason) 64
   Taylor, Mary 64
   Taylor, Robert 64
Taylor family (Wesleyan) 69
   Taylor, Thomas 73, 190,
      214 n. 108
Taylor, John (coroner) 199,
   201, 202
Temperance Hall 116, 202, 208
temperance movement 16, 17, 71,
   184–5, 200–3
Ten Hours Bill and Act (1847)
   206–7, 208
Test and Corporations Acts 72
textile bleaching and finishing
   66–7, 70, 96 n. 48, 127, 210–11
Thistlewaite, Rev. 37
Tholfsen, Trygve 181, 191, 201, 208
Thomasson family 60, 63, 64
   Thomasson, John Pennington 64
   Thomasson, Thomas 64, 74, 75,
      87, 88, 110, 114, 115–16, 118,
      123, 135
Thomis, Malcolm 12
Thompson, Dorothy 117, 130
Thorpe, Ellis 65
Toleration Act (1689) 60
Tomlinson, Messrs. (cotton
   spinners) 190
trade unionism 14, 20, 130, 132 ff.,
   138, 151–2, 153, 179 n. 86,
   219–20
   and Chartism 132–5, 209 n. 8

in building 163–6, 177 n. 64
in coalmining 169–70, 178–9
in cotton spinning 157–8,
   190–2, 208
in engineering 162–3
in tailoring 166–8
traders 9, 25, 26, 48–9, 74, 195, 207
Trinity Act (1813) 60
truck: anti-truck campaign 42
Turner, Henry 190, 205

unemployment 114, 145 n. 74,
   161–2
Unitarians 60–5, 67, 69, 72, 73–4,
   82, 94 n. 33
'unstamped' press 133, 195

vestries 29, 30–9, 44, 49, 77, 78, 82
volunteer movement 92

Wallsuches 67, 186
Walmsley, Joshua 183
Walsh, Robert 199
Warden, John (gardener and
   Chartist) 110 ff., 128
Waring, John (tailor) 47
Webb, Sidney and Beatrice 11
Weiner, Martin 57
Wilson, George 74
Winder family (Unitarian) 60
   Winder, James 34, 60, 74, 78, 84
Winkworth, Stephen 64
Wood, Joseph (tea-dealer) 110, 116
working-class consciousness 8, 9,
   11–14, 17–21, 126, 171–3, 223
   and political radicalism 127–38,
      218–21
   and Reform Bill agitation 42–8,
      49, 107
Worsley 65, 168

For a complete list of
Keele University Press and Ryburn
books in print, please write to
Keele University Press, Keele University,
Staffordshire ST5 5BG, England